Bound

Boundaries and Motherhood

Ritual and Reproduction in Rural Maharashtra

DEEPRA DANDEKAR

zubaan

zubaan

ZUBAAN
an imprint of Kali for Women
128B Shahpur Jat, 1st Floor
NEW DELHI 110 049
Email: contact@zubaanbooks.com
Website: www.zubaanbooks.com

Published by Zubaan Publishers Pvt. Ltd 2016

10 9 8 7 6 5 4 3 2 1

ISBN 978 93 83074 50 1

Zubaan is an independent feminist publishing house based in New Delhi with a strong academic and general list. It was set up as an imprint of India's first feminist publishing house, Kali for Women, and carries forward Kali's tradition of publishing world quality books to high editorial and production standards. *Zubaan* means tongue, voice, language, speech in Hindustani. Zubaan is a non-profit publisher, working in the areas of the humanities, social sciences, as well as in fiction, general non-fiction, and books for children and young adults under its Young Zubaan imprint.

Typeset in Baskerville 11/13 by Jojy Phillip, New Delhi 110 015
Printed in India by Repro India Ltd., Navi Mumbai

Dedicated to the memory of
my own 'child interrupted'
(17 February 1999, KEM Hospital, Pune).

Contents

Acknowledgments

I am grateful to late Professor Sharmila Rege for being my first real mentor. It was at Krantijyoti Savitribai Phule Women's Studies Centre, Pune University that I first began to think of myself as a woman with agency. I am also grateful to Zubaan Books for providing me with the opportunity of publishing this book.

I thank Bhargavi Davar and Karthik Venkatasubramanian for providing me with research opportunities at Bapu Trust. I express my gratitude and deep, lasting and enriching friendship for some close colleagues from Bapu Trust, whom I had the opportunity of learning from. I specially thank Madhura Lohokare for an enduring level of reflection on intellectual matters and for providing me with support and further fieldwork opportunities at Ghodegaon.

I am indebted to Professor William Sax, Karin Polit, Gabriele Alex and the team of doctoral researchers at the South Asia Institute, University of Heidelberg, who influenced my research deeply during the time of study in Germany. At home, I am indebted to Professor S.R. Walimbe, Professor P.P. Joglekar and Professor V.S. Shinde for their support in the research and writing and submission of my doctoral dissertation. I especially thank Dr Abhijit R. Dandekar for investing particularly in my thesis and the various kinds of fieldwork and photography ventures that its research and writing involved. I thank my friends at Deccan College, Pune, who carried out fieldwork with me in various capacities and supported me lovingly.

I learned an enormous amount from the public health sector

and the ICICI Foundation for Inclusive Growth, Centre for Child Health and Nutrition, Pune, where work inputs broadened my political perspectives on women's health. I especially thank Shilpa Deshpande, Rahul Sarwate, Dr. Shinjini Mondal-Sharma and Dr Mohan Deshpande as colleagues from ICICI Foundation, from whom I learned greatly about the Public health system, training and health policy. I learned a lot from the Jeeva team, Dhanashree Gurav and their incandescent research passions on midwives and home birthing. I want to thank my friends from ICICI Foundation, who warmed some of those very emotionally stricken and final days that I spent in India.

I thank all my field respondents and informants for this book. I never forgot them for a single moment, while writing this manuscript, even as there was never much of a 'moving on' from the subjectivity that invented this research in the first place. I remain grateful to Kusum Karnik and the Shashwat Sansthan for helping me articulate and develop my analytical approach towards political struggles of my field area just as I thank Mai, Rekha and Lata for fostering a feeling of home for me in the village.

I express my loving gratitude for my parents, Dr D.K. Bhattacharya and Dr Pratibha Bhattacharya, whom I would have dedicated this book to if I had not addressed it elsewhere: to the shared journey with childless women and to the invisibility of child loss. I express my special gratitude for *pishi* (aunt), Mrs Deepti Sengupta, for always remaining emblematic of courage and fortitude; Ajay Sawarkar, my brother, for being an idol of strength, *Tai-maushi* (aunt) and Shivaji Uncle Mrs Vijaya Ramalingam and Dr Shivaji Ramalingam, who have constantly showered their special prayers and love upon me. I do of course thank all my family, even if I have mentioned only a few by name here, who have constantly wished me their best.

Finally, I thank the titan of emotional endurance who has helped me to take courage in passing through the most pervasive 'curtain' that separated my life into halves, leading to the creation of that unrestricted and undemanding space, which finally allowed me to understand 'what really happened'. Thanks, Torsten!

PROLOGUE

An Introduction to Dreams about Birthing the Impossible

I would like to define my primary engagement at the beginning of this book as one that describes motherhood as systemically constructed through childbirth/child-loss goddess cults, represented by the Satvai and Maulya in rural Maharashtra, as marginal and associated with village inhabitation boundaries. I begin this prologue with the most poignant aspect of my fieldwork: women's dreams, even as I end this book with dreams in the epilogue, which are mine. These dreams represent, to my mind, the suffering associated with the goddess cult in the lives of childless and motherhood-less women and contribute to a discourse of 'child loss' that is as powerful as the discourse of childbirth, both constructed academically to create a predominant view of women as fertile and birth-giving. The recounting of dreams that I have elected to begin this book with, depicts childless women and motherhood-loss/child-loss to be that eternal shadow-land of womanhood that each childbirth and motherhood is equally imbued with. Childless women or witches and mothers are like the reflections of goddess dyads themselves, representing the fluid relationships between pure and impure forms.

My women respondents often spoke of dreams that linked goddesses with important indications or premonitions about their children and the purity of their reproductive lives, which were at the same time threatened with affliction (ritual diagnosis pertaining to their experiences of child loss, subsequent childlessness or the inability to have either children or more specifically sons). These dreams were like a hotline between goddesses and married women, who were still considered of reproductive ability. However, in order to understand these dreams, a little needs to be explained first about these goddesses and the systemic manner in which they preside over motherhood-loss in my field area and the prevalent discourse about how performing their rituals averts and heals from affliction, even if these afflictions are sent by the same goddess to women who are deemed impure.

Goddesses 'harm' and 'heal' women at the same time, curing them from the very afflictions that they send as part of a punishment and a reminder of their moral duty of motherhood and purity. Women who are afflicted by the goddess for having become impure, therefore, perform healing rituals and for this purpose come into contact with margins and boundaries of village inhabitations where goddess shrines are located. They are themselves considered peripheral to their marital clans, until their moral recalcitrance is not considered purged and they are not cured of what is considered impure, resulting in the subsequent birth of sons. Village goddesses presiding over childbirth primarily protect village clans (women's marital clans), securing them with male inheritance first by 'converting' and recruiting the women married into them as pure mothers and wives. The womanhood, wifehood and motherhood duties and domestic labour that goddess rituals create within these converted and 'colonised'[1] women thereafter, concentrate on producing a subjectivity of non-owning[2] valour among them in relation to husbands and sons, since they are themselves created as 'owned' through rituals. Feelings of overwhelming attachment with one's own biological sons are considered to go against the welfare of the clan unit, since it might

[1] Kashibai Kanitkar (Kosambi 2008) was the first writer of the nineteenth century, who explicitly stated that women were colonised within patriarchal clans.

[2] The term 'ownership' when concerning children is problematic, as pointed out by Lee Schlesinger, Michigan (personal communication at the 15th International Maharashtra Conference, Arizona State University). What is meant here is a translation of '*maza*' (mine) that is very rarely proclaimed by women, when referring to children in contrast to *amche* or *aple* (ours).

instil a sense of competition between agnatic women and their children, which is considered to benefit the enemies of the clan, since these rituals create sons as clan and land 'owners' and their mothers as owned by marital clans and lands as its progenitors.

My respondents always pointed to the *Ramayana* while explaining the quality of this 'competitive' motherhood. Overwhelming emotions of personal attachment to one's own son (a form of affliction and cannibalism) could only be traditionally known to those outsider hostile women, who knew the inside of one's body, like the midwife. In mythical times, Queen Kaikeyi's secret sin of overwhelming attachment to her son, that even went against her marital clan's interests, was known to her maid and midwife, Manthara, who could exploit this knowledge to her own benefit against her enemies, Kaikeyi's husband Dasharatha and the whole Suryavanshi clan, whose downfall was wrecked because a weak queen, too attached to her son, confided about it to an outsider, a midwife, who was a secret enemy of the king's clan and the state (thus making the whole unhappiness of King and Lord Rama a mistake about motherhood). My respondents felt that interactions between a mother and a midwife needed to remain distanced and mediated by the mother's marital clan to avoid any breach of interest against the clan and to avoid secrets being exchanged during intimate services that were provided in 'body-solitude'. This also minimised the chances of accusations being levied against both mothers and midwives in the future if something went wrong during childbirth.

In her ethnographic tome on motherhood, *Death without Weeping*, Scheper-Hughes (1993) interrelated reproduction amidst poverty to an alternative idea of motherhood as one that was full of ambivalence in contrast to more bourgeois notions of it, that constructed it as soft and encompassing. The motherhood paradigm for women within my field area was also one of crisis, due to its own internally conflicting bourgeois nature. The insistence on the motherhood of sons in my field area was created through the aspirations of strengthening dominant caste demography in the village itself, only for the motherhood bond to be denied for women as impure in a bid to hark back to a tradition of being distanced from sons (in the Ramayana style), which was an equally idealistic bourgeois tradition of denying women ownership, since they were themselves owned by men, marital clans and castes within patriarchy. Their ownership was further promoted as their purity by goddess cults that had to be preserved and restored in order to escape affliction. Pure motherhood and denied and martyred motherhood, as reflections of bourgeois traditions of childbirth relationships of labour between women and the owners of their fertility, fitted in with its soft and encompassing nature promoted by the market of motherhood ideals that dictated servitude, purity and the ownership and protection of both mothers and children by men, their clans and dominant castes.

Women in my field area were colonised as wives and mothers and gained status when they succeeded as mothers of male heirs that cemented their own 'owned' status within clans. They suffered, on the other hand, when they became childless or widowed, while at the same time competing with each other to remain encompassed and protected as esteemed and prized clan possessions. They failed at achieving this as childless women, as they faced domestic violence or remained marginalised when undergoing loss and lived in fear of being abandoned, performing rituals constantly when they fell ill, unable to grieve at child loss because they felt guilty for their illnesses and affliction diagnosis received from various ritual healers making them feel lesser women or faulty clan possessions. Reproductive illness and mental illness diagnosed by doctors, hierarchically superior in their social world, only added to the misery of affliction diagnosis, making them feel increasingly like failures. Their bodies and the sense of its well-being was produced as disciplined labour and an absence of this could not be experienced by them as freedom from gendered labour.[3] Freedom itself was understood as a form of abandonment that was considered to be a result from illness and affliction instead.

In fact, the recent claim that traditional healing shrines and their rituals 'healed' systemically battered women (as refuted by

[3] Foucault (1979) describes the way in which punishment and its threat leads to the establishment of discipline and the incorporation of labour.

Venkateswaran 2014 and Dandekar 2014a) is one way in which the processes of gender violence and casteism were further reproduced and perpetuated, whilst masquerading as 'cultural', original or autochthonous within nationalist political regimes. Individual narratives of justice received within contexts of ritual healing are often tautological, and concern justice surrounding alliances with larger clan/caste groups and patriarchal morality. Pro-tradition fieldwork narratives that I have encountered often demonise the politics of caste and gender, sabotage discursive formations of categories such as outcastes, the unhappy, the childless, the widow and the outsider within social mainstreams; without any desire to explore individual experiences of suffering systemic traditions quite conveniently. Social scientists may go a step further by refuting the existence of the individual within traditional healing contexts almost entirely and identifying the self instead, amidst collectives of socially defined identities. The claim that rituals may constitute a form of 'healing' and justice has been suggested by William S. Sax and others. Though situating arguments about rituals within techniques of altering the self in his book *God of Justice* (2009: 235–47), he explains the manner in which modernity and democracy have generally failed to efface pre-modern subjectivities such as ethnic or religious ties. He claims that if anything, these ties have become stronger within modernity.

My book, however, seeks to contest the manner in which modernity may not just be a temporal or a dualistic concept seen in contrast with the pre-modern, especially for my women respondents undergoing child loss and motherhood loss. Modernity and the subject of social and legal justice that is beyond the goddess's clan and caste-centric tradition of dharma is also a clash of values about freedom from caste and gender recruitment of the female body for reproductive and sexual labour and ownership, that as a social and political movement is simultaneous, equally accessible and powerful. The observation of a failed modernity does not take the dominant caste-centred nature of modernity's implementing regime into consideration when lamenting its failure. The failure in its implementation is not a failure of values. In fact, it is on the basis of such 'modern' values as free speech on which even the arguments of those advocating for tradition being the best way out for Indian women steeped in violent personal lives are actually based. I will revisit these discussions in detail further on in the book.

This prologue is, however, about dreams. Women recounted their dreams to me, expressing their pain and fear of failing their motherhood goal quite vividly and wrenchingly. In the beginning I thought they were sharing material for interviews I had requested them for, since they already knew about my research. Later, it dawned on me through our conversations that they expected me to 'understand' these dreams better, since I was myself childless and motherhood-less. In their opinion I must have had or be having similar dreams of child loss, since they believed me to be afflicted. And I became a participant in dream-building with them as their affliction diagnosis of me became a part of my interaction and affective world shared with them, even as the whole research for this book took on its own reality.

These dreams were deeply complex, and shrouded in painful fears and anxieties that were specifically about reproductive failure. Goddesses in these dreams appeared malevolent, punishing and ferocious, shaming and blaming women for infant mortality. Many women consulted healers about their dreams, even though most healers remained embedded within systems of clan and caste alliance that made them choose between women and their clans, based on the index of dominant caste-based support lent to poor healer families in the village, when interpreting dreams. For example, many lower-caste healers were often used as pawns by upper-caste clans against their women. On the other hand, upper-caste women often viewed lower-caste healers as those who worked witchcraft against them with the help of other ambivalent or jealous insider competitors within their family or by other witches. Healers and women (if we viewed them temporarily as categories, even though these were only categories of convenience for researchers) were interrelated in a complex manner through the mediation of dominant castes and their clans. This wasn't an easy relationship for women.

The village childbirth goddesses known as the Satvai and the Maulya provided leadership for the motherhood role in the village by constituting it's very opposite. Through their own image of women's afflicted and impure form, they became repositories of women's problems. Their shrines were situated outside village boundaries in marginal locations, while they absorbed afflictions away from women through rituals that were supposed to make women acceptable to their clans as fertile mothers. On the other hand, it was these very impure goddesses, who were supposed to send 'errant' women afflictions that marked their impurity and revealed them as public defaulters. Once women performed rituals, they were supposed to be healed of the problems that the goddess had sent them as punishment, even though they were always in a sort of quarantine of relapse possibilities that the rest of their clanswomen (daughters and daughters-in-law for example) could inherit. Therefore, it was a circular process of absorption and distribution, punishment and healing that took place simultaneously between women and goddesses. The punishment of the goddesses was always aimed at women for the non-fulfilment of the wifely duty of clan reproductive labour, which was an indication of women's physical defiance at being biologically owned (through their uterus after marriage). This is why the symptoms of affliction were supposed to manifest themselves only after marriage, even if the affliction may have taken place earlier.

The impure Satvai and Maulya were, therefore, often considered low, wild, sexual and powerful themselves, but non-owned and ascetic at the same time, as they were considered to be without menstruation, family or children; these were the very same qualities expressed by women ritually diagnosed as afflicted. Their shrines were situated on village boundaries, where women were supposed to lay down their children and their feelings for these children, encompassed in ritual goods and food dedicated to the goddess.[4] Women who were converted and 'colonised' with the help of these boundary rituals by the Satvai and Maulya—who terrified them—had to thereafter lead their lives as docile and

[4] Masilamani-Meyer (2004) discusses the topic of 'the outside' or the wilderness in the context of deities acting as guardians of rural communities in Tamil Nadu.

fertile mothers and wives, inside the village boundary with their children, as the goddesses remained 'outside'.

Childbirth rituals served to separate sexuality or asceticism (considered an active male domain) from reproduction and wifehood (a passive female domain), leaving the overlap between sexuality and fertility to goddesses within the ambivalent space of a village boundary and all those who were the ritual agents or healers of the goddess and therefore, also the agents of that boundary and its power. Those who became afflicted by the goddess also fell into this boundary space between women and goddesses and were considered to become impure like lower caste healers themselves, as these afflicted women performed rituals with the latter's help, with the purpose of being re-absorbed into the category of pure women and leave the boundary zone. These goddess agents, usually considered of a lower caste were often treated as sexual labour and produced as androgynous in Maharashtra. They were more often than not, ritually dedicated to the goddess's cult, since they were traditionally kept away from land entitlements in the village interior and lived in separate colonies that were also outside the village boundary.[5] Hence, goddesses, while being female themselves, were not feminist at all; they were intensely masculine, sexual and ascetic champions of patriarchy, imposing reproductive labour and clan servitude on their female subjects in order to protect the security and inheritance of upper-caste village clans.[6] Their cults also enforced ritual servitude on the lower castes they had to serve the upper castes through the duty of healing and cleaning their villages and afflictions in order to

[5] Viswanath (2015) provides a detailed description of endemic landlessness and poverty among those denounced as lower castes in what she terms as the 'Dalit difference' in post-colonial India that has its roots in systemic discrimination and violence against those, who were once considered too low to be even included within Hinduism. She goes on to describe the way in which Dalits are now being incorporated into modern post-colonial Hinduisation drives in India to politically out-manoeuvre other religious minorities, demographically.

[6] Volumes such as *Is the Goddess a Feminist* (Hiltebeitel and Erndl 2000) discuss popular debates about how Indian goddesses could be considered part of women's empowerment movement.

purify the village and its owned aspects (women, material goods, children etc.). Goddess cults afflicted both castes if they did not perform their prescribed gendered duty: upper caste women for their childbirth duty and lower caste women for assisting in upper caste childbirth duties by healing away obstacles to it and establishing purity. Goddesses were, thus, the actual mythical mode of patriarchal oppression through affliction-punishments and healing and prevention from the same afflictions sent.

Also, it was not that women stopped having afflicting dreams after giving birth to male children. These afflictions and their stigma remained residual and dormant within them, often to be inherited by other female family members and often to resurface, since the fear of their sons dying to the clan and they being blamed for it remained strong. Till their sons were married, when the responsibility of their longevity could be passed to their wives, women remained responsible for their deaths. This manifested in a relationship that was defined through women's role separation from male children and husbands as service and care providers and their relationship of competition and hatred with other women (often daughters-in-law) who eventually took over this responsibility. The constant threat of affliction, witchcraft accusations and ritual diagnosis of cannibalism in case male members died were ways in which women were owned by their marital clans. Women's nightmares continued irrespective of healthy children and a living husband as a kind of half-afflicted consciousness that ran parallel to everyday reality, a kind of secret affliction within silent everyday but capricious normalcy. It was a world of constant worry and tension for their sons and husbands as their lives revolved around their menfolk. Their existence had the possibility of seamlessly transitioning from being an auspicious wife and mother one day to a childless, cannibal widow the next.

As I began having my own nightmares (a mixture of dreams I began 'borrowing' from my village friends) and began sharing these with them, they began sharing an even more overwhelming variety of dreams with me till the two became inextricable. In my dreams, I carried a heavy box with mysterious contents that I felt ambivalent about. I was always exhausted in my dreams and worried about what I carried. I felt perennially saddled by the box and would try to lose it at airports, bus stops or railway stations. But each time such an opportunity presented itself, I would also feel very guilty, afraid and anxious, and believed that people investigating it later would be able to trace me through its contents. In some of my dreams, I ate parts of the box to lighten its burden, but I remained unable to find an opening to unpack it. The dream made me feel deeply fearful of the goddesses and my research in the village.

Many women in the village shared their dreams with me as they accepted me as a half-insider to their circle. Maybe, following the tautological cycle of healing rituals, I allowed myself to dream with them, letting my fears merge with theirs; I wanted them to accept me and I wanted to be part of a society of women, even if there was deep competition and non-acceptance there for all the feminist ideas that I thought changed my life but did not change theirs. Although these dreams dragged me back into my own body and its losses, essentialising me to my reproductive body and role; I am thankful for the time I spent with my respondents and for being able to write about this relationship that women made with their bodies, their babies and goddesses. A collective consciousness developed around these dreams and us dreamers, and our sharing lent richness to certain narratives that evolved out of them.

The Dreams

I would divide these narratives into the following five types: the reptile type, the family type, the breastfeeding type, the divine punishment type, and the sexual type.

The first type of dream, the reptile type, was mostly concerned with the anxiety of the aftermath of birth and the fear of producing a non-human, undesirable and unrecognisable child (despite sonography). Women would dream of giving birth to a reptile or a snake, or many intertwined snakes or conjoined reptiles. Sometimes, these would be malformed or non-discernible from each other, headless and limbless, a mass of bloodied flesh moving uncoordinatedly and making crying noises. The women were sure these were monster babies. Sometimes they would crawl away very fast and as soon as they were born, dig a hole into the ground and disappear into it, or they would climb up a tree or jump into a well, or just wander into the village, where others would discover them and kill them cruelly (burning, drowning, burying alive). Most women would feel extreme and visceral revulsion for these beings, along with a wrenching pain and anxiety about them. Some of them said that their mind would be full of the sound of these crying beings who wanted to drink their milk or blood. Some of them said that they were afraid of suddenly coming upon these beings in reality and were scared of apparitions; they almost felt stalked by them. In another variation of this dream, women gave birth to excreta; they woke to cradles full of excrement and dirt. They feared that the midwife would tell their families about these monster children and excrement, and they would then be accused of witchcraft. No amount of placating based on a normal sonography report (and not all families could afford one) helped these anxious women to calm down, since the world of goddess afflictions and healing rituals was more real for them in terms of the fear of giving birth to unwanted babies than obscure machines that claimed to see actual babies within the stomach.

The family type dreams were concerned with the fear of agnatic clans claiming the child after separating it from its mother. In this dream, midwives or groups of women (imagined as the Maulya goddess) would play with new-born children and then proceed to eat them from the cradle or attack the cradle after paralysing the mother. The actual figure of the child would often remain inconsequential within the dream.

I found women displaying maximum reticence with the group of dreams I called the breastfeeding type, which revealed their ambivalence towards the new-born. They dreamt that babies would suckle them dry and dead or, conversely, blow up their breasts instead of suckling, till their entire body would fill up with air and burst like a balloon. When I asked them whether incidents such as what happened in the myth of the demoness Putana and the punishment she received at the hands of baby Krishna could actually happen to real women today, most of my respondents made the association with the Putana story only after I pointed it out, while others said that these dreams could be an aspect of affliction.

The fourth type of dream was the divine punishment category, in which the woman would be faced with a journey down a long road, where people would be able to look down upon her from above. Sometimes, the end of the long road would open into a river, where garbage could be seen overflowing onto a street. The dreaming woman would be walking down this road with a heavy bag in her hand, feeling exhausted. The goddess would be following her wherever she went, and they would always end up on the same road. Some of the women fell, unable to dispose of the bag, while for others the bag would split open to reveal a monster child, a reptile or excrement.

The sexual type of dream revealed a fear of childbirth. It concerned the anxiety of birthing in public, resulting in the exposure of genitalia, and the shame associated with this. Women dreamt of being surrounded by public during labour and of their inability to control the situation.

I remained disappointed with both ritual and medical diagnoses of these dreams (mental illness or affliction), since both these types of diagnosis mutually validated each other within patriarchal systems that produced women as faulty pieces, wherein practitioners remained working hand in glove with dominant caste clans in eliciting reproductive labour from their owned women. The dreamers were neither afflicted nor mentally ill and neither did the majority feel 'healed' by the intervention of either doctors or healers, since the dreams continued even as sons were born to women. Most of these dreams described women having the 'wrong' kind of unwanted children or products that were not acceptable to their families and that made the goddess denounce their bodies as shamed and impure, even as they tried to hide these monster children that they could not even view as valid enough to be babies, only to be discovered as malefactors. Neither could the mothers protect or love these children, even as they could not 'own' the acceptable sons desired by their clans that they gave birth to, as their own body-extensions. And they continued to dream despite having had sons.

These were dreams about reproductive labour that were existential and systemic to women's lives. To diagnose the trauma of female colonisation within patriarchy as 'affliction' or illness in the first place would, in fact, reproduce patriarchy, wherein the recruitment of reproductive labour and the ownership of women within clans and castes as mothers would be naturalised. All those considered resistant and deviant by this naturalised order would be considered afflicted and ill and handed over through clan consensus to healers and doctors (who pretended to sit outside systems but were actually its protagonists, giving out verdicts of affliction and illness) as dysfunctional. Dreamers suffered enormous emotional poverty and existential insecurity, since they were constantly on the verge of loss and abandonment and could never overcome the system that kept them in deprivation as owned, unless they died in order to become goddesses/ancestors themselves.

The whispers about the goddess's ritual (*paach-pauli*) and treatment (*golya* or pills) that constantly pervaded the atmosphere between women merged together to create a conglomerate of both illness and affliction, since both paradigms were equally patriarchal.

Affliction Understood as Feminism

I came to enter this uncomfortable cohort of ill and afflicted women as soon as my own child-loss experience and childlessness became known to village women. Everything I said thereafter was immediately interpreted in the light of my affliction diagnosis. I was entering an unhappy alliance of sorts among women who were either already nearly excommunicated (sent back to their natal families) or desperately performing rituals (they could not take part in auspicious collectives and functions during this time) or facing excommunication due to some personal crisis or fear as a result of which they drew closer to the peripheries of their clan. It was a painful and ambivalent subjectivity, a category that many women hated, since they competed with others as 'better off' when they shared their difficulties. They tried desperately to cling to their clans, even as 'better' women came to fear them for spreading the affliction of childlessness through contagion. Even as this became a source of further pain and fear to them, this competition was spread by them to others who were considered 'worse off', without compunction.

The excommunication, marginality and clan peripherality was extended in my case to my interest in carrying out feminist research (*baikanche hakka* or womcn's rights) that pertained especially to women's reproductive control. According to my village respondents (many of them friends by then), my feminist thoughts (part of my affliction, according to them) disturbed my attitudes to my own marriage and ideas of childbirth (*sansar karne).* It was *kop* (the goddess's anger and affliction) that made me do something as terrible against dharma as to view women as separate from their marital clans, to think of women's individual control over the female part of the body that would result in deviant behaviour such as prostitution and love marriages (*anachar-durachar*) and to think that worshipping goddesses was superstition (*andhashraddha*). To be a feminist was, therefore, according to them a form of immorality, since it signified a woman, who did not want to share control or the right over her body and children with her marital family, her husband or natal family; to be a feminist was to therefore be a woman without relationships and love. I sounded like the goddess's afflicting form standing outside the village periphery to them, since individual control over body was only allowed to the goddess, as she was an ascetic but became afflicting for normal married women, who had to allow clan control over their bodies to be included and protected inside the village. To share body and labour with the marital clan was for my respondents, a way of demonstrating love and care and a way of eliciting love in return. The husband's violence or the goddess's affliction was definitely painful, but it was also, ultimately, a form of guidance (*marga-darshan*). A feminist (as I described it to my respondents) could not be imagined by them as an auspicious married woman (*suhasini*) at all and being a *suhasini* was the most important eligibility criteria for survival within society for them.

Even though many of the childbirth rituals I documented were public, since they involved communal spaces associated with clan and village physical boundaries, most private families sponsoring them wanted to keep me out of their homes, fearing I would infect the new mother and baby, since I was considered inauspicious and afflicted. This balance of public and private was often difficult for both of us to achieve. My resultant data has been somewhat fragmentary, as I sometimes got just 'outside' stories and sometimes only the 'inside'. I got very few 'whole' pictures and even as I got some, there was great individual, regional and caste variation across them, which is part of the limitation of conducting feminist fieldwork within patriarchal settings as women operating within the same culture that encompasses themselves and their research. Instead, I bring more female-centred insights into my study, since not many women hid their life stories and experiences from me or justified themselves, as they almost took for granted that I must already understand the details of reproductive affliction and illness. Neither were the afflicted and stigmatised hidden away in villages from me like the mental hospitals and institutions outside Pune city that were bureaucratically out of reach. These afflicted women did not need to be hidden away, since potential loss hung over each woman as she tried to shield herself from the 'evil eye' through witchcraft preventive rituals. The goddess was part of village hierarchy among my respondents and childless women signified a moral rupture in society that encountered women whose bodies refused to yield to reproductive labour and clan ownership. The afflicted lived as the blamed scapegoats within society and were present in nearly every family as real and potential malefactors. They did not need special asylums to go to; their daily lives held an invisible inertia binding them to their fears of failure as they hung on to the poverty-stricken edges of their families with nowhere else to go, sometimes pulled to the inside when they briefly succeeded and sometimes pushed out again when another female competitor succeeded.

Frustration

In the beginning, sharing these dreams and experiences with my village friends was exciting, since it constituted an apt beginning to a collective fieldwork journey. These dreams did afford me with immense understanding of systemic violence. But what frustrated me over time was exactly the 'other-worldly' quality of these goddess experiences of affliction (whether they took place in dreams or visions/trances). The fact that systemic oppression and its suffering took place and was allowed to occur only within dreams and trances, which were split off from the same systemic oppression within everyday waking hours, debarred women from actively negotiating with injustice in their 'real' and 'waking' relationships. The surreal and other-worldly, associated with the goddess, constructed a division between itself and an imposition of silence created within the periods spent outside dreams and trances. Women did not and could not articulate experiences of systemic oppression outside the other-worldly. They only recounted specific acts of violence that were socially accepted as violent and which were unconnected with either their dreams or any idea of what systemic oppression could constitute. They recounted dreams in isolation of these acts of daily violence and failed to link them. Systemic oppression remained inarticulate, expressing itself only in dreams and afflicting trances that expressed the suffering of the female body as reproductive labour, separate from all that was tangibly happening to them. It was within the silences about small acts of violence and ownership in waking hours (apart from the recounting of afflicting dreams) that the dualism of women's acceptance of reproductive labour and its suffering within marital clans lay. Dreaming or trance, within this context, became an act of compensation or coping rather than of healing and it perpetuated and strengthened systemic oppression.

I am not trying to point to dreams as an analytical category in terms of a psychological framework that detects mental illness. I am instead attempting to point out the very prevalence of compensatory spaces that lie culturally embedded at the core of traditional cults that researchers mistake and eulogize as alternative forms of agency, while making a sociological analysis of tradition as celebratory. These compensatory spaces are themselves a deployment of conservatism that create the philosophy of the latter as inclusive and romantic, when actually producing domination, exploitation, labour extraction and subjugation as an expression of validity, love and dharma. It is the very valour and discourse of belonging generated by these ritual performances in public that serve to emphasize the ownership of persons that remould and silence the experiences/expressions of those allowed to suffer violence when protection is removed, the moment ownership and colonization is abdicated. Thus ritual cannot 'heal' without perpetuating the oppression that it creates spaces for, while mitigating and resolving conflicts in duties and the social indoctrination of persons into labour. Many women I worked with lacked a grief-related language for speaking about child loss, child death and childlessness, apart from mainstream expressions of dharma, fear, repulsion, guilt and contempt presented to them by rituals, even as they recounted dreams and mystical experiences to those they considered as afflicted insiders.

Women often had very little help from outsiders or people they could reach out to with their difficulties. While healers, doctors and neighbours were often aware of their crisis, they remained wary of being accused of interference in 'other people's private matters', even though this did not deter them from intervening at other times. Clans often became moribund arenas of oppression for vulnerable women: newly-wed women shouldering new marital relationships, new villages, domestic labour, hitherto unknown sexual roles and sudden and seemingly unending reproductive duties. Ritual and medical practitioners hardly ever went against dominant caste clans as a policy, and both treated battered and oppressed women as either afflicted or ill and therefore responsible for their own condition—as defective pieces, without holding the clan responsible, as far as possible. Very often women were sent back to natal families as a last resort, where the husband would later be invited to 'negotiate'. The accepted language of marital violence, while speaking to women, always surrounded battery, alcoholism, poverty, dowry harassment, ill treatment by marital clans, and the husband's impotence, while the production of women's bodies into units of domestic, sexual and reproductive labour remained inarticulate. Non-consensual sex, lack of control over reproduction and domestic labour were viewed as part of marriage and were never negotiated with, just as impotent husbands were hardly ever accepted lovingly for their other redeemable qualities, since the fear of women being socially blamed for not having performed reproductive labour remained the greater fear.

Neither were women who dreamed or went into trances automatically 'spiritual', with access to the sublime. Vieda Skultans (1987, 1991) demonstrates the way in which women in the Mahanubhav temples of Maharashtra undertook afflictions from their family members as a form of labour to compensate for their low familial status and gain esteem through ritual function and duty. Many women in this 'preventive borderland' zone of taking on healing for their family or community often become mediums (*zhad*) of their clan goddesses, a feature they usually inherited from other senior women in their family instead of child-loss afflictions from the Satvai (many women inherit healing traditions from purer clan goddesses in order to mitigate childlessness afflictions as a ritual mechanism—and this replacement usually takes place to keep further affliction relapses at bay). Goddess possession among them, therefore, becomes a mark of purity as they become traditional mediums and take over the labour of healing, precisely because these replace the possibility of future affliction, securing for their clans and themselves a relative position of security that stands in good stead for them if their smaller clan unit falls into penury. These women can then always perform ritual labour of healing for their larger clan, riding piggyback on the former and providing them with ritual labour in times of financial crisis in return for economic support.

Clarifications

Writing this book would remain incomplete without a few clarifications. One of my past mentors[7] has already pointed to discrepancies between the aims of ritual performers and what I, as a researcher, may want to interpret in a ritual.

[7] Sax (2010) writing about ritual efficacy.

I must point out here that although I myself shared ritual diagnosis and shared both disbeliefs and beliefs in the goddess, being located within my field area; I drew my own conclusions about Satvai rituals just as every woman or informant privately and collectively did, sharing what he or she 'really' felt about my research only in safe forums or trustful exchanges. These too changed over the time that I was in field, based on their changing personal relationship with me. Everyone I spoke to had changing public and private views and opinions about the implications of cults such as the Satvai's in terms of gender, caste, poverty, space, and ownership and how all of this was politicised through rationalism, health policy, nationalism (history and culture being deployed) and its meaning for clan reinterpretation that was useful for controlling women, childbirth and marriage (in its existent form). The expression of their opinions and its emphasis and endorsement always varied in terms of their 'political stakes' entrenched within a certain view important for their village life, just as mine does for my analysis. There were many layers to it.

Even as I discussed my research concerns with my respondents (such as the link between goddess rituals and local politics) and continued to explore women's various ritual aims (laying down something intangible and intense that I called motherhood along with their babies at boundary shrines) that could be different than my research agenda, I came to realise that this proposed dualism between their aims and my interpretation of it would remain eternal without conversation and opportunities for personal re-discovery and transformation of both their aims and my research.

My respondents expected me to be 'different' in my research, while they also expected me to be the 'same' because of my childlessness and it was difficult for me to separate how different or same I really was, apart from what they felt about me, because I was transformed by them. The other way round was true as well: they were what I had expected all along in terms of their rituals and beliefs in the Satvai and Maulya, since that was why I had chosen them for my study after all. But they were also very different as women than what I had expected them to be; since not only had my research transformed them but I had begun dreaming about the Satvai too. This interaction between South Asian/South Asianist—feminists, would have to remain entangled and messy because these described political, personal, sometimes painful and somewhat poetic relationships along with being academic ones, where expectations were always transformative. I realised that unless I stopped making dualistic differences between their interpretations and mine, both our beliefs would calcify, without our thoughts giving each other the opportunity to transform ourselves and I would end up perpetuating a colonial form of writing a one-sided narrative about 'them' that none of them would ever be able to recognize, even if someone translated parts of my book into Marathi. I would simply have to let go and make my research endeavour a relationship.

The second clarification is about the two kinds of motherhoods I am discussing: one is obviously that of an attachment kind, laid down and ritually given up at boundaries by women and the other that is taken up and assumed as a valorous role/labour/duty, that construct women as socially successful among a group of other clan champions, deserving of status. It was the latter avatar, emerging out of the laying down of the former that allows clans to own children as clan inheritors and women as progenitors of inheritors. This first 'motherhood' given to the goddess by new mothers at village boundaries did not represent the subjugation of a powerless, naïve and natural motherhood either. It was this motherhood that the goddess consumed and absorbed through ritual food and items dedicated by women, that made them the 'real' protectors of village children. The goddesses imbued with this biological motherhood of women had to be nevertheless distanced from babies and kept outside village boundaries, lest they too turned cannibal in their attachment of babies. And they did!

Satvai afflictions predictably conjure up reportings of the goddess cannibalizing the infant. The appeased and distanced Satvai of the village on the other hand became the powerful and omnipresent, albeit far-removed, benefactress of all legitimate clan children associated with the village thereafter. In this way, each woman's motherhood constitutes the Satvai's motherhood and the Satvai rituals constitute women's motherhood status in order to distance the malevolence of biological attachment from the baby. The distancing of the mother and her attachment from the baby is considered to give it life and social existence. Pure mothers become valorous labourers with a split off sexuality and attachment that is dedicated to the goddess, even as the malevolent goddess absorbs this sexuality and motherhood at these boundary shrines, growing appeased, distanced and retreating to protect the baby from the cannibalism this attachment causes. Any disturbance in the hygiene between the separation of sexuality/ attachment and fertility among women is understood to result in affliction sent by the goddess; a result of a mother's contamination and too much attachment for the baby.

The final clarification is about using what are accepted nomenclatures about 'upper', 'lower', 'dominant' castes, the word 'community' and their names, etc., in this text, which unless disclaimed as not being so, have a certain genesis and political history of development that have served to subjugate large sections of society. The use of these should not be read as validations of condemnations, biases, socio-political constructs and as a support for systemic and structural hierarchy by those privileged like me, who have enjoyed writing this text. The use of these terms is not an unquestioning act of casteism or discrimination, as if I have shared in the condemning experience of what I write. It is these shared experiences that have in fact motivated me to write this book.

CHAPTER 1

Locating Method and Fieldwork

When interpersonal relationships in fieldwork become fraught and complex, they are best left pliant for channels of communication to remain open in order to make space for empathy and mutual transformation. I took feminist ideology and politics about women's right to their own reproductive and sexual body into my fieldwork and this became part of my relationship with my respondents, influencing and increasing my sensitisation to how issues of childlessness 'motherhood-loss' could become transposed to concerns of women's individual control over their interpersonal relationships within marriage. My relationships with my respondents also served to illuminate the ethics of carrying feminist ideology into fieldwork, since I could not 'other' the village women as 'respondents', being childless myself and sharing their condition. My concern of associating reproduction with women's individual control over their own bodies and relationships drew different responses of great depth from them, even as many disagreed with my views and tried to 'convert' me to their own, as ways of balancing power between my research and our interpersonal relationships (I even came to perform Satvai healing rituals at their behest).

As already mentioned in the prologue, my feminism and childlessness was mutually interlinked by them and became mutually counterbalanced as I came to be socially understood in my field area as afflicted. This, while acting as a form of transparency between us, as it allowed many women to confide about painful experiences that had increased their own burdens, also exerted pressure on me to become part of their hierarchy by subverting the power that my 'doing research' on their life posed.

My feminist concerns opened a confidential window between my respondents and me that enabled reflection on issues in their life that they in turn, considered feminist, such as: unfulfilled desires surrounding educational and professional aspirations; the desire for a nuclear family and personal relationship with their husbands, the desire to live separately from the joint family; the desire for personal toilets, especially during menstruation; the desire for expensive sanitary towels rather than using home-made materials that had to be repeatedly washed and dried in secret; the desire to wear nightgowns and other clothes apart from the sari at night; the desire to be free from domestic abuse and alcoholism perpetuated by male family members; the desire for paid domestic help, especially during pregnancy; the desire for hospitalisation in special clinics (that gave pain-relief injections during labour and performed 'cesur' or caesarean) during childbirth; the desire for riches and jewellery and kitchen implements; the desire to be able to go out with their husbands to the marketplace in order to publicly demonstrate their marital intimacy and lastly, a desire for more celebratory functions organised at home that would provide them with social status in the neighbourhood. They wanted me to understand their desires even as they felt angry with and jealous of me for having had access to all these things and yet not appreciating this freedom and for having become a 'pheminishta' despite of it.

As I moved to Ghodegaon village, the equalisation that they sought to make in order to survive my research and me, (the personification of the quaint and ungrateful), was brought about by identifying me as 'afflicted'. Each conversation about their desires and complaints about 'a woman's life' (which they wanted me, as a feminist, to understand) ended predictably with their declaration of my marital relationship as complicated (which allowed me to live alone in a village without husband or other marital relatives, without a job, with my own money, for an obscure research project on childbirth—instead of having my own children—to fulfil a 'selfish' ambition of a PhD). My childlessness declared as my own fault was accompanied by sympathetic curiosity about my then husband, who was considered very kind hearted for having tolerated me. Some even demanded to see my marriage photographs to ascertain the validity of my 'married' status and associated claims.

Remaining constantly in empathetic[1] 'engagement' with my respondents did result in burnout and 'transference' and counter-transference (to use psychological parlance), as I often escaped to Pune for reprieve. However, I tried to view my research engagement, even in the most difficult of moments, as an effort to create self-reflexivity in my writing about power equalisations between me and my respondents. Even though it became difficult to separate strands between what my respondents thought of my research or political concerns and what I thought about the Satvai and motherhood and their views about the goddesses and rituals at various points, the differences in our views and resulting tension did prevent my research method from becoming unidirectional as it transformed me and my 'respondents' both in terms of our politics and friendships.

It was a painful and challenging process for my respondents to have their life and beliefs researched and critiqued by me. That I could do this at all was due to the difference in our social background and the similarity in what childlessness meant for all women across the board, irrespective of social strata, that simultaneously allowed them to diagnose me as afflicted to counterbalance those power differences lying outside the reproductive sector. They questioned my private life decisions and my personal qualification for engaging in research on childbirth and childlessness almost continuously on the basis of my afflicted status, since they had to accept, on the other hand, that I was urban, had cash (rather than grain), was a Brahmin (upper caste) and had greater access to forms of education and power associated with social mobility that they lacked.

My fieldwork relationships became fluid and often conflicted, as village women and I shared mutual anger, affection, suspicion,

[1] I have elaborated on feminist research methods as empathetic engagements elsewhere (Dandekar 2014b).

trust, resistance, and compliance simultaneously. We were not 'others' to each other and yet often angry with each other, as we came to view mutual disparities between us as unfair, often discussing the real and moral reasons for this at length. My respondent's participated in my research quite actively than simply sharing information with me, as a lively negotiation with patriarchal mine fields in the village ensued between us.

The Goddess's Pain

Questions about the goddess's pain arose when one of my few male informants arranged a secret meeting for me with another special informant (a visitor to the village) towards the end of my fieldwork. This special informant was supposed to be of great importance, especially since he always visited only briefly (like giving darshan). According to my informant, who introduced me to this special informant, my 'work' would remain incomplete without this important interview that explored the goddess's pain (*daivivedana*). He thought it would redefine my research focus, hitherto wasted on women and their child-loss experiences.

The special informant spoke to me for a very short time in a dimly lit room, saying that he had agreed to such an interview only at my informant's request and that his information was of a classified nature. During our conversation, he mostly remained focused on his mobile phone, refusing to make too much eye contact or disclose his identity. He did not want to be photographed or taped since he claimed his work was divine and secret; he said he did not want his identity to be either misused or exploited by political enemies.

He began by telling me of the goddess's pain and how much she suffered when she killed demons (like women killing reptiles in their dreams, I thought), since they were, after all, also living beings and a part of divine creation, but who had grown demonic. He continued to speak in metaphors about how the goddess shared this pain with her special 'emissaries'. He finally exposed the nature of his own 'career' to me, disclosing that he was one such 'emissary' (*doot*) of the goddess. He said he had been in the goddess's 'army' in two battles (I am reading these as riots here) in a row (he called these *varya* or ritual journeys) and had accepted the goddess's choice in making him one of her fighting arms as part of his life's mission on the basis of dreams he had received from her to take up arms (*shastra*). He said that he also went into a trance several times, while holding sacred battle implements belonging to goddess idols that confirmed his dreams to be a 'call' and this (trance with battle implements) had been a tradition since the time of Emperor Shivaji (I am not sure where or whether these skirmishes or battles or riots took place; he, however, seemed to be known and respected for his status, according to my informant). In the interview, he concentrated on how this secret service rendered to the goddess, had made him grow in his spiritual understanding of not just her power, but also her compassion and pain. It was an experience, according to him, that he had increasingly come to share with his other comrades, although not all of them were as evolved as he was. He, like them, shared the goddess's pain that was born out of the violence necessitated by performing her duty which was simultaneously connected with deep compassion. He said that this violent duty made him perform umpteen acts of compassion and healing as well, which he did with as much sincerity as a doctor performing surgery. According to him, healing entailed violence, since demonic forces causing evil possessions had to be killed and eliminated through an act of force. These acts, both of violence and of compassion, saved dharma from demonic influences. He spoke euphemistically of demonic influences primarily concerned with 'evil', that could also be read as outsiders (*baherche*), whom he likened to bacteria (*jantu-jivanu*) that had to be killed using medicine if the body were to survive an epidemic.[2] He said he could no longer consume meat because it was a part of goddess *nivad* (ritual offering: *naivedya*) and sacrifice when she came to defend and purify society.

He also claimed to be interested in more people like himself and wanted to conduct his own independent research about them

[2] The paradigm of village goddess cults and epidemics can be co-opted easily within the framework of violent nationalism.

and not concentrate on the demonic, who posed as victims of the goddess's violence. He said that researching victims' experiences (like I was doing) was a way of subverting the goddess and creating martyrs out of the demonic. Experiencing the goddess's pain, according to him, could make people devout and spiritual social workers rather than corrupt politicians. In the end, he said that he had also suffered the goddess's pain. He said he remained ill for months after each violent 'encounter' (*samhaar*), with mysterious illnesses full of headaches, fever, nervousness, mood swings, nightmares and trances. No doctor had been able to treat him of the goddess's pain.

After this interview (that numbed me), my informant (who had introduced me) clarified some of these standpoints and the irrelevance with regard to my research on childlessness and immorality as we debriefed. He explained how the benevolent goddess was forced to take on a malevolent form (*ugraroop*) because of an increase in corruption and immorality among women in society today. This, according to him, was due to the targeting of good women by bad and corrupt women, which then served to turn the former away from the path of righteousness. Therefore, the goddess had to swoop down with afflictions on good women to show them the righteous and moral path and correct them, and people like the special informant were created as the arm of the goddess to destroy bad women for whom no chances of redemption ever existed in any case.

So goddesses and their armies worked in dual ways to simultaneously eliminate bad women and correct women in order to finally destroy sin and evil in society. Good women were, therefore, only misled by bad women and they weren't really bad or corrupted at their core, whereas bad women, who, posing as their sympathetic allies and sisters, inveigled their way into the former's trust, like the demoness Putana, only to harm them. Only a god like Lord Krishna, or his avatar, like Emperor Shivaji, or someone like the special informant, could kill such demonesses. The good women themselves were too simple to kill Putana on their own, precisely because they were good women. This special informant was not dedicated to the goddess like a healer. I asked my informant after this interview, if the former was ritually dedicated. My informant reiterated indignantly that he was like the goddess's general, a small king! A Kshatriya! Not a Matang!

The goddess's affliction sent to village women was, therefore, still an act of benevolence reserved for good women, since it proved that they still had a possibility of healing and being socially re-assimilated, the affliction acting only as a stigmatising mark of their deviance that they should be careful to veer away from relapsing into in the future. For the bad women facing divine punishment or the special informant, on the other hand, only the unspeakable and annihilation lay in store. Furthermore, my informant felt regretful that the administration (Maharashtra *shasan*) supported many bad women and others who protected them, before making proper enquiries into their real intentions. This only obstructed the path of religious and morally purifying activities, such as what the special informant carried out, which put the latter in fear of getting arrested, even in the face of traditions laid out by in Maharashtra by Emperor Shivaji in the past, which constituted the real law of the land. Many bad women like the demoness Putana got a free reign and protection nowadays from the government, surprising the innocent Yashodhas of society, while the protecting Lord Krishnas were blamed as criminals. He lamented on the nature of *Kali-yuga* (the fourth cosmological phase of time that appears at the end of a cyclical chain of the Hindu concept of never-ending time that starts with the Krita-yuga and is followed by the Treta-yuga, the Dwapar-yuga and finally the Kali-yuga) and exhorted women to be more careful about whom they befriended first, before complaining of affliction and violence. Still, he felt confident that the goddess was there!

For my informant, maintaining morality was not just the responsibility of women but also that of men. If women were moral, men would find no one to distract them or to engage in immorality with. It was primarily bad women with state protection, who tempted both good men and good women into immoral behaviour. It was within this context that he located increased incidences of sexual violence against women within society. According to him, if bad women stopped tempting men, sexual violence against them would automatically reduce. If women were married off at a young age, as was done in earlier times, both affliction from the goddess and violence against them would automatically reduce. He felt that the violence against women that newspapers were constantly writing about was actually deeply associated with the goddess's pain and was metaphorical (*pratik*) for the way in which society was losing control over women (who were turning bad and losing their moral balance or *tar-tamya*) and their moral goodness. He felt that the village goddess afflictions that I was vehemently opposing actually helped clans regain morality.

According to him, the Satvai automatically helped to abort children of immoral women. As a corollary to the same logic, all children of immoral women would always be aborted as a result of affliction, thereby recasting each woman suffering childloss (through ritual diagnosis) as immoral. Speaking further of female infanticide, he said that it was one of the most cruel methods of re-establishing dharma. Society had rediscovered a way of controlling rising immorality and corruption among women, with no other alternatives left to reform women but to limit their numbers. Regretting female infanticide, he said it was the only way for poorer clans to have sons as a way of maintaining morality, correct forms of inheritance and purity in their clans (so that their property could be protected from the negative intensions of bad women, who would inveigle and fool good women). Therefore, female infanticide could be viewed as a kind of family planning.

These interviews glorified a kind of 'khap' alterity in the villages where I worked with a shade of victimhood that sought to decriminalise patriarchal violence, while imbuing the goddess cult with it, which simultaneously constructed this patriarchal violence as moral, righteous, eternal or timeless, ahistorical and all pervasive. The goddess came to be used as an empty signifier[3]

[3] Laclau (2005) uses the concept of empty signifier to demonstrate the ways in which political demands within a populist state unify and consolidate themselves under a banner that acts as a public mask for it. This banner may have no independent virtue or may shift to suit the populist demand, often being associated with nationalistic concepts of tradition and history in a bid towards justifying the demand.

for a fierce and populist militant Hindutva that sought to split female sexuality from reproduction and bad women from good women, while legitimising both the destruction of female sexuality and the production of marginalised motherhood. Though riots are considered an urban expression (other respondents said that there had been no riots in my field area), goddess shrines in Maharashtra were best expressed as rural 'roots' in my field area, lending both these expressions (riots and shrine worship) associated with goddesses internal continuity. Urban clashes and rural shrine strongholds become contiguous extensions of each other, lending each other force, as those in the 'special service' of the goddess, functioning in urban areas 'touched base' with their clan shrines in villages in order to perform special rituals or *abhisheka* in order to gain ritual and moral power from their rural roots. The existence of strong linkages between rural and urban militant mobs was garbed, moreover, by the constructed value of a rural-urban divide that was more part of vote bank politics than an actual denial of fluidity between agrarian and industrial sectors.

It is now paradoxically the deconstruction of such a rural-urban divide accepting poverty-related migration to urban slums as a public health issue that finds reflection in ways of teaching the urban and rural poor models of 'behaviour change communication' when defining them as either superstitious or traditional and alternatively as data collection havens. The economic and ritual nexus between upper or middle class and upper or middle caste urban families and rural landed elites, remains on the other hand obscured and masked. Many moneyed, upper-caste families continue to share a vibrant relationship with their rural counterparts that is based on land ownership and clan rituals and deities and this relationship is often camouflaged by an essentialisation that describes rural as 'traditional' and slum-based urban cultures as an extension of this rural as laboratory conditions in transcultural relational shifts that obscures the nexus between richer clans and their cults. The narrative of eradicating superstition among the poor fluctuating with the narrative of celebrating rural traditions as alternative knowledge, emphasises a nationalist politics of rural vote lobbies for extremely rich agriculturalists that extends itself into urban clan and caste groups.

Connerton (1989) reminds us of how tradition may be used to negotiate identity within political frameworks. In applying his theory we come to understand how modernising departures of communal violence are co-opted into grand narratives and constructions of the past. This intensely contemporary and political adherence to the past views tradition as healing, pure, good, and restorative in order to serve a populist agenda. A distinction needs to be made between the various social groups that view this performed tradition differently, since it has diverse political implications for each one of them. The constructed suffering of an ambivalent and 'eternal' goddess in my field area replaces the actual suffering of real women, becoming the epicentre of a battle about motherhood, wherein patriarchal systems refuse to engage with the bodies and emotions of women, even while gaining complete and manipulative control over their destruction.

Sax (2000: 263) asks his readers to tread carefully while analysing the violence of goddess cults as displacing mechanisms that mask the violence of men. In my field area, however, one does encounter the way in which goddess cults actually mask patriarchal violence in the garb of traditional rituals. The goddess cult exhorts both women and men to become protectors of marriage and motherhood; to purge themselves of their own sexuality from within, even taking the risk of annihilating corrupting forces from without. While the Satvai may represent the spectre of corrupt sexuality from within, with her shrine outside the village boundary, it is the demon or sacrificed beast, and through it the lower-caste body, who represents the spectre of corrupt sexuality from without, who also (by virtue of caste) undertakes healing duties for upper-caste women. 'Communal' and caste battles, [4] extolled by stories of the Devi Mahatmya, are repeated in order to ask society, constitutive of both men and women, to purge the evil of female sexuality from within and without, since it is predictably

[4] Butalia (1998) describes the manner in which communal differences become racialised first in order to legitimise sexual violence.

only within the inter-communal and inter-caste sense of sexual interaction that male advance is reinterpreted as both demonic and constitutive of sexually transgressive (unlike Lord Krishna). It is only because the demonic in this case is identified as lower caste and equalled to animal that the goddess, as a good woman, upholding upper-caste marriage, gains victory over him. My respondents never imagined, for example, that they could complain about marital rape in same-caste relationships. However, till today, marital rape does not count as a cognisable offense within Indian courts. Neither did any of them construct the romantic interest shown by men within the same caste and class as molestation; this was romance for them. In answer to my questions about why the goddess killed a man who wanted to marry her, they made clear that first, the *mahisha* was a demon and second, she was already married to Lord Shankara. When I pointed to how Radha was married too, they always answered with how Lord Krishna was divinely playful (Lila) and how he was a God.

Coming to a closure on this section on issues of rural-urban interaction based on the question of healing, there are entire academic strains of thought (Marriott 1990) that have associated the idea of rural homes, ancestral land and native village as embodied aspects of identity in modern India, that produce individuality as shared, dependent and 'dividual' (in contrast to individual). Traditional concepts of travelling to native 'homes' and the natal village (that may be close to traditional healing centres) have further gained importance (in the light of individuality theories) in academic debates about healing (Nichter 2001).[5]

In my field area, however, goddesses send afflictions to women who forget their village, in order to punish them and remind them of their real roots, sending them a 'call' (*bolavne*) to return to their natal villages, where they are supposed to perform rituals in order to gain relief from afflictions that were sent to them in the first place to admonish them for forgetting their roots. According to my informants, no woman, if she was morally good, may be allowed

[5] Nichter (2001) speaks about the healing properties of 'homecoming' in contrast to biomedical care.

by the goddess to think that she was above other village women, even if she had left them behind (as a result of her circumstances), for the city. If she did this, she was taught a lesson when the goddess sent her an affliction, 'puts a ring through her nose' (*nakat dori*) and pulled her back into the mud from where she came (*shen-mati*), or demonstrated to her, her real status (according to which she is disallowed from 'owning') however plush (*alishan*) her city house may be. According to my informants, the goddess's affliction (and ritual) is an equaliser among her devotees (*sarvanna saarkha karte*).

These articulations were perfect examples of rivalry between women. My respondents in the village, who competed endlessly and mercilessly with each other for 'comforts', feeling angry with each other's ungratefulness for having 'owned' more than the other had access to and hoped that the goddess would take away from those who had more, rather than give to those who had less, since blessing was only constituted by the distancing and removal of punishment or affliction. There was a fear about how women through their ownership of comforts would themselves evade ownership and become free from it. Being roped through their noses was the hope that these women would be owned again by the goddess cults that were emblematic of dominant caste-clan ownership of capital, persons, produce, labour and land on the basis of ancient traditions based on the purity of the owned product that led to its belonging and identity.

However, the emotional category of returning to the native village (and/or shrine) does not take place in the case of many castes that do not traditionally own clan property entitlements or ancestral villages, farms or shrines and associated healing catharsis connected with a return to it. Since such phenomena can be accessed only by those that already enjoyed the legacy of land ownership (demonstrated mostly through presiding goddess allegiances), the matter of catharsis is often extended to urban homesteads as well, where shrines to village clan goddesses are built with equal care in order to fulfil rituals, since urban-rural landed families have enjoyed a lot of internal continuity in Maharashtra as well. In many other cases, especially in the case of poorer and often lower-caste families, wherein migration to industrial areas as labour has taken place four or five generations earlier, the question of returning to native villages (and presiding goddesses), where there had in any case been no property to inherit becomes a fraught contention. Many such families have already lost the memory of their native villages or clan goddesses. Many such families ritually 'undertake' new goddess cults (preferably coinciding with a *jatra*/annual festival of the goddess) once they gain some economic stability (Kalu-*bai*/ Mandhardevi is popular among lower-caste families of the western Maharashtra region, for example), which allows their clan to strategically negotiate with their peers of the same caste or other similar castes for activities such as intermarriage. Their 'return' meetings of reunion during subsequent goddess's *jatra*, either at her *tirtha-kshetra* or during her clan rituals, have little to do with returning to ancestral villages for healing, since the adopted cult does not concern the village at all (the many thousands of people assembling at the *jatra* of Kalu-*bai*, for example, hardly belong to Mandhargaav, which is the village her cult formally presides over). These reunions concern the formation of clans, problem-resolution of conflicts within clans, the generation of new conflicts at many instances, and celebrations that mark auspicious occasions such as childbirths, marriages and inheritance.

Although Nichter's (2001) observations may be ethnographically noteworthy when researching certain specific regions, organised differently, they do not apply to the landless, such as large populations of women or lower-caste sections of society in Maharashtra, who do not traditionally own village interior land and are notionally demarcated as village labour by goddess cults. The social location of the poorer, the female and lower-caste sections of society are therefore more associated with mutual bonding and internal competition that is concerned with the consumption and distribution of ownership and resource entitlements, even as members often harbour a burning rage, expressed in outbursts, for differential treatment than the rest of the 'group' that becomes the subject for conflict during reunions. Ritual practices that consolidate the return to the village are more of a venture among upper or dominant caste families that have moved away to urban areas in the past but seek through ritual means to re-establish contact with land and resource ownership in the native village for political and financial purposes, even if they have built the shrine of the village deity in their city home already.

As far as the shared nature of 'dividuality' is concerned, the theory is very pertinent to rural Maharashtra, even though it does not address the concerns of interpersonal rivalry embedded therein, in addition to the personal labour commitment that is morally upheld by the goddess cult within rituals that every woman individually fulfils. Every woman, even if surrounded by jealousy or rivalry and the goddess's punishment, that forces her to stay within the group of *suhasini*, undertakes the commitment of becoming an owned and pure object for her marital clan or of commencing with reproductive-based labour. Every mother is individually produced and has an individual journey of negotiation with the formation of dividual groups through goddess rituals, even as sexuality is sought to be separated from fertility, attachment to children is sought to be separated from motherhood and regions inside the village and outside its boundary are separated to designate pure and impure castes. She assumes this individual journey in all her decisions, interactions, relationships and her circumspect body that remains conscious, even when sleeping. Her entrance into 'dividual' networks is individual and there are conflicts and communication on this journey of the self that are often heralded by marriage and motherhood.

Equalising Research

My research was often challenged on grounds of it being 'unscientific' or 'biographical'. These critiques were based on the similarities between my personal trajectory and that of 'afflicted' women or the idea that I had decided to undertake the research as a result of personal experiences. This revealed deep fractures of distrust about feminist research and feminist empathy, by turning the deeply resonant feminist slogan of the late 1960s, 'the personal is political', on its head to suggest how in this use it was actually the opposite. Such critiques valorised subject-object divides, placing the highest premium on making divisions and classifications that are popular in the natural sciences, wherein the distance between the researcher and the researched would ideally be of the greatest value. By implication, all politically motivated research, wherein researchers were experientially situated within action-oriented explorations (with a rights-based agenda), and where data could be used as political intervention, would then fall into the trap of being reinterpreted as inauthentic and opinionated. Finally, suppressing the researcher's voice that intermingled data with experience in an arena that valorised research based on 'othering' experience, became an effort at eliminating 'over-representation' of the same subject under research that produced competition between those representing it, based on how much these 'representatives' could access and experience their subjects, which in this case was considered to constitute their power. All research method with the uncontrollable other, assumed to be 'true' only when distance between subject and object is the greatest, devolve into fieldwork handbooks that emphasize on managing difference and extracting data optimally, where personal transformation and empathy can be minimized and the rational and necessarily outsider researcher can be safely extracted from outsider-insider conundrums.

But just as research and researchers, who could not access experience, eliminated competition within an academia that had to therefore extoll subject-object divides, there was also an equally strong experiential world that could not access research and activism and therefore sought to eliminate its danger. My village friends lamented the absence of dharma and the onset of Westernisation in women like me that had led me away from my path. And though I found it strange, many of my academic colleagues 'understood' the point of view of my village friends when I recounted my field work experiences to them, since they had already come to assume the presence of subject-object divides within research. The two halves fitted perfectly as I often discovered internal continuity between the parochialism of worlds that were more concentrated on eliminating dangerous competition than being interested in sharing and transformation, even while professing it.

Splitting a study from its experience and scholarship led to the production of its subject as a masculinist and positivist arena; this because the society surrounding the study would grow to be positivist and mutually associate and collaborate to form knowledge that would be deemed higher than researchers bringing in feminized experiences. Feminized knowledge would be seen to be lower and created as 'exotic' in the conceptual imaginaire of a caste system of wisdom both within fieldwork and academics. Gender discrimination within academia and fieldwork would then become as subtle as research methods, accessible field networks and researchers, who would adopt patriarchal empiricism and natural science approaches, even while researching gender as a topic.

Never has this difference between intellectual discourse and experiential research been as explicitly and aptly flagged off than in Uma Chakravarti's (2006) description of the anti-Mandal agitation in Delhi University. She describes how upper-caste intellectual academicians with caste prerogatives towards empirical knowledge production mourned the demise of merit due to proposed caste reservations in university jobs. Since lower-caste sections of society were traditionally denied access to empirical knowledge making, the anger towards the bill (among the upper castes) was directed at the introduction of Dalit and other lower caste experiences of marginalization, and their bodies that had borne the brunt of traditional discrimination into academia as non-knowledge.

During my research interactions, I have found a kind of awe emanating from some intellectuals such as social workers, school teachers, and medical practitioners (especially working in Adivasi areas) about traditional practices of the body located within social contexts that were poverty-based and lacked access to medical services due to systemic elimination from meaningful and sustainable benefits. The body practices of marginalized groups were identified and imagined as valorised arenas of traditional and pre-medical practice that as yet had potential to serve the poor. The poor and the underprivileged were therefore first being created as 'exotic' with autochthonous and pristine knowledge and then later created as deemed unfit for modernity, with the state being too cruel for their 'lost' world. The problematic of this view remained centred on how the faulty modern state and medical systems were almost treated as 'givens' (as if these social workers and teachers were themselves not a product of modernity). Indeed they were seen as a justification for supporting poverty-based systems that were labelled valourous, cultural, aboriginal and autochthons, without any insight about the colonial and orientalist bent of this approach. Accordingly, the Adivasi became eternally pronounced the victim, elementally unfit for modernity, while the state became the eternal oppressor and the school teacher/social worker the eternal hero; this was a soft nationalist model that was best represented by the initial congress party kind of politics in post-colonial India.

By doing this, both modern medical systems and traditional systems were moreover produced as static and socially non-invested in transformation. Maybe it is noteworthy that conserving this stativity itself remains a powerful researcher's goal, when opposing all social movements towards equality and human rights, since the latter is conveniently constructed as 'development' (as a result of foreign/western conspiracy or a leftist ploy or then a new-liberal right wing development). At the basis of it lies a refusal to engage with how social movements, with their history of civil liberties and reform in India, still struggle to create multiple choices for women in distress.

What the mourning of absent merit in Indian universities—the elimination of experience-based research in the high echelons of university life in the West or the support of alternative medicine for the poor and the downtrodden in India—actually mask are upper-caste or racist fears of being forced to interact with the underprivileged body of experience at an equal footing that deconstructs masculine institutional knowledge, superiority and its associated and competing entitlements. It represents the disguised fear of different kinds of research and knowledge being allowed political access to counter-influence the hegemony of intellectual discourses that valorise positivism, dualism, subject-object separations and the naturalisation of the state and its various hegemonic practices that seek to simultaneously institutionalise gender roles, caste superiority and poverty through convenient and transient separations and merges between what are sometimes medical and sometimes ritual treatments as forms of the politically 'given'. Moreover, academic casteism, where the experiential knowledge of gender, caste and poverty would be consistently erased from knowledge production, constitutes a form of violence that even masquerades as a critique of colonialism itself (since equality as a value was introduced within the Indian constitution as a result of Westernization), as it contradicts with Jyotiba Phule's definition of the 'Tritiya Ratna', wherein the writing of one's own despair mixed with the collective experience of oppression becomes knowledge.[6] I struggled for power equalisation within the research and academic world of the university, where I felt baffled to find a foothold as a South Asian/South Asianist, a female-feminist and a childless woman working on childloss, claiming epistemic validation based on personal experience along with my academic writing, which made my research amidst conflicts, oppositions and confusions often very circular.

Power equalisations of research within fieldwork were an extremely dynamic part of research as well. As already mentioned, village women demanded to look at my wedding photographs as proof in order to decide whether they would grant me entry into their personal lives as someone 'normal'. Many of my village friends could not empathise with a research question and researcher who simultaneously shared and questioned the collective experience of childloss and goddesses. Even if my ultimate goal was research, the fact that I, as a Marathi married woman, had not accepted my personal situation as afflicted and wasn't trying to have a baby but was trying to write on childlessness and the goddess instead, travelling to potentially dangerous shrines with cameras but at the same time having dreams like them and living an ambivalent life. It put many of them in a situation of internal conflict and confusion, while understanding their own biography and recounting their personal marital relationships to me. For many of them, supporting my research

[6] Chakravarti (1998) describes the social reformism spearheaded by Phule in her book, *Rewriting History*.

meant allying with my feminism, problematising the opinions their clans held about them (i.e. an absence of dharma), allowing alternative emotions portending social danger and possibilities of further affliction by associating with someone already considered afflicted. Many of them feared facing clan violence due to their open support for me, which was implicit in the very articulation of my politics, research and the visibility of my non-normative choices. Their public withholding of support, often resulted in the development of a somewhat clandestine relationship between us in which they simultaneously confided, argued, resisted and remained ambivalent about my feminist politics and my analysis of the goddesses they worshipped.

This complex relationship became a process of equalisation between my respondents and me. They resisted the research deeply, subjecting me to stiff discrimination on the basis of my childlessness, attempting to counterbalance my research, which alienated them from their experiences of child survival, by interpreting it as a result of a personal and biographical failure of the same on my behalf. Our friendship grew only gradually and was vulnerable to mechanisms of return interpretation through reversals and responses made within unequal power dynamics. I became part of their relationships with other women outside the paradigm of clan, and though this was dangerous, it was also interesting for them as their curiosity was concentrated on a vicarious and often a voyeuristic inquisition of my choices. This process took collective ownership of my research by altering its contextual hinge, changing it from research about childlessness to research about mothers and fertile female communities that combined sexuality, reproduction and its social approval. I could enter this group only through the performance of healing rituals of the goddess myself, even though all those accompanying me already knew of my lack of interest in having children. The ritual was my threshold to becoming included in their group as a marginal member, as it did for many, which I came to realise only after I entered such a group!

It was finally a process that required that I renounce my research agenda in order to accord increasing primacy to women's groups and motherhood by participating in 'real-time' concerns such as performing my desire to be a mother that would gain me social inclusion. It was through these groups that I came to understand how each 'fertile' woman, celebrating child survival within these mother-wife communities, lived under the eternal fear of childloss, reproductive failure and childlessness (as she desperately tried to avert it ritually) which would have subsequent affliction and medical diagnosis repercussions associated with it if she failed, taking her further down a spiral towards domestic violence and possible marital abandonment. Being part of a fertile community was therefore, hardly temporary or transient for women when they performed life-stage rituals averting child mortality, moving from one life stage to the next as ritual theorists such as Victor Turner (1977) or Arnold van Gennep (1977) suggest. Women were potentially never free from the constant fear of their son's deaths and the stigma of cannibalism this would bring upon them. Mothers faced the sudden abyss of childloss and associated domestic violence and crisis in marital relationships even amidst celebrations of fertility, as the spectre of childlessness always loomed in the background, like the goddess across the boundary who would punish them at the slightest mistake. Childlessness, with the associated ritual diagnosis of witchcraft, was therefore on the same spectrum with child survival and the fertility of auspicious women. This cultural contradiction that projected differences between wives/mothers-cannibals/afflictedwitches then actually served to mask women's lack of control over their own reproductive bodies that kept them within the subjectivity of ritual control and morally positioned them as the reproductive labour force of their clans and castes.

It took me time to understand women's needs to make contradictory life choices, effecting small betrayals, while engaging in relationships of seemingly unnecessary control as mechanisms for rational, strategic and subversive agency, even though they enjoyed power through their participation in patriarchal institutions. My village friends were consumers of patriarchal institutions as part of the internal structures of the village, which were interwoven with localities and neighbourhoods, and many boundaries in-between.[7] They effected the strategic utilisation of patriarchal structures just as equally as they fell victim to it, through their negotiation of it and their need to counterbalance power structures.

Goddesses equalised as well. I was told off at the beginning of my fieldwork by a healer, who was a medium of the Satvai of Koldhawde village, while she was in a trance, possessed by the goddess, about how I could not research 'her' cult as easily and arrogantly at my own will without the goddess's permission. Being a goddess, she was beyond research, since a research stand defied belief while justifying the researcher's childlessness. She told me that she would also test my motives and faith before she allowed me to continue researching and would visit me in a dream or a vision in the next weeks in order to notify me of 'her' results regarding my 'application'. The result never came. I did not receive either permission or forbiddance in any allegedly supernatural form, though I had some uncomfortable nights awaiting the verdict. I came to see my apprehensive waiting, my fear of the medium and my affliction dreams themselves as means of power equalisation.

Deploying Nationalism

Running into nationalist discourses when gathering information on goddesses from sources other than the experiential becomes somewhat of an inevitability, although this is not to be treated as an excuse when one's research agenda becomes co-opted within right-wing politics. My research became co-opted within the search for information on 'local' (*sthanik*) 'Marathi' 'folk' (*lok-*

[7] De Certeau (1984) describes the way in which everyday practices subvert the hegemony of the city, its planning and its architecture, by consuming it in unplanned and contradictory ways. I came to understand this theory in the context of my fieldwork within the larger purview of patriarchal institutions, wherein the many structures of clan and caste translated themselves into village spaces and the associated rules pertaining to the boundary and the goddess and her mediums. These spaces were consumed in many planned and unplanned and seemingly contradictory ways by women, mediums and non-mediums, who constituted its owned consumers and labour.

daivat) 'village goddesses' (*gram-daivat/thana*) and soon became a nationalistic enterprise in the eyes of those who were beyond, or unconcerned with women's experiences of child-loss affliction (mostly men). My new informants became interested in how the goddess had been an ancient tradition in Maharashtra from the time of Shivaji Maharaj (*Shiva-kaalin*) and even before, from the time of the Pandavas (*Pandava-kaalin*). It was claimed that the Pandavas were the first to bring civilisation to these parts, known to my informants as the *Dandakaranya* (Western Ghats), even if the latter area is generally identified as the Vidarbha region. Many male informants from the village entered my research at this point, as it widened to encompass areas outside local experience to a nationalistic and diffused enterprise, as they told me of how the Mahadev Koli from areas around Bhimashankar were descendants of the local hero Babruvahan, who had accidentally killed his father Arjuna (according to the *Mahabharata* story), not knowing of the secret alliance between his mother Chitrangada and the Pandava King Arjuna when the latter was in exile. They told me of how the Ghod River emerged in red colour, bathed in the blood of Arjuna and was 'healed' only after the Koli Babruvahan received a boon from the Koli goddess Ulupi to bring his father Arjuna back to life (it did not matter to them that the story of Babruvahan in the Mahabharata is supposed to be located in Manipur).There was actually a Koli village in the nearby mountains, I was told, where this battle between Arjuna and Babruvahan was supposed to have taken place, called Tirphad (euphemistically supposed to be named after the word *chirphad*, meaning, in Marathi, 'to tear apart'!).

I found out that my informants knew about some important Natha texts (non-specific, since I could never find these references in libraries) that mentioned goddesses and their afflictions, which they had translated to signify the antiquity of the Satvai cult as part of Maharashtra's traditional grandeur. Discussions about these goddesses, whom they believed were 'none other than the Satvai', opened up discussions about the subject of goddesses, and the politics of healing and childbirth with many other people in the village.

This nationalist enterprise also soon became uncomfortable, even though many of my informants were kind and helpful. My research soon became subsumed under the general desire for conservatism about preserving culture for posterity against outsiders and Westernisation, especially as those with access to positions of power in the village began to see my enterprise as something to strengthen the preservation of ritual documentation and filming within their region so that my research could be read by outsiders to view the grandeur and traditions of rural Maharashtra and the contribution of their village in preserving this. One of my benevolent informants soon used our discussions as a way of publicly voicing his political opinions on how 'low' goddesses were worshipped among the 'backward' (*magas-varga*) as contiguous confirmations of their mutually low status. These common reinterpretations that insidiously deploy nationalist readings of religion and history remind one of how archaeological expertise is utilised for clinching right-wing political agendas (Bernbeck and Pollock 1996), such as in the case of Dwarka (2004), Ram Sethu (2008) or Ayodhya (1992).[8]

The knowledge of textual references on goddesses in the Natha texts (however tenuous their connection to the Satvai) by those who are outside even the possibility of child-loss affliction strengthened the hegemony of the prevalent Satvai affliction cult and its rituals over those susceptible to affliction diagnosis within an ever stringent patriarchy of *kali-yuga*. As pointed out by Bell (1992: 197–223), ritualisation may be a source of authority for those who are able to influence it without getting afflicted (against the 'other' category of the afflicted/'afflictable') so that they can assume a position of local hierarchy against the afflicted/'afflictable', which in this case translates into being able to create hegemonic concepts of tradition and to finally objectify their superiority through the knowledge of texts that they transpose to village goddesses in order

[8] The utilisation of Hindu elite and upper-caste archaeologists for solving communal issues through scientific investigation indicates the changing nature of democracy into populism, where tradition and modernity are no longer separated. According to this axiom, being a traditional nationalist is modern and scientific.

to produce knowledge. This conveniently reinforces notions of women's reproductive labour within dominant caste-marital clans.

My discussions with male informants about Natha texts revealed a rural and local Hindu subjectivity that considered itself to be 'Kshatriya'. A 'landed' subjectivity, it was closely tied to the Brahminical caste system. All Maratha, non-Dalit and '*balutedar*' clans (that had rural traditional land rights) could technically effect this reinterpretation into the Kshatriya caste category if they converted to vegetarianism and ritually adopted higher-god/goddess clan worship, involving deities from important *shakti-peetha*. It was the same process that now relegated the rural Brahmin presence to the past and the contemporary Brahmin presence to urban areas or foreign countries, while cultivating reinterpretations of class, education, urbanism, and professionalism as part of an overarching caste hierarchy. Caste hierarchy, nationalism and patriarchy became unquestioned values and discourse while working among the non-afflicted/'afflictable', since they considered it natural that I would be educated, rational and non-superstitious, which made them view me as somewhat more masculine than the women of the village. They themselves, on the other hand, took on Kshatriya status and I became privy to many discussions about how and which '*jati*' could be understood as the Kshatriya caste based on vegetarianism and common gods with urban Brahmin families. The non-vegetarian '*jati*' became similarly grouped together with the OBC category (Other Backward Caste), even though they shared Brahminical deities in the village as well. I was asked to mediate in relationships on behalf of the many men among my new informants, whom I also befriended, since I was considered educated enough to understand their side of the situation with regard to their relationships with women better, since I was somewhat considered to be in a grey zone between men and women. They found it acceptable that I travelled to and photographed different Satvai shrines and they encouraged me to expose the backward superstitions among women and the lower castes, while documenting the real 'folk' history and 'folk' traditions of Maharashtra for Western educated people to read. They exhorted me to refer to how the Natha texts, which also considered goddesses like the Satvai to constitute lower caste practices.

My new informants accompanying me on these photography forays banged open doors of shrines (that they considered 'lower', superstitious and insignificant) as they laughingly held up ritual offerings made there by women, so that I could take better photos. They recounted how they went to these shrines as children in order to eat this ritual food and how 'nothing ever happened to them' (in order to demonstrate that the taboo against eating ritual food was a superstition), while I contrasted these stories with women's warnings about my bravado and how my pride would ultimately come before a fall. What my informants failed to appreciate was that it was within the context of patriarchy and its caste politics itself that they were produced as superior and systemic beneficiaries in contrast to 'backward' women, lower castes and the uneducated, whom they were so contemptuous of, whose 'lower' location made them automatically 'afflictable'. It was assumed that I would join all my informants in condemning those who were *magas-vargiya* (the poor women, the lower castes in the village along with the uneducated). Many of my informants invaded the micro-contexts of rituals within domestic spaces by trivialising them, even while the women from those households objected to my presence. This sudden enthusiasm about my research left me feeling alienated from the women, who would otherwise have never invited me for childbirth rituals in their homes, since they considered me afflicted. I felt guilty about their resentment and simultaneously came to appreciate anew the enormous entitlement and ownership my new male informants experienced within the collective domestic spheres of their village.

Gaining information from the Natha texts about goddess cults soon led to discussions about Hindu male militaristic powers, gained through asceticism and yoga, a topic that Pinch (2006) also explores. My new informants regaled me with stories from the Natha texts that described the saint's violent anger born out of spiritual powers that could control others through alchemical prowess and how the saint Goraksha Natha gave a woman a boon to have a son. They told me of how much contempt the

Natha saints had for the goddesses (whom they identified as the Satvai), since Goraksha Natha, the great Natha saint, was able to counterbalance the inauspicious power of low goddesses by his masculine valour and thereby diminish their importance.

With saints (yogis) having traditionally originated from among the lower castes, the Natha *pantha* (sect) and its equally powerful traditions of magical rituals had the possibility of altering village goddess traditions and the spectre of affliction that they held for women, despite the interpretation of Hindutva masculinity that following such a sect effected amongst my new informants. Excited, I paid a visit to a Natha *panthi* yogi's (a saint from the sect) ashram (hermitage) with an informant's family near Bhimashankar. The meeting took place in absolute silence and hushed respectfulness as the yogi refused to speak to anyone. I was informed after the silent meeting that though the yogi accepted visitors, he maintained a vow of muteness that was the source of his spiritual purity. Moreover, he had never touched a woman (after having become a *sanyasi* or ascetic in childhood) and spoke only in sign language. I could obviously not introduce my research in this other-worldly environment and felt deflated about nothing changing in terms of the goddess.

Coming away from Bhimashankar, I mused about how village goddess affliction cults had carried on parallel to, and simultaneously with, the saintly-magical-militaristic traditions of the Hindu Natha *pantha* and had not become altered by it as women kept suffering their childlessness stigma, even if the texts, claimed by my informants, recounted acrimonious relationships between Natha saints and goddesses. The Natha saints and their ashram, with its proximity to one of the most important *Jyotirlinga*'s (shrine for Lord Shiva), Bhimashankar, in Maharashtra, that had been celebrated by King Shivaji, had assumed the heights of 'Shaiva Brahminism' in their ascetic claim of virile masculinity that was associated with militarism, which within Maharashtra wasn't outside the context of being Brahmin and becoming linked with Parashuram either. The Satvai continued to afflict women, even as the Natha yogi became another kind of a silent and masculinist and militarist Brahminical paragon, outside the reach of women suffering childloss and relationship difficulties. Women could not even speak to such a saint, who was too pure and far removed from their reproductive worlds that were considered too impure and polluted.

Superstition and Belief

Knowledge of rationalist movements and their discourse about superstition and rationalism, [9] when it came to performing clan-based goddess rituals, was located within parameters of education, class-based access to it, and an ability to resist clan interpretation of a woman's childlessness within it, which was simultaneously based on questions of caste. There were gendered divisions within the same clan that upheld patriarchy in different ways: women following clan rituals upheld it differently than men from the same clan, who upheld education and class among upper-caste members of society, as rational. Although this gendered division of upholding patriarchy differently seemed ridden with internal contradictions, it actually served to purify and strengthen patriarchy within the same clan by demarcating roles for each person who could claim to be 'rational' simultaneously. Similarly, though poorer families within a larger clan may be condemned by its patriarch as backward, superstitious and ultra-rural, they constituted the ritual bulwark of its larger clan, the poorer women acting as mediums or providing 'impure' labour (for childbirth for example), when women from its richer sections suffered affliction or were in labour.[10] They were rounded up and provided economic sustenance during times of affliction-crisis or illness, when they were summoned to provide support to the richer units within the larger clan. They acted as the outer ring to the clan, similar to how the lower-caste inhabitations formed an outer ring to the inner core of the village inhabitation during epidemics from outside,

[9] Quack (2012) has written an extensive ethnography of the rationalist movement in India and Maharashtra.

[10] I have explored circles of empowerment within clans based on poverty between its sub-units (Dandekar forthcoming).

serving the latter and providing it with labour and protection in times of need and depending on it economically in return. At other times however, they were condemned as backward, uneducated and superstitious.

Thus questions of belief in the Satvai came to actually replace questions of belief in her ritual for many women for whom being rational was as important as adhering to a clan and its goddess, just as replacing the goddess with belief in ritual (as a child-conceiving mechanism) became more important for women who laboured for their clans and depended on the clan's goodwill. Beliefs and rituals came together and then again split away from each other, depending on the negotiating power that every woman had with her clan. Ritual was performed by everybody to gain social acceptability within groups of women and wives and mothers. Beliefs or fears might continue even if the ritual was dropped due to religious conversion into neo-Buddhism (as an example). This resulted in an ambivalent situation: educated women performed Satvai rituals to satisfy clan members and to enter women's groups that celebrated fertility as a part of clan tradition, without necessarily believing that the ritual would provide them with a child, especially in the absence of sex. They often claimed the rationalist verdict when they felt more secure with their marriages and clans when rituals celebrated them. Within interviews, they often negated blind faith in ritual cults, exhorting the importance of clan unity and society that attending functions and celebrations fostered instead. On the other hand, I had more than enough respondents confiding in me about how performing rituals without a belief in them backfired, since it constituted an act of betrayal to the goddess and was against the believing and worshipping clan. They felt sure that the goddess would recognise the heart of a lying person confronting her in ritual. It was considered akin to leading others astray (*labaadi*) and other social evils that emanated from harbouring clandestine and manipulative subjectivities. These views were obviously competitive views expressed by those women dependent and abused by their clans, when they resisted or criticised other women in comfortable marital and clan relationships, who could 'afford' to be rational and who did not need to take the real brunt of constant rituals to prove their purity and labour allegiance and ownership to marital clans. In those instances, wherein women, dependent on their clans, came to fear the goddess and believe in the latter's power to dismember their biological connection to their new-borns, the ritual did have the desired effect of transforming them into clan labour, owned members and marginal mothers under the threat of childloss and impurity denouncements. Many women, dependent on their families constantly prayed that the regular rituals they performed would help them conceive and better their situations at home. Theirs was a desperate situation, steeped in domestic violence. And this was sometimes irrespective of their sexual relationships as they came to believe increasingly in magical stories.

There were, however, other 'superstitions' in my field area that originated from health practice, which concerned the 'immunity' of the lower castes and the poor, even though the poor (mostly belonging to depressed castes) constituted the primary clients within health centres. According to this superstition of 'immunity', poor women and children were considered to have higher resistance against disease and infant mortality than richer women from dominant castes. Poor and lower-caste women were also considered to have a stronger fertility, a stronger capacity for manual labour (despite decreased access to nutrition) and a violent nature. Their supposedly naturally unclean habitat and lack of hygiene was viewed as the basis for this biological and inherited 'immunity' that allowed them to resist illness, even if this was contrasted by an overwhelming amount of poor patients in clinic outpatient departments (OPDs). This superstition, apart from being deeply casteist and anti-poor, was one that clearly contradicted all health research, demonstrating a clear indication of association between poverty, its social determinants and infant/ maternal morbidity/mortality.

This health superstition of 'immunity' was further directly associated with the casteist notion of 'affliction absorption' that imagined the body of the lower caste, especially producing it as the gendered body, as an icon representing a combination of the warrior, sexual/fertility provider and labourer of the village, through an absorption of epidemics and dirt. I was repeatedly told how the 'fact' of 'absorption' has traditionally motivated space and settlement planning in a modern village: of how lower-caste inhabitations are located outside upper-caste, core village areas, so that the former becomes exposed to dangers and epidemics coming from both the inside and outside upper-caste inhabitations first. They were then understood to 'absorb' these dangers through their peripheral and absorbing powers, remaining immune, militant, resistant and violent to these attacks, without letting these afflictions spread as diseases to vulnerable upper-caste areas, where resistance, absorbing power and immunity to disease was missing.

The notion of lower-caste immunity and fertile absorption of disease created the transfer of epidemic carts ritually from the boundary of one village to the boundary of the next, wherein another member of the same caste would take over the pulling and transfer of the cart during the epidemic as part of caste-based traditional labour even today. In the case of the midwife too, who always belongs to a lower caste, she is usually invited to cut the umbilical cord during childbirth, clean up the afterbirth and wash clothes till the mother is out of birth impurity. During childbirth the primary aim of her presence remains this 'absorption' of birth impurity released during the moment of separation between mother and child during the cutting of the cord. By absorbing this birth impurity into her body she prevents afflictions from spreading to the upper caste clan members (especially the new-born) deemed 'pure'. The midwife is herself understood to remain immune to this impurity due to her lower-caste and 'absorbing' status that is consequently considered non-'afflictable' in nature. She becomes a ritual recipient of gifts and food in return for her ritual duty. A lower caste healer is afflicted only if she does not answer the goddess's duty or 'call' to heal upper caste women in the village.

In the case of trance, which has been viewed by some feminist scholars, such as Ram (1991), as 'embodied' experiences of power, these mostly involve the labour of lower-caste women in my field area, who are supposed to absorb the goddess's sexual heat into their bodies, which is considered released during her annual village festivals (as noted by Kinsley 1986). These sexual trances have made lower-caste women traditionally available as sexual labour to upper-caste men as part of their caste duty and burden, demonstrated by the swinging and display of their body and hair in an uninhibited manner. Goddess possession among women is therefore a form of caste and clan labour, as healers and mediums of the goddess who 'absorb away' impurity and afflictions of both upper-caste women and men, as part of their caste duty and labour, when they express the goddess's capacity of 'heat' and power that is generated by the village boundary (I will discuss the village boundary in more detail in the subsequent chapters below).

A male *bhagat* (healer of the goddess), whom I once interviewed, imagined a female healer as a form of a boundary goddess (*vesi-varchi-Mukta-aai* or the goddess/mother Mukta of the boundary[11]), a village cleaner of epidemics, broom in hand, sweeping away infectious pox scabs as a form of performing traditional duty. Whenever there were illncsses in upper-caste clans, lower-caste women from the village were invited for meals, so that their presence could absorb the affliction away from these clan homesteads. Seeing them begging ritually (*jogwa*) for oil, salt and flour in the villages, a method that would feed them and avert afflictions for the upper castes, was a common phenomenon. The sustenance derived by lower-caste families in the village, therefore, rested squarely on the provision of cleaning and 'absorbing' affliction from upper-caste clans, while freedom from guilt for this amidst discourses of caste and gender equality among the higher castes rested on the casteist notion of the inherent fertility, strength and immunity of the lower castes and the poor that is shared by the medical fraternity.

A female healer/medium of the Satvai I once interviewed during fieldwork confided in me about the enormous menstrual

[11] Professor Anne Feldhaus was to later tell me in the context of one such discussion of how the late Professor Sontheimer (from Heidelberg) had identified the popular rural Goddess Mukta-*bai* from Maharashtra as a docile form of Mari-*aai*, the pox goddess (15th International Maharashtra Conference, Arizona State University).

cramps and severe bleeding she suffered. She explained to me of how these problems were sent by the Satvai as a sign/mark of her ritual servitude of absorbing similar afflictions from other women into her own body. She had not been totally free of the after-effects of upper caste women's affliction after all, because of years of 'absorption' labour (*kaam*), though she had had no problems with having children due to her caste-based immunity and the goddess's blessings. According to her, if she had stopped this work, the goddess may have really punished her by child-loss/childlessness or by making her totally infertile. It would be by stopping her duty that her affliction would have come to her; these symptoms she suffered for the last so many years, though painful were just a mark of the goddess's blessings for her, that acknowledged her 'absorbing' duty for which no medical help was necessary (even though I offered to take her to a private doctor).

On the other hand, I interviewed a woman who had gone to help with childbirth in homes outside her clan (midwifery), despite belonging to an upper caste (Maratha). She was forced to relinquish this work, even though she was a skilled midwife, due to a ritual diagnosis of goddess affliction that stopped her from this impure task, due to which she had incurred *vitaal*. She told me how, after she had lost all her hair and developed dark marks on her skin, her clan Satvai had told her (in the medium's trance) to stop meddling in other clan childbirths, since it would bring her clan only *vitaal* and caste shame (*jati cha maan harvel*). The goddess punished her for breaking caste rules by taking away her beauty instead (*Maza roop gela!* she complained!).

Domestic Violence

For many of my male informants, goddess cults and being traditional also provided women and children with belonging and respect. Caste systems were also good according to my upper-caste male informants, since they provided poor people with occupations, ritual roles and social duties and defined respectful interaction. According to them, it was exactly the dissolution of gender and caste roles that was leading to joblessness, suicide and unhappiness among people in cities, apart from role confusion brought by feminism among women. Even though many of them agreed that people were treating women and poor people and lower-caste families badly, they also felt that this ill treatment was itself a corruption of what was prescribed treatment. Without knowing it, they were telling me exactly what I believed in, about the implementation of progressive values and its differential importance for each person, who would decide her values for herself, before those who had never struggled for modern values in the first place decided to throw it away, on women's behalf, along with all the hard-won freedom it introduced, by denouncing it as colonial in origin.

My male informants who believed patriarchy and the caste system to be beneficial on the other hand, sought to mirror what they believed was an imposition of modernity on pristine and static Hindu Dharma, by imposing claims about the traditional that were equally reinvented within modernity and populism. What was viewed as being outside this tradition was then conveniently denounced as a tradition of another outsider or exotic variety: a colonial or Western 'tradition', which in the context of the right-wing politics also became equally constructed as a form of decadent superstition from the West. At one level for many of my male informants, who were extolling the virtues of upper caste purity, it did not matter which constructed 'superstition' they denounced and consumed simultaneously. It was the same for them, whether they denounced the superstitions of the lower castes more, despite going to the latter's part of the village for purposes of their own or whether they asked me to get them imported gifts from Germany, while denouncing 'the West' as superstitious and without culture.

According to many of my traditional-modern new informants, women needed behavioural discipline. They needed to be stopped from ill-treating their family members and breaking up clans into nuclear units by mimicking what they saw in TV serials and generating internal fights in the family to live separately with their husbands. These informants saw the goddess's affliction as an opportunity for convincing women to become amenable to clan discipline by diverting their attention to having children and uniting with the joint family with a feeling of loyalty instead. The goddess, in her own way (according to them), helped clans and also helped women by securing them and their children with a sense of belonging that kept everyone in the larger family together through the birth of sons and by the generation of multiple and plural motherhoods for all women and children. This, in their opinion would ultimately keep Indian values and culture together. Good women, who became mothers for all their clan children, had a lot of respect in their clan, caste and village, and the goddess herself, who was venerated by all clans, was made from the souls of women, who had died while completing their valorous village duty. According to my informants, I was overlooking the pain of clans, many of whom were driven and provoked into acts of violence by their errant womenfolk (mother-in-law against daughter-in-law, for example). My informants did not agree that patriarchal systems (*purushasatta*) positioned the lower caste, the poor and women as labour by pointing to individually powerful women who were also champions of patriarchy, like the goddess in the village. They asked me not to sympathise with afflicted women in the village as this caused problems for them. My new informants told me of how many women used affliction rituals as an excuse to run back to their natal families and blackmail their marital clans for giving into their demands, never agreed upon at the time of marriage in the first place (Freed and Freed 1993).[12] They did not agree with the question of women's sexual and reproductive labour and ownership or that of women's domestic labour, even if it was in addition to agriculture or outside work, since they claimed that it wasn't any different to the physical labour of men. Women's

[12] Complaints about 'fleeing women' also locate domestic violence and affliction together within the larger discourse of married women as migrants in their natal and marital homes within the virilocal marital structure. Both Palriwala and Uberoi (2008) and Sax (1991) points to migration in terms of opportunities for 'belonging', 'gaining' and performing politically correct actions and duties in association with earning inclusion within marital relationships. Freed and Freed (1993) also write about a preponderance of possession symptoms among newly married women, who experience existential tension about their new responsibilities, experiences and subjectivities.

grief about failing to perform reproductive labour or sexual labour, when they considered themselves to be defective pieces was compared by my male informants to physical handicaps among men, due to which the latter, too, sometimes became burdens for their families. This had to be obviously treated as either illness or affliction or both. They were dumb founded with my proposition that handicapped men being abandoned or ill-treated by their families or the question of caste was itself a feminist issue along with the question of how the wives of these men underwent double oppression in a society where a woman's status was measured by the status of the men she was owned by.

I, for my part, could only contrast this with haunting images of afflicted women, provided to me by my women respondents, depicting childless weeping women at desolate places near riversides, doing their household washing while wishing for death, only to have the hovering goddess nearby grant them their wish, taking them into the swirling waters. The search party arriving at the spot later on would only find the half done household chores, some green bangles, turmeric, vermillion and a rag of her sari left behind, which they would reverently carry home and worship henceforth. No one in her clan would henceforth be allowed to use the same sari colour; the colour would be reserved only for her shrine as a special mark of honour during ritual offerings. The place of her disappearance would become a cult spot for the goddess thereafter as the clan would build her a shrine, where people would make dedications to appease her pain and anger.

The realisation of margins between the goddess's violent discipline and domestic violence were really thin, hinging upon punishment for non-performers of sexual and reproductive duties, sometimes acting as evidence of their mental and reproductive illness and constituting the grounds for marital abandonment at the same time. Goddess rituals were supposed to transform women into illness free, sexually responsive, reproductively functional and suitably sane clan members, who would fulfil all labour roles and duties to become *suhasini* and participate socially in their collective family tasks. Many disagreements among women within the clan centred on unequal respect for work and the financial contribution of their husbands to the unit. Leaving the clan without their husbands, even within the context of domestic violence, was too far from the reality of their lives and this was the chink within which goddess rituals fitted themselves. Women feared the possibility of marital abandonment, viewing themselves as dependent on their natal clans as single and abandoned women. Clan violence, domestic violence and the goddess's violence merged into one in the case of childless women or those experiencing childloss, as they desperately shelved their grief and kept performing rituals in order to conceive male heirs. Unable or disallowed from grieving, women only experienced fear of affliction and guilt as failures for crimes they hadn't voluntarily committed. In their clan-dependent state of being primary upholders of its inheritance, many of my respondents became incomplete persons, seeking personal and social identity only through their roles of being successful clan progenitors. For them, clan violence, goddess violence and the concept of discipline became inseparable from 'love' as a form of intended welfare, guidance and possession by clan members, husbands and goddesses, as many explained how rituals held out a possibility of being protected by clans and goddesses, even if violently so.[13]

It is not that senior women remained outside the purview of clan violence or were forever safe from the violence that they too perpetuated on younger women once they were widows or had lost their functionality and power within clans. Hierarchy that effected separation between women within the same clan made domestic violence and revenge mechanisms on individual old women possible, when the tables were turned and widowhood came to older women. And this, despite the much claimed discursive power and status that the aged are supposed to hold over the young in India; it was startling how suddenly old women lost power to the wills of their daughters-in-law in the insides

[13] Foucault (1979) writes about the way in which discipline and productivity is produced through punishment. This argument can be applied to the manner in which afflictions understood to be sent by goddesses helped extract reproductive labour from village women.

of formally represented family life in the village when younger women came to power and 'avenged themselves'.

Finally, it was the perpetuation of the clan as a valorised cultural unit that perpetuated the dominant caste and continued to perpetrate violence on women and created them as perpetrators and agents of it, as fundamental rivals and enemies of each other. The agency of marriage songs that Raheja and Gold (1994) point to, in my opinion, rather indicates an effort made at hierarchy and competition production among women of an extended clan and of equal castes that displays public power through gendered performances of control over the female body, collectively claimed at the site of marriage by women, using the metaphor of marital sex and childbirth, where consent is enforced and its absence naturalized.

Fieldwork

I was requested throughout the writing of my doctoral thesis to not just write in different kinds of languages, but to also write in different languages. I was also enjoined to aim and locate my thesis within fixed disciplines, epistemologies and interpretive frameworks that would aid in its understanding, even though my attempts in this singular direction resulted in terrible confusion. My research used multidisciplinary and interdisciplinary methodological frameworks that could allow me to articulate a meta-discourse for a collective experiential world, based on empathy. However, this is not to say that this book represents any total experience, wherein I would attempt to fix the boundaries of either motherhood or motherhood-loss finally and once and for all. I am not endeavouring to assume the position of a ventriloquist shaman for my time, age or concern, that would ultimately play back into a single voiced nationalist or 'culturalist' discourse about my field area either. At the same time, I could not really provide a mono-method perspective to a conundrum of conflicts and ambivalence that the relationship with my respondents/informants and an exploration of primary and secondary materials came to present. Also, I did not want to write about my subject in a way that would leave the politics of my research undefined and rob the emotion of empathy that became the corner stone of my method.

My biggest struggles came to surround a sensitive understanding of the almost 'given' category of 'woman' that did not necessarily include its association with any other forms of dynamism, such as caste or poverty, region or lifestage, engagement with labour, ownership and reproduction or trauma, within discourses of development or culturalism. I could not identify with middle-range feminism either: a reformist standpoint that created women's empowerment out of traditional caste labour and duty, plucked and stated outside of its historical and regional context and instituted in comparison to modern clinical practice (hitherto critiqued) that suddenly became produced as a benchmark of potentially good science. These practices were imagined outside operative socio-political structures such as intra-clan hierarchies, dominant caste village politics, vote bank politics and resource allocations within health sectors just as medical practice (while comparing) or cultural contexts of practice (whether traditional or clinical) that were elite, which were selectively left out while critiquing either tradition or modernity as decadent and superstitious. I floundered over my language and its pitch as I sought to define 'feminisms' (a multiple and multifaceted struggle that encompassed caste and poverty-based struggles; a movement defining the rights of the underprivileged, who are structurally and systemically organised as lower within patriarchal hierarchy). Women embedded in structural hierarchy, facing distress, indeed made myriad choices that seemed contradictory to those outside their condition. But all these choices had strong internal logic and continuity that answered to their complex circumstances of multiple pressures and roles and thus constituted the best alternatives for them, since their situations often had very few inbuilt exit routes to it, even though they had recourse to compensatory and coping mechanisms in their lives, such as possessions, trances and dreams.

The fieldwork for this book was mostly carried out within rural areas surrounding Pune (Ghodegaon, Ambegaon tehsil/taluka or sub-district), Pune city (Taljaislum) and Osmanabad district (Chivri, Tuljapur tehsil/taluka). Although caste-based groups in both areas were largely the same, dominated by Marathas, the Adivasi society (Mahadev Koli, considered as a Scheduled Tribe in Bhimashankar, and the Pardhi, considered as a denotified ex-criminal tribe in Osmanabad) in these regions were fighting different kinds of battles with the state and the dominant castes.

While the Mahadev Koli, though accepted by caste society, had an embattled relationship with the Maharashtra state department for forestlands, the Pardhi continued to be feared as antagonistic dacoits (*dakus*) by villagers at Chivri, which only intensified their poverty, due to the fear and stigma of traditional robbery and forest hunting attached to them. While the Mahadev Koli lost their battle for forestlands with the state and have become integrated within caste villages over time (even though some purely Koli villages do exist), the Pardhis continue to battle with the state for resettlement and protection from police raids and violence (since they are picked up by the police and tortured for every crime in the region and treated as scapegoats, whether they are really guilty or not). Their goddess cults reflect this difference as well: just as the KoliVan-*devi* (forest goddess) from Ahupe (worshipped as the Satvai by some) was benevolent, the Mahalakshmi of Chivri, considered a Pardhi clan goddess, was considered extremely violent, demanding the sacrifice of an embryo taken from a sacrificed ewe.

I also carried out a brief part of my fieldwork on home birthing at Taljai, an urban slum in Pune[14] that was mostly inhabited by poor migrants, mostly of the lower caste, known as Matang, hailing from rural areas around Solapur district. Most of them today are engaged with businesses and shops of waste recycling in Pune. To deal with 'waste' or *kachra* and sweeping and cleaning is considered a traditional Matang occupation in rural areas of Maharashtra that allows them to be popularly imagined as cleaners, immune 'absorbers' and healers of goddesses such as *Veshi-varchi-Mukta-bai*. Such healers (as has already been described above) are imagined as persons with brooms, cleaning remnants of epidemics such as pox away, since they are constitutionally considered to be of an 'absorbing' and 'immune' nature by the upper castes. Their

[14] Facilitated by Dhanashree Gurav and the Jeeva team.

migration to Pune city has neither changed their rural ritual profile, nor their occupations at places such as Taljai, where they perform the same village duties in cities instead. Many of the families in the slum kept in contact with rural goddess cults from their villages and had ritually 'dedicated' their children to these cults as *potraaj* (ritual agents of the goddess). While many at Taljai recalled their experiences of home birthing and self-birthing, the economically more stable spoke of going to hospitals, even as they reported loopholes within both medical services and traditional midwifery within their interviews. Poorer families still practised home births and self-birthing that involved long hours of waiting and concepts of instilling 'purity' in the birthing woman in case she got 'stuck' (*adhleli*), since it was nevertheless believed that it was women's impurity that caused illness and the other way round as well: ill women must somehow have encountered impurity, either intentionally or accidentally. Since the whole of Taljai slum was mostly a Matang inhabitation, which was somewhat homogeneous, the midwifery practised over there did not develop as a competitive caste duty between clans that involved impurity (*vitaal*) 'absorption' of the goddess's affliction or 'immunity' of contagion amongst each other.

Instead, midwifery became a neighbourly favour between friendly women that was based on sharing personal experiences of childbirth, when women unable to go to the hospital required last-minute help.[15]The experience of social stratification was more homogeneous at Taljai slum (in terms of caste and socio-economic background), as many of the inter-caste, and its co-dependent, structural hierarchies concerning economic sustenance, so rife with the exploitation of lower-caste families in the villages where I did my fieldwork, seemed almost abated. Although I did not stay long at Taljai, it made me feel that midwifery could almost be practiced more safely in a social context where neither caste nor

[15] Encouraged by my fieldwork with Gurav, and van Hollen's (2003) ethnography, I made a small joint presentation on home birthing outside cultural or institutional hegemony at the first International Conference on Qualitative Research in Nursing and Health in 2010 in Chiang Rai, Thailand.

class stratification between the birthing woman and the midwife was so sharp. Issues of female impurity and their ownership by men were however universal and unavoidable.

I have discussed different issues in the various sections of this chapter that have outlined concerns of what doing feminist fieldwork on a shadowy part of reproduction, childloss, in rural Maharashtra entails. These sections include the goddess's pain that is linked to a section on domestic violence for women that comes a little later on. I go on to discussing the pitfalls of nationalism that are often counterbalanced with the moralism associated with rationalist thought and the definitions of superstition and poverty and an engagement with how different 'communities' and groups are constituted by violence perpetuated against them, first by others and then as forms of resource-struggles, identity politics and struggles against violence (feminisms) by themselves. Lastly, I have tried to express the difficulties feminist research and women researchers doing feminist research run into, when expressing political frameworks within academics, when they face accusations of being opinionated.

CHAPTER 2

Silence amidst Babble, Women's Relationships amidst Discourse

Michel de Certeau (1984), in 'The Unnamable' chapter of his book *The Practice of Everyday Life*, explored the impossibility of articulating death within cultures that generated mechanisms for its repression, in which death itself became 'obscene' (hidden, transformed, celebrated, and obscure), as a result of which the dying person in turn came to be almost considered immoral. This axiom is aptly demonstrated by the obscenity of childloss and the immorality associated with women stigmatised for it within affliction cults of village goddesses, such as the Satvai and the Maulya. The longevity and health of a child and the 'good' and successful value of motherhood in my field area was associated with easy and speedy childbirth, where the mother was deemed moral, brave and of high virtue when she suppressed the expression of labour pains decorously (expressing only what was culturally acceptable) and turned the event of childbirth into a social occasion for others, who sat chatting around her, even as they assisted her. Expressing what came to be understood as 'exaggerated' articulations and expressions of pain, that interrupted normalcy, were associated with possible inauspicious events, women's weakness, impurity, possible medical crisis and fears of childloss and the spectre of the 'obscene'.[1] Suppressing the articulation of 'too much' labour pain

[1] Patel (2007: 395) has demonstrated how articulations of any untoward fears concerning the negative outcome of childbirth are silenced during labour in her ethnography of childbirth in Rajasthan.

and the bearing of it in a stoic manner that would in fact have the beneficial result of avoiding 'self-scaring' and facilitate easy and speedy birth, became a popular conversation for pregnant women in my field area. These were also associated with notions of good female behaviour linked in turn with valour. Every woman wanted to be redeemed from birth impurity and immorality by supplanting her birthing pain with childbirth and child survival or, in their words: exchanging the labour cry of the woman with the birth cry of the child. Rairkar (2007: 451) recounts the story of the origins of the Banana tree, in which the birthing woman (belonging to the Matang caste), after giving birth to a male child (born out of an illegitimate union with a Brahmin man), dies by jumping into fire and ultimately becomes propitious for upper-caste society by becoming the auspicious banana plant by fulfilling her ritual duty/ feminine labour by presenting society with a male heir and it is her death that is venerated in the Holi festival.[2]

Women suffering childloss and childlessness continue to be treated as social outcasts within their clans and on many instances suffered ritual affliction diagnosis of cannibalism and witchcraft (unless they were able to have sons thereafter) for this along with a battery of medical diagnosis that on many occasions did not help to alleviate their ritual diagnosis. They came to be located within a marginal grey zone, associated with goddess rituals, as they sought 'healing' or reintegration with their marital clans, under the explanatory rubric of having undergone childloss or childlessness in the first place, sent by the goddess Satvai as punishment for their immorality and impurity (of being unable to separate female fertility from masculine sexuality, an androgynous mix allowed only to the ascetic goddess). Souls of women who had died in childbirth, on the other hand, attained valour for having joined the goddess Satvai for having fulfilled their gendered duty of motherhood as her retinue (especially if their children continued to live), while sharing the goddess's infamous upper hand for the first time in expressing their repressed pain and anger

[2] Rairkar (2007) has provided a minute and detailed description of childbirth rituals, celebrations and midwifery in rural Maharashtra.

against the society of mortal women, who were as yet fallible and punishable for mixing sexuality with motherhood, ruining the purity of female fertility and becoming faulty as owned persons for their families.

Childbirth goddesses of rural Maharashtra, the Satvai and the Maulya, the latter also known widely as the Sati-*asra*[3], as ancestral goddesses of women, as souls of women dead in childbirth or the 'mothers', as they are euphemistically named—for saving the lives of sons—were similar in their conceptual essence to the Sati, or women who died with their husbands, heightened probably by claims of Rajput linkages in western India, as also demonstrated by Guha (1999).[4] Like the Sati, the Satvai were also associated with the impurity of pain and anger associated with an untimely death that became transformed into a virtuous sacrifice to save the afterlife of husbands, as is described in some detail by Harlan (1994). But in the case of the Satvai, their lives were concerned more with the virtue of saving their sons in childbirth, as part of their marital duty rendered to their clan to preserve its male members.

Goddesses and women were therefore separated from each other through a kind of hierarchy that transformed women's deaths in childbirth into their power over mortal women that then allowed them to express their grief and rage at untimely death (in childbirth) and anger as goddesses, who championed and upheld clan inheritance of village property among sons from dominant castes. Women-turned-into-goddesses thus presided over the longevity of sons, who inherited clan property, while this whole process of transformation between women and goddesses hegemonised mortal women, as goddess cults acted as agents of patriarchal modes of land and capital ownership, inheritance, distribution, hierarchy and labour allocation and speedily came to represent symbols of neo-feudal and violent nationalism. While

[3] Feldhaus (1995a) has explored many shrines of the Sati-*asra* in Pune district of Maharashtra.

[4] Harlan (1994) discusses how women change into goddesses within Rajasthan through the Sati's curse.

the labour of upper-class and upper-caste mothers was concerned with the purging of sexuality and the undertaking of childbirth duties to preserve female fertility, the labour of lower-class and lower-caste healers and goddess mediums lay in the absorption of impure sexuality from upper-caste women in order to facilitate better motherhood among the latter, so that lower-caste women could perform the caste duty of 'healing'. Consequently, lower-class and lower-caste women were constructed as dirty, impure and sexual, and their trance activity within goddess cults primarily marked their labour and sexual availability for the upper castes of the village as 'immune absorbers' (as explained in the chapter above). Their reproductive disorders became constructed as part of their caste duty and their progeny were viewed as inheritors of the same labour (even as girls were viewed as inheriting their mother's reproductive duties, afflictions and all) along with its associated duties of cleaning and absorbing. Prevalent casteist superstitions in the mean while absolved itself of any guilt about hierarchy and inequality by ascribing the lower-caste body with myths of immune power, fertility and strength. While upper-caste women were required to protect marriage institutions and property inheritance by restricting their sexual availability to their same-caste husbands, lower-caste women engaged in healing and were at the receiving end of demands of sexual labour in addition to reproductive labour for their own clans and cleaning labour for the village, within enforced contexts of poverty, low hygiene and poor health. The Satvai cult, remained outside the periphery of the village, guarding its insider clans from errant women married to it from outside villages, by punishing them with afflictions and teaching them how to remain loyal to their marital clans as owned feudatories through ritual propitiation. They also linked lower caste members outside the village boundary to village servitude under the threat of punishment, who would help errant village members to belong better to its pure interiors by 'healing' them and absorbing affliction. They represented all that the centre was not: wilderness and the connotation of both excommunication possibilities for women who kept within its boundaries, who in turn undertook rituals in order to prevent this excommunication.[5] As pain-repressing and life-affirming goddesses,[6] the Satvai and the Maulya propitiation resembled a form of female ancestor worship, since their cult was known to include the souls of women who had died in childbirth or virgins' who had died before they had a chance of getting married or having children, among rural dominant castes of Maharashtra. Their impure forms come to represent the opposite values considered desirable among fertile and living village women, as is demonstrated by Kripal (2000). Women 'distanced' the goddess from them and their babies in rituals, just as the shrines and the lower caste agents of the goddess were always located far outside the village boundary.

Yet it is not only local discourses in rural western Maharashtra that render certain aspects of the Satvai cult 'obscene'. These discourses intersect with various academic, state and public sphere discourses that construct Satvai worship or goddess worship in various ways. Below, I will discuss five such discourses that outline: notions of purity and impurity that are linked to the body; public health discourses concerning child and maternal health; rationalist and feminist critiques of 'superstition'; the valorisation of rituals and 'tradition' as 'alternative knowledge'; and historical and archaeological ideas concerning goddess worship in rural Maharashtra. Each of these discourses serves to further obscure and render 'obscene' questions of women's labour, ownership and the question of their association with childloss and female impoverishment.

The Impure and Celebrated Body

Celebrations of purity, childbirth rituals, social customs and functions connected to female fertility, goddesses and their close

[5] Masilamani-Meyer (2004) discusses the affinity of village guardian deities of Tamil Nadu with wilderness and asceticism, associated with areas outside village boundaries.

[6] Schuler (2009) has made a detailed documentation of goddesses concerning dead mothers, virgins and safe childbirth within ritual texts from Tamil Nadu.

'blessing' sort of association with women, along with its academic documentation; especially the exploration of historic relationships between goddesses and epidemics (such as the seminal research by Apffel-Marglin 2008) constitute a powerful discourse about women and 'positive power' in South Asia that produces goddess cults as pro and proto feminist. Healing and trance are (within this light) interpreted as ritual journeys that effect transformations within participatory collectives such as regional, religious or linguistic belonging, cult, clan or caste 'communitas' (as suggested by Turner 1977) and the performance of multiple modes of selves that adhere to gendered or historical subjectivities that are then linked to selfhood or political identity (Sax 2002). Yet, even as 'healing' remains an arresting arena for social analysis, the main aim of this section remains dedicated to uncovering the rather more mundane and 'daily' preventive rituals of impurity (*vitaal*) that women invest considerable energy in, in order to actually prevent the necessity of such hugely and socially visible affliction-healing predicaments.

The Satvai and Maulya shrines lying outside village boundaries are avoided by women independent of ritual context. Menstruation marks their peak vulnerability period for affliction, as inhabiting the innermost recesses of their home (the kitchen, rooms for family deities or *dev-ghar* and the family toilet) also becomes taboo for them. Their movement in the village, especially during menstruation, exemplifies the impurity discourse by mapping out their movements and charting out a time-space surveillance regimen for them inside and outside their homes by all village members that keeps them on the margins of both (the home and the village, by disallowing them inhabitation of both its absolute interior and exterior). This grey zone of surveillance then constructs the household as part of the village, connecting its boundary with its multiple 'interiors' and with a 'grey zone' as surveillance area for 'afflictable' women in-between, where both village members and goddesses become active agents. The Satvai is supposed to act as a kind of divine policeman for women in this grey zone, especially during women's menstruation, making some times of the day and places taboo for women to be out visiting, when unchaperoned. The Satvai is understood to become mobile from their shrines at these special times of the day (such as the afternoon) and roam the village streets looking out for errant and unchaperoned menstruating women in order to afflict them. Ritual contact with the goddess, on the other hand, who otherwise afflicts when encountered outside the ritual context, therefore functions as moral 'inoculation', whereas accidental and afflicting encounters with the goddess indicate women's moral recalcitrance for not having learnt the social rules about sexual morality that necessitates adherence to surveillance during menstruation. Women during menstruation are therefore advised to keep to their private chambers and venture out in public spaces for only specific tasks in the company of other women at certain times of the day and only if necessary. They may not enter the family kitchen, cook or perform daily rituals for clan deities or use the family toilet (they must use public toilets) and on no account must they travel or wander to village boundaries, near the shrines of the Satvai and the Maulya either. There is however no *vitaal* if they associate with their husbands or children in the course of inhabiting their private chambers.

Menstrual impurity has been explored by many anthropologists (such as Bennett in 2002), but according to my respondents, menstrual impurity or *vitaal* was at its most heightened when the possibility of immorality was also at its highest. According to my respondents, women had to gate-keep their own bodies in accordance with Satvai-Maulya taboos of keeping within the marital family in order to avoid affliction(that took place through *vitaal* or impurity), while the goddess herself was tightly vigilant about recalcitrant women. Childbirth goddesses were said to send cobras/*Nago-ba* (considered to be spirits of male ancestors, also her minions) into the village at night, who would then search the garbage of every household for the evidence of women's impurity or *vitaal* (incurred in the public exposure of such a potent witchcraft medium such as vaginal or menstrual blood). The *Nago-baw* is said to go blind upon coming in contact with menstrual blood, should a woman have carelessly disposed any clothes soaked in it. He would then punish her for witchcraft and this careless immorality of also exposing her availability for impregnation (sexual availability and public disloyalty against husband and marital clan) by afflicting her with barrenness (witchcraft and female sexuality being closely associated). Only the husbands of menstruating women, the only persons, who don't suffer from the woman's *vitaal*, are in fact even encouraged to initiate pregnancy during the wife's menstruation. One of my respondents grew angry with me as I told her of how initiating pregnancy during menstruation was biologically impossible, when she was trying to convince me, in turn, of how a son conceived during his mother's menstruation lives to become a future king; it was all about the right 'utilisation' of menstrual blood for clan purposes that would avoid wasting such a potent medium for witchcraft and anti-clan and anti-village purposes.

Discursive indoctrination into affliction prevention is initially characterised by segregation during menstruation that publicly marks women's ownership by marital clans, followed in quick succession by the celebration of fertility by those clans and the success of female morality that has already removed impurity or *vitaal* from motherhood and established pure fertility. The celebration of this purity is first initiated during puberty and repeated all throughout pregnancy and postpartum along with preventive rituals against affliction. It is usually this back and forth between fearful rituals performed at village or significant inhabitation boundaries and celebratory functions back home that serves to separate women from their own control over sexuality and biological fertility. By splitting up female sexuality and reproduction and likening sexuality only to the masculine, the androgynous or elder and widowed agnatic women, female pliancy in heterosexual marriage is further fused with female fertility, the idea of being owned, women's marital reproductive labour and gender roles with caste and village allegiance is entrenched. Further, this plunging back and forth is shared with an entire community of other married women with sons, who seek to attach belonging with this internal separation, and who in turn become constructed as pure and healthy because of their living male progeny. They are known variously as *savashne* (*suhasini*) or *helkarni*, who form an upper-class group of dominant caste, pure, fertile and visible village women. The goddess discourse is not just repressive of pain by marking women systemically susceptible to affliction as impure, it is also repressive of pleasure for all those exposed to affliction, since the potentiality of 'healing' rituals only disciplines them into certain limited sources of pleasure that are elementally associated with power. While the association of the Satvai and the Maulya as 'out of boundary' phenomena for married women in the village places female power outside the experiential arena of women in the village, teaching mortal women to be afraid of affliction, the association of being 'outcastes' for healers places village women in a position of esteem for lower caste women, as the Satvai cult stratifies both castes of women against each other. The repetitive transitioning of women between segregation and celebration, between impurity, its prevention and the celebration of purity (when affliction seems staved off), ultimately serves to separate female sexuality and feminine experiences of the body from the actual female body that just becomes tantamount to a masculine product, making reproduction a clan and caste perpetuation exercise in purity, legitimation, inheritance and ownership. *Savashne* (*suhasini*), or *helkarni* and the agnatic group of upper-caste village clanswomen, who act as the many mothers and wives of village clans, then form a dominant caste of matriarchs on their own, who form a powerful cohort of patriarchal agents, like a second rung to the goddesses themselves, and dominate the articulation of data, providing researchers on gender with the maximum political networks and access in the village, even as they eclipse inarticulate women and survey or correct the latter's expressions almost constantly. This powerful cohort, constituted by successful mothers, mothers-in-law, visiting daughters and fertile daughters-in-law, often invited to each other's rituals, also judge and decide on the fate of inarticulate and invisible childless others, as they gossip over the range of moral downfalls in the village. They speak easily about replacing the new-born's biological ties of blood (with the real mother) with social ties of milk (with agnatic mothers) and ritual ties (with the goddess).

The transition for women to become good mothers and avert childloss is thus manifold: first, as a mother, a woman transits into 'pure' biological motherhood (cleansing herself of *vitaal*); second, she transits into becoming a social mother for all the children of her clan and distances herself from biological possession towards her own new-born in order to avoid childloss, and dedicates the child ritually to the goddess instead, allowing other agnatic women to initiate milk relationships with her child within celebrations, just as she is expected to do with their children (effecting a pendulum swing of first transiting into biological motherhood and then out of this into social motherhood). Lastly, she must maintain a distance from all those who have been incapable of any of these transitions in order to avoid child-loss affliction, sent from the goddess herself; for this she must perform preventive rituals of the goddess to 'inoculate' herself protectively. The ideal of agnatic and clan motherhood that first necessitates the biological birth of a child and then the biological separation from it, based on concepts of duality between blood and milk, produces motherhood as a feudal duty itself that is rendered to a divine child/future king that borders on adoring devotion (bhakti) and renunciation of personal claims of ownership on what is hitherto a biological extension (*potcha gola*). Motherhood is instead replete with the duty of labour provision and the valour gained through the association of duty that creates its failure as affliction and illness and a failure of village citizenship and dharma that is judged by the goddess.

A powerful example of how blood and milk inhabit exclusive cultural domains in the mother's body, with milk representing purer motherhood qualities in comparison to blood that is considered more ambivalent, associated with witchcraft, sexuality and cannibalistic tendencies, lies in the affliction of milk in women, i.e. an absence of lactation. Women unable to breastfeed are considered afflicted by the Satvai, since it is believed that breaking the taboo of engaging in sexual encounters during the postpartum birth impurity period, wherein mothers are supposed to concentrate almost entirely on breastfeeding, leads to the drying up of milk in the maternal breast. This becomes a matter of shame and exposure for most women (despite malnutrition and the genuine inability to produce milk in their bodies), as they have to perform rituals for the Satvai, offering her small earthen vessels of milk, requesting her to release 'their milk' and forgive them their sexual immorality and misconduct. Afflicted women have in any case to undergo a long ritual process of 'owning up' to their mistakes, as I have explained in my earlier research (Dandekar 2009).

Moreover, affliction is considered an inherited stigma among families even after it is healed, constructing immorality among certain clans women as almost genetic. There is marked absence of celebration within families suffering intergenerational traditions of affliction that concentrate attention on avoiding bad luck and objects that may re-introduce calamity within the clan. These objects, or those made of various natures or specific colours, known as *dharjin*, are considered to be reserved in honour for specific clan ancestors, who may have died an untimely death, reserving these objects for their honour, in return for protecting clan welfare. These objects (such as cradles or certain flowers or sari colours) or performing certain celebrations remain unlucky and out of bounds for other clans women, since it has been respectfully reserved for the ancestor with the untimely death, who has turned into a clan goddess. *Dharjin* remains similar in essence to the Sati's '*Ok*' described by Harlan (1994) when referring to trajectories of deaths in families where women died as Sati, leaving behind wishes that certain objects or acts of purity and celebration be reserved only for their consumption after they died in a manner that was heroic, unless they wanted to incur the wrath of the Sati.

Lastly, the body is claimed in more ways than one within the various cultural expressions that incorporate labour within paradigms of love and honour. Anthropologists (such as Raheja and Gold 1994, and Gold 2000) have explored the expression of sexuality and sexual consumption within women's songs during marriage and childbirth celebrations, insinuating that gender oppression is merely an ideological performance, counterbalanced with spaces inside patriarchy, where women actually express sexual desire. I believe these to be non-inclusive readings of the gendered body in relationships, female sexuality and reproduction, since women's life operates differently in my field area of rural Maharashtra. According to my observations, the ownership of the female body is harnessed within clan labour and ownership at ritual sites of patriarchal institutions such as marriage, which witness the deployment of lewd and explicitly sexual songs associated with the female body as an expression of clan hierarchy and its access to broaching the female sexual and reproductive body and its control that is introduced through joke, song and celebration. To premise that women were having a suitably dormant and pliant public life to comply with conservative norms and a roaring secret life of private sexual desire and fantasy (expressed suddenly in song) is just another patriarchal exemption from guilt that even justifies right-wing criticisms of women's so-called secret, rising immorality and subsequent afflictions that dehumanises women. In many of these song performances, women took on a masculine role vis-à-vis the new mother or the new wife who is expected to become pregnant, claiming access to her body and reproductive labour within marital relationships as part of enlisting her body within the clan. They demonstrate how they could breach her boundaries by claiming her body collectively and effacing her individual control over resistance. Physical changes were viewed as valour and the satisfaction of food cravings (*dohale*) viewed as reward for providing the clan with a male heir, even as a woman's discomfort, 'feelings' or experiences about these physical changes were viewed as unnatural or 'overacting'. The actual extent of changes in a woman's body and the laying of claims over her pregnancy were completely naturalised, even as many pregnant women felt increasingly alarmed by these changes and could not really accept them as 'normal' as they grew increasingly afraid and had nightmares. To theorise that women only performed gender oppression within rural society is as dehumanising as to hold that women 'acted out' pregnancy discomforts and emotions in a world that openly laid claims to their body and its ownership, along with the product they were about to give birth to, while they privately harboured a different/unknown and imagined sexual agenda, that would only be re-invented by those outside their empathetic circles.

Poverty and Policy

Working briefly in the public health sector[7] helped me understand the caste- and poverty-related biases inherent within maternal and child welfare policies operative and executed in Maharashtra under the National Rural Health Mission (NRHM). Just as children were constructed as legitimate and social members of their clan and society by producing biological motherhood itself as social through goddess cults, public health policies also sought to place children as subjects of the state first, by valorising mothers and female community health workers in the village (such as the accredited social health activists or ASHAs), who helped in operationalising maternal health policies of the state[8], as its feudatories. Maternal health and childcare policies, such as the 'Janani Suraksha Yojana' (JSY), designed predominantly to target poor families and bring their reproduction under state surveillance (in return for financial incentives to both the mother and the ASHA) are mainly governed by the ASHA. Financial incentives are paid to families and ASHAs alike for effecting institutional deliveries within public health clinical settings, despite their often less than adequate infrastructural medical facilities within interior areas. Financial incentives, however meagre, have conversely had the effect of turning ASHAs into state agents, struggling to secure maximum payment and state validation, even as these irregular and sporadic payments hardly suffice to make their status commensurate with employment. ASHAs continue to complain

[7] Centre for Child Health and Nutrition (Pune Branch 2010–2011), ICICI Foundation for Inclusive Growth (Mumbai).

[8] Female community health workers or ASHAs are supposed to be literate women, to be held accountable to the village (with some amount of primary education), chosen/instituted from among the married/widowed women of the village, nominated by the gram panchayat or the various government village councils for community and child health working in the village. Though they receive performance-based financial incentives from the NRHM, they can be held responsible by the village council, its various committees and various villagers for failures in their tasks in the same way as women held 'errant' can be held responsible by their clans socially or by goddess cults for afflictions of child loss.

of ill treatment at the hands of both village peers and village doctors/auxiliary nurses and male health workers at the Public Health Centres (PHCs) at public grievance hearings. Further, ASHAs continued to face competition from other health workers (such as child-nutrition workers or 'Anganwadi Workers'/AWWs) in the village, who work under different overlapping government schemes and struggle to compete for financial incentives. So, not only does the ASHA undertake the state's responsibilities imposed upon her, facing social pressure at the same time, she also becomes a link person for effecting the policies of influential health sector activists[9] interested in bringing about revolutions in home-based childcare responsibilities that they personally remain unacknowledged for, as women undertaking the traditional duties of childcare at home. This allows the state, on the one hand, to further withdraw from service delivery, even while paradoxically having engaged in a genealogical critique of neonatal care at home/home birthing/denouncing the midwife (as unhygienic and superstitious) and extolling clinical settings as the best method for reducing neonatal and maternal morbidity and mortality. On the other hand, it is finally the class, the so-called 'scientific rationality' and caste as location of specific forms of health sector activism that serves to suddenly create home-based neonatal care or HBNC as acceptable, even as it further produces the ASHA within gendered roles that are not too different than the ways in which the goddess cults originally produces mothers as primary care takers. The function of the ASHA follows the example of Foucault's executioner (1979: 51) : sharing the infamy of the people he oppresses (since the ASHA is chosen from one of the village women and has no escape routes), when facing the sovereign, and being oppressed in turn by both the sovereign and the people he controls, on behalf of the sovereign.

State surveillance over birth in return for financial incentives and inclusion for poor families within the government did not, however, yield so much and so easily even to the poorest of clans,

[9] Personal communication, Shilpa Deshpande, former head, Centre for Child Health and Nutrition, ICICI Foundation for Inclusive Growth.

since benefits such as JSY were accessible only to a layer, who were deliberately constructed as the subaltern by the state. For example, to become eligible for government inclusion within financial incentive schemes such as the JSY, mothers had to possess officially valid government documents of proof, namely postal addresses, caste certificates and poverty certificates. In addition, they had to live in areas that made it possible for them to access regular antenatal care (ANC) and postnatal care (PNC) that would allow PHC (Primary Health Clinic) clinicians to update their registration cards, recording their regular visits. Women became enlisted in government schemes through check-up regimens and through the provision of valid administrative documents that could prove details such as the caste of their parents or father, ration cards, electricity bills or school-leaving certificates that could prove a written name, postal address and so on. These also constituted some of the essential criteria for procuring Scheduled Caste (SC) or Scheduled Tribe (ST) certificates from the *tehsildar*'s office (office below district level), which were then used to procure other cards such as below poverty line (BPL) cards or ration cards. These cards alone made them eligible for financial incentives under the JSY scheme upon institutionalisation in PHCs (for two days) and PNC, irrespective of the quality of the services. Groups that were nomadic, or homeless—those living in slums without postal addresses, migrants, refugees, or those unable to produce BPL cards or ration cards, those without any formal education or without knowledge about their caste (such as orphans or people of a mixed caste, as an example)—were obviously debarred and considered 'obscene' according to the state. The JSY constructed its own subalterns, which were indeed only a lower-class segment of the dominant castes, and served to uplift them in order to demographically strengthen the position of the dominant castes and certain mainstream groups that included 'settled' STs, who would mimic dominant castes by following state policies, even though they would remain within caste hierarchy (since financial incentives for SCs and STs were different). Further, state policy under schemes such as JSY supported only two children and the mother would have to be of a certain age (above 19) to receive financial incentives for her institutional delivery, the actual amount decided in accordance with the development index fixed for her district and in accordance with her tribe or caste status. Both she and the ASHA would miss their incentives if even a single document or precondition/proof of eligibility was missing. Childbirth became an added government scheme-associated pressure of moneymaking that clans and community health workers became involved in, as if the tension of giving birth to a long-living male heir was not bad enough for mothers, without the government replicating similar processes of reproductive labour and state ownership of women's bodies that sought to locate dominant castes as its demographically majority citizens.

Having two children (preferably sons) whose institutional birth was paid for by the state, and that too in the absence of inadequate attention paid to temporary methods of contraception (apart from condoms distributed by the state, the male inclination towards the using of which remained abysmal according to many of my respondents), abortion remained the most popular method of contraception (I have known respondents who have had up to nine abortions) that deliberately precluded the birth of daughters. Families and marital relationships tried to take as much advantage as possible of women's legal right to abortion and state policies such as JSY that were assisted by village ASHAs to circumvent the issue of temporary contraception (dependent on men) and the birth of girl children (an increased use of abortion), despite a law against sex selective tests.[10] All sorts of informal ritual methods, sign language, euphemisms and 'advice' continued to be used to communicate the sex of the child, especially outside clinics, even as clinicians could not avoid having vibrant social relationships with their patient's families within rural inhabitations. Government schemes and women's legal rights to abortion were therefore being cleverly subverted and used against them by the very clans that claimed to love and own these family members, or on whom women and children depended financially and physically

[10] The Pre-conception Pre-natal Diagnostics Test (PCPNDT) Act in India banned sex-selection tests identifying the female embryo in 1994.

when pregnant and young. Fighting for or against any of these causes at a universal or general level remained impossible, since it would always be outside of their situational context of potential abandonment or abuse, wherein its dangers for those socially vulnerable would have to be carefully evaluated. A rising number of institutional births then actually also reflected its shadow land counterpart of possibly rising rates of abortions that were actually daughter deaths couched in the language of women's legal right to abortion as a result of contraceptive failure. This as 'data' will always remain statistically unproven due to the way in which close social relationships between rural doctors with political connections worked in association with dominant caste clans with connections to larger networks of powerful caste lobbies that were linked to vote banks. These in turn worked hand in glove with healers connected with influential religious groups, who exerted pressure on women to need sons in order to redeem their personal poverty and avoid the diagnosis of being defective or faulty and avoid a subsequent future of abandonment and abuse and instead gain purity and valour.[11]

Many of my respondents preferred removing the legal ban on sex-selective tests in order to reduce the trauma and number of abortions they underwent. They wanted to avoid all the violence, domestic abuse and the consciously deployed malnutrition that they and their girl children were subject to, when the latter was allowed to take birth. Some women recounted being violently beaten after being accused of 'cheating' when they had daughters contrary to ritual prediction of a male embryo, while others spoke of being forced to cut down their new-born daughter's nutrition and breastfeeding. Ritual healers obviously tried to escape what would be understood as the clan's private matters by further diagnosing such women's wombs as swindlers (*dagaabaaz*), having given birth in contradiction to the healer's diagnosis of all the right signs for male embryos in their wombs.

Sex-selective abortions were the lesser evil according to my

[11] Weigl (2007) demonstrates the way in which clan reproduction within a Delhi slum is mediated more through poverty than religion.

respondents, since the legal determination against the female foetus would serve to cut down the domestic violence and torture of women and expose the social truth of discrimination against women as it existed, without pretences. They felt that if the ban was removed, they would get to know the scientific truth know the foetus's sex rather than depend on the divinations of capricious healers, who would possibly grow afraid and blame their wombs in the end if things turned against ritual preordination in any case. In this way, if they knew the sex of the child in the second month of pregnancy itself, the abortions would also grow easier and speedy, without the child getting the opportunity to grow in the womb, reducing their guilt and grief. This would also avoid miscalculation and ritual mis-diagnosis and blaming. They told me of how a woman in the neighbouring village of Chaas-Narodi had been misdiagnosed by a travelling healer to have a daughter and the aborted foetus after a terribly traumatic medical procedure at Junnar, after the first trimester had finished, had apparently been male. The family had searched for the healer but he had run away by then and everyone was grief stricken but nothing could be done. But on the other hand, there would be no daughters born any longer, which in any case no one wanted (according to my respondents). Since accepting this publicly was equally painful, problematic and embarrassing, some of my more angry respondents felt that they had to bear the brunt of keeping social dignity intact (*Samaaj tyancha*! *Jeev amcha*!—Their society! Our lives!).

The biggest NRHM demand underlying JSY institutional births and its financial incentives lay in the banning of midwifery by labelling it unhygienic and irrational. This demand of banning midwifery did not lie in the understanding of the practice as casteist or discriminating against women that extracted feudal labour from them, putting lower-caste women into hierarchical and 'absorbing' relationships with 'upper-caste' women. Instead it viewed midwives as uneducated and illiterate women, whose traditional ways were irrational. The argument of being unhygienic was, in any case, simple enough to be overcome, as many community health workers and ASHAs themselves demanded to be trained in scientific methods of midwifery in one such meeting I attended at

Mukhada, Jawhar (district Thane, Maharashtra), claiming to need such clinical training as part of their community work. The NRHM problematic of it lay in its denouncing of midwifery on 'scientific grounds' that was unsubstantiated since ASHAs were assisting in crisis-based childbirths in their own villages in any case, and since the roots of this NRHM denunciation lay in its somewhat colonial frameworks of 'scientific rationality' as superior.

The actual problematic of midwifery practice lay in its lower caste duty of 'impurity absorption' that I have delved in, in some detail, in chapter one and not in its rationality or hygiene. An ASHA too suffers pressure from her village, since the government holds her accountable for her village women's health just as the goddess cult holds the midwife accountable to the upper-caste clan and women in labour, whom she serves. If she is not 'absorbent' enough, the child may die and the clan may accuse the midwife to be a witch. Similarly, if the ASHA does not serve the public health system well enough, the pregnant woman in question may not receive adequate government health services and she may be blamed by both the village government institutions and her village peers: the dominant caste clans. The problematic is the hegemonic network of feudal servitude within which these women are bonded to their village in both cases, when childbirth is in fact a complicated process that can turn into a crisis at any moment, even with the greatest of doctors, ASHAs or midwives at hand. The problematic lies in how the difficulties of the ASHA may mimic those of the midwife because of their location as village women, who are part of its belonging and susceptible to its pressures and witch-hunts[12] without any possible escape routes. Though discussions about retrieving the midwife's power retain interest in her considerable skill, even as such positions seek to combat decadent government positions about the midwife's irrationality and absence of hygiene (Chawla 2002; Sadgopal 2009), the problem of her caste- and

[12] It brings to mind cases such as Bhanwari Devi's, a community health worker from Rajasthan, who faced terrible violence as she became involved in struggling against gender crimes in her village (*Vishakha & Ors vs State of Rajasthan & Ors* on 13 August 1997).

gender-based labour that concerns the powers of absorbing impurity as a ritual duty for the goddess unfortunately seems to remain outside the ambit of discussion.

Midwifery, even as it remains a great resource of experiential and technical potential among women, cannot be 'retrieved' as long as it remains entrenched within caste and religion, as a system of hegemonic networks and feudal labour extraction that is strengthened by government health policies and which bolsters dominant castes. We would never be sure whether we were retrieving individual knowledges or whether we were strengthening caste networks, clan dominance and religious alliances! Moreover, the 'knowledges' midwives had were thickly interwoven with patriarchal concepts of the female body as owned in marriage and female purity that led to successful delivery, even as these remained located within women's relationships with their marital clans in addition to their punitive relationships with goddess cults.

Moreover, to 'retrieve' these as alternative resources for the production of how or what we understand as knowledge today would require an intensive exercise in decoding and contextualising these practices deductively, while locating them within what are understood as other acceptable sciences today that are themselves undergoing processes of redefinition, rediscovery and change. Therefore, in the attempt to 'retrieve' midwifery and criticise hyper-rationality, we would have to first hegemonise the same hyper-rational science or indigenous science in order to hold it as a paragon-like framework and a reference point, which in reality is a cultural product and undergoing transition quite heavily itself. And even thereafter, we would only be able to point at similarities. We would never be able to establish demonstrable linkages and continuities between traditions of the body that indeed have completely different genealogies of caste and impurity on the one hand and anatomy and physiology on the other. Maybe it would be more worthwhile to understand the relationships between women and midwives as mystical, transitive, worthwhile, esteemed and personal, while at the same time recognising and respecting how these remain different for every woman and, finally an issue for feminist research, rather than medical anthropology.

Rationalism and Feminism

Rationalism as a social movement has a long tradition in Maharashtra, and the Maharashtra Andhashradhha Nirmulan Samiti (MANIS/ANIS), very active in science awareness programmes in rural Maharashtra (Quack 2012), has become a powerful grass-roots movement in my field area. Some of ANIS's important contributions include pointing out the rampant social exploitation of women (battery, molestation, rape) happening at the hands of healers and fake god-men, when the latter, as agents of the woman's marital clans, harass, rape or humiliate her at the latter's behest. This is especially so when childlessness becomes a major clan concern, wherein a clan may not want to reveal or expose the concerned woman's husband's impotence or sterility.

The flaws of the movement are, however, concerned with the conflating of 'superstition' (under which term trance and spirit possession are especially targeted) with issues of attention seeking and mental health disturbance that are sought to be rooted in social exploitation among and against lower castes, women and the poor. The same definition therefore can be extended towards constructing upper-caste practices as the really religious (and not superstitious), since these are not based in exploitation or the exploitation underlying them may be intra-caste, intra-clan and silenced personally among seniors. Furthermore, upper caste religion may have systemic acceptance with state and government holidays and constitutional rights of religious freedom attached to them, while superstition may become produced as a mental health and social exploitation issue. ANIS ends up making rigid differentiations between religion and superstition based on caste and class, even while denigrating those who are 'superstitious' according to these terms as being either victims or criminals, which in either case produces them as being unfit citizens. It's a complex position that harks back to Western scientific models without the reflexivity of viewing science and its problematic engagement with racism, violence or consumerism as cultural products, whether in the past or the present. ANIS has targeted all lower caste cult practices defined by it as superstition that are exploitative, even while remaining silent on the validity of what constitutes religion and its use within politics by the state. Neither has the movement afforded sensitivity to an absence of economic possibilities for poorer and lower caste groups and families who, while remaining outside dominant castes and economic security, survive at the very bottom of structural hierarchy and depend economically on dominant castes and elites. Like government policies or then like the goddess herself, it repeatedly targets a social section and invalidates its citizenry that can ill afford any financial leverage to be able to change their existential poverty, enforced doubly upon them through caste duties and denouncements of superstition and backwardness by social movements such as the rationalists.

According to the ANIS logic, lower-caste and poor women are responsible for the perpetuation of systemic exploitation(or they are simply attention-seeking victims, who have mental health problems) and their attitude ultimately act as obstacles to science, which, in turn, is the only conceivable path to achieving rational and scientific nation building. There are no available economic alternatives viable within their rationalist frameworks for those belonging to the lowest rung of caste hierarchy, dependent on dominant castes for subsistence and safety within villages, in exchange for ritual favours, which for many lower-caste families remains the only feasible option, especially if they inherit the traditional rights to healing at a shrine and can earn something from it. ANIS judges the way in which poor healers and midwives subsist economically within villages, ignoring rural social structures of caste, while extoling 'freedom' from superstition, without probing deeper into what the real economic alternatives for lower-caste populations living within urban slums constitute.

The rationalist argument on gender, when addressing possession and mental health, is not unlike earlier anthropological theories resembling peripheral cults propounded by I.M. Lewis (1978) that considered possessions to be arenas within which peripheral members of the community, such as women, expressed their grievances for gains that they were otherwise socially denied. ANIS has likewise rediscovered possession as an arena for reforming its target community of superstition, based on an identification of peripheral communities, even if such an assumption itself is unscientific and unsubstantiated. Many persons, including men from the upper class and urban and dominant castes, engage in trance and possession activities, for example, albeit in non-typical formats of '*dhyaan*' that cannot be easily identified by ANIS members as superstition.

In any case, if the ANIS viewpoint were to be believed, it would amount to the following functionalism: socially oppressed lower caste women, fully recognising their condition as systemic oppression and unable to solve their problem in any other viable manner but the culturally recognised one, deliberately manipulate the possibility of solving their problems through trance and spirit possession, while remaining completely insightful about how this would result in the desired end. They would then deliberately 'become' mentally and emotionally unstable, using possession cults as ways of attention seeking and gaining empowerment temporarily within their clans, assuming that once their demands were met, the possession fits would automatically subside (which is also unsubstantiated). This theory would also make most possessed women atheists and rationalists at heart, since they would have to enjoy an absence of belief in deities a-prior, in order to know them to be false, so as to manipulate a trance and bring on fake possessions (this is unsubstantiated too).

Further, there were rationalist feminists within the fold who viewed trances and possessions in terms of what these 'represented', in terms of new age body practices, curiously after removing these first and entirely from contexts of caste and gendered labour. Viewed as empowering, healing and freeing body movements that subverted patriarchy and expressed female physical oppression within it, these theories (critiqued by Clark-Deces 2008) obviously allowed rationalist feminists to identify with their own New Age ritual healing practices that mimicked trance.

These theories, however, do not explain the occurrence of afflicting trances for women that indicate certain fault lines within society as Michel de Certeau (2000) analysed within the context of Loudun. The social fault lines in terms of goddesses in charge of afflicting large swathes of population with rampant epidemics in the Deccan were similar when compared to the plague in medieval Europe, even as Dhavalikar (2002) describes goddesses emerging in the enormous ecological and epidemic-related catastrophes of medieval Deccan as part of providing an eco-historical explanations for the origin of afflicting goddess cults in the pre-modern period. Just as the nuns at the monastery of Loudun started showing signs of possession that demonstrated fault lines of a society growing religiously rigid, when in the grip of an epidemic and its terror, the fault lines of rural Maharashtra rigidified feudal labour of caste and gender stratification in the face of epidemics to perpetuate competitive property ownership[13], inheritance and demographic power among dominant caste clans as well as notions of dharma that conflated with the longevity of sons, even as children died in medieval droughts and epidemics.

The point of interest, however, remains focussed on why affliction cults such as Satvai and Maulya still remain popular in rural Maharashtra, even as the pandemic proportions of epidemics that were once considered to cause infant and maternal mortality now seem abated. Since the material base that produces ritual propitiation of these affliction goddess cults in rural Maharashtra as cultural or traditional forms of 'rationality' (that have since transited into realms of superstition) no longer lies within historical contexts, its material base must shift to lie more within the fear of witchcraft and its opposition to patriarchal ownership.

Women seek to 'inoculate' themselves against this witchcraft with the help of affliction-goddess cults, when the latter turn into protectors of the village through transformations affected in a 'combination' of witch-like women, who are propitiated to act as gate-keepers. For those who base themselves more within the non-rural, it is the sister or the 'purer' counterpart of the Satvai, the goddess Jivati, who has entered the realm of rational religion in urban Maharashtra, worshipped on every Friday of the *Chaturmasa* by Brahminical women, as the goddess Satvai passes into the lower realms of impurity, non-acceptability (as religion)

[13] Anand (2005) demonstrated that the *Balutedari* system of occupational ownership gradually transformed itself into the caste system within Maharashtra.

and superstition. The Satvai is a reformed witch, only propitiated to protect, even as she is understood as cannibalistic, while the Jivati, her counterpart, is considered pure and Brahminical (explained in the next chapter). The material realm of Satvai propitiation therefore has also changed, since not infant mortality but witchcraft and female immorality has become the new fear. It is this fear of witchcraft and witches that turns the womb and the soil barren, makes kingship and feudal duties impossible and renders patriarchal pillars of ownership and inheritance out of the question. Each woman, by virtue of being considered non-owned or without marriage is understood to manipulate her reproduction and reproductive fluids from within herself and consequently be therefore capable of witchcraft and the cannibalism of children and men. It is through allowing the rightful ownership of her body through marriage and childbirth rituals that women's control over their bodies and their bodies are split away, harnessing the latter as a fertile field for impregnation within patriarchy. Women are also taught to harness their wombs to this labour and feudal duty by remembering the separation between their control over their body and their body, as they come to morally view all female exercise of will over it as sin. They try to avoid situations in which their bodies may turn rogue, witch, barren, afflicted and cannibal with the help of goddess cults that hold out the possibility of avoiding transformation and facilitating splitting and fragmentation.

Alternative Knowledge

The critique of colonialism and modernity and the consequent valorisation of traditional systems purportedly repressed by colonialism and modernity as alternative knowledge and agency mechanisms, is a powerful discursive mode that in contradiction to its own critique of modernity, continues to retain the language and value systems of modernity, secularism, democracy and free speech. Relationships between the modernist state and its colonial legacy become a cause for anxiety among nationalists valorising tradition, even as concepts of tradition within right-wing ideals of modernity that view caste as occupation, unrelated to hierarchy and exploitation, are sought to be expressed.[14] Indeed, nationalists have invited the state to rationalise tradition as modern, rather than conceptualise modernity as a form of rationality.

Campaigns in favour of how traditional systems worked best within contexts of poverty and health activism—for example, in favour of midwives and traditional healers as perfect service providers within resource-poor regions, failing health service sectors and poor communities as a form of 'alternative modernity' run the danger of supporting two very dangerous suppositions. First, they implicitly accept the recalcitrance of the state health-care service provision (mostly used by the poor) as a 'given', by offering other alternatives to it (which they claim, have stronger chances of cultural success), instead of strengthening the state and helping to remove its biases and corruption (the real obstacles). At the same time, the view holds the poor responsible for their 'culturalism' that is deemed to be beyond medical care, when citing how cultural methods work best for them, which then comes close to the rationalism-superstition-oriented denouncing of the 'native', poor and lower caste, whenever a crisis befalls them. Moreover, the guilt for the poverty of the Adivasi is redeemed by the arguments of her 'exotic' and oriental nature that might never respond to the state's modernity, while research among her autochthonous habitat may bolster her pristine and changeless image that might remain in continuation of colonial research, even if formally contradicting its learnings.

Second, advocating for different kinds of health systems that the rich and the poor access differently, as a matter of being free from hegemonic systems of oppression operative within their lives, becomes problematic from the point of view of every individual's universal right to health choices. When there are no availability of choices, there are no choices! The rich can afford both private medical care and traditional methods equally, since class and

[14] Cf. the statements of Yellapragada Sudershan Rao, the chairman of the Indian Council of Historical Research (ICHR), concerning the supposed workings of the caste system in ancient India and the furore they created in July 2014 (Mukul 2014).

languages of modernity and liberal education may provide for powerful escape routes from gender and caste hegemonic structures for them, but since the poor cannot even access acceptable public health services in many cases, hegemonic traditional practices that are rooted in caste and gendered oppression hardly constitute health choices for them, since these are not just availabilities but enforced clan decisions on their bodies and they do not allow women, especially those from the lower castes, either freedom from labour or social mobility.

The Supreme Court introduced strictures on traditional healing centres in India after the Erwadi tragedy in 2002 in which some 'patients' housed within a Muslim healing shrine, a dargah, were burnt alive in a fire that broke out there because they were chained to the walls within the building.[15] The Supreme Court's move of questioning traditional healing centres attracted criticism from mental health activists (Davar and Lohokare 2009) against the state, as they used this opportunity to demand better services within state institutions that, according to them, also violated the human rights of patients, while they sought to view the rituals at these traditional healing centres from a soft psychological angle (such as being bonded to God, a psychological commitment to healing and so on) that is, completely interpretive and impressionistic. They demanded that ritual healers be integrated within state health delivery systems because they introduced a traditional form of psychology that had indigenous and cultural roots, [16] as they compared traditional healing centres to psychological healing from various theoretical perspectives and new age body practices that relieved psychological stress in friendly religious formats. This approach, though innovative, creates problematic parallels between the two systems of psychiatry and ritual healing (assuming that rituals heal in the first place, rather than integrate

[15] Manicom (2008) discusses the healing centre at Erwadi in Tamil Nadu using the Foucauldian analysis of institutionalisation, while seeking to separate traditional healing from the exotic, locating it instead within the discourses of colonisation that pits mental distress as the opposite of civilisation.

[16] Somewhat along the lines of Kakar (1982) in *Shamans, Mystics and Doctors*, who explains the psychological benefits of traditional healing methods in India.

people, who want to move out of oppressive mainstreams back into it), considering both as equals and their trajectory of origin and development in India as linear. Such parallelisation refuses to probe deeper into issues such as religious belonging and the communal division that such grouping forms—political lobbies based on religious fundamentalism, local power structures of gender and caste and poverty—while making easy parallels between the two systems based on popular psychology and poorly comparable research methodology. Finally, such parallels again ignore the way in which it is ultimately the language of science, psychiatry, cross-cultural methods (based in colonial encounters and early anthropology) and modernism that are still hegemonic within theoretical frameworks, while deciding on the 'scientific value' of traditional healing practices.

Added to this is an intensification of what I understand as right-wing paradox: the state would now have to provide institutionalised non-clinical health services (considered traditional) within arenas that already had access to traditional healing practices and shrines by integrating traditional healers within state service delivery as recognised religious leaders with control over the errant bodies and minds of those lower within the hierarchy, such as women. In short, a modernised tradition would validate rituals formally as part of a state-sponsored technique of healing. This would then allow state health service delivery and health budgets to withdraw from areas where ritual healing centres would thrive. Nandy (2004), on the other hand, holds that shamanism is an act of state subversion. The view of integrating traditional healers or healing centres into the recalcitrant modernist state is then a formula for a right-wing religious state that withdraws from health services for the poor, where shamans (if they are indeed against the state) are co-opted into becoming state supporters, where only the rich have health choices and they become state supporters too, and where social hierarchy is deepened impossibly to shut off all escape routes in terms of health choices for those at the lower rungs.

As a discourse, the notion of alternative knowledge claims that indigenous history of associations between traditional practitioners and goddesses, for example, can be separated from its colonial construction without needing to understand how the shaping of concepts, such as tradition, are deeply entrenched within postcolonial modernity.[17] Theories about ancient connections between goddess cults and midwifery become reinvented within modernity in order to justify images of idyllic tradition and retrieved knowledge resources, which in turn run the risk of becoming co-opted into nationalism. A dangerous right-wing academics of validating 'traditional' practice as science runs the risk of proclaiming patriarchy as 'healthy' by searching for parallel practices in some or the other reinvented medicinal tradition (after intensive academic decoding exercises) and transposing all social conditions of structural hierarchy and caste to non-political subjections of medical materialism (such as how fear of the goddess is actually an ancient fear of disease and so on, for example).

The ironic obliteration of the poor and poverty by traditionalists is best expressed by Mary Douglas (2004) in her paper, 'Traditional Culture: Let's Hear No More About It', in which she demonstrates how the rich delude themselves when they claim traditional practices as instruments for healing, even while advocating its use for the poor. Since elite advocates of tradition are not entrenched within societies where these practices form part of exploitative and hierarchical structures, all they have access to, on the basis of which they advocate these practices, from outside the location of these practices, are its superficial and purported similarities (and that too in alleged effect) with new age practices that they use as instruments of healing, transposed to a different context.

An important layer of repression operates at the level of academics that upholds the discourse that designates regionally dominant castes as 'subaltern' and valorises their practices as 'traditional'. This construction participates in a form of repression, wherein the experiential articulation of loss is obliterated and becomes 'obscene' in the all too familiar way.[18]

[17] Chawla (1994) has outlined the ancient relationships between goddess cults and midwives, for example, and continues to describe, along with Sadgopal (2009), the practices of midwives as science, according to Ayurveda.

[18] Chatterjee (2012) has revisited the nature of the subaltern analytical category, questioning its veracity as misleading within subaltern studies.

This discursive repression has its real roots in political networks with regional dominant castes that extract labour and develop its own authoritative understanding of 'birth' and birth attendants for example, that simultaneously renders child and maternal mortality and morbidity and issues of exploitation in association with birth attendants opaque. Propagated by scholarship ensconced in a dominant caste-associated nationalist enterprise of retaining domestic culture, it results in the perpetuation of caste politics that supports patriarchy, wherein women are owned and face social ostracism when their bodies don't comply with such demands. 'Healing' discourses surrounding goddesses are, as discussed above, centred on the cultural value of impurity (*vitaal*) or, according to Professor Guru (2013), centred on the 'social ecology of dirt' that justifies and rationalises the avoidance and condemnation of those identified as impure.

Ultimately, apparent differences between the non-articulate or 'obscene' and the exotic and dominant (the articulate 'data providing' subalterns according to academic discourses about culture) are themselves constructed as hierarchically inferior to those who formulate the discourse, even as they seek to control the process of knowledge production. Within discursive exigency, however, the inarticulate however, falls entirely out of data and become 'obscene' when not producing seamless monochromatic depictions of culture that could match texts and sculpture for those constructing them as subaltern, timeless and exotic. They run the danger of falling out of power nexus as individuals as well, when they can no longer be heard or understood within academic parameters or language, since they fall outside the empathy and experience of both researchers and their nexus with the dominant subalterns.

In summation therefore, it would only be dangerous to transpose 'specialist' healers with 'ancient knowledge' into modern clinical settings as technicians or merge traditional healing with modern medical practice, since these healers operate their knowledge very much within paradigms of purity that are in turn located within religion and caste, just as modern clinical settings operate according to hierarchies of class and Western education. Western-educated, rich and usually upper-caste doctors at institutional helms would hardly entertain midwives with 'traditional skills', unless the entry route of a religion-based nationalist lobby was used for this inclusion. Even according to my interviews at the Taljai slum, Pune, where I spoke to women who were experts at self-birthing, the concern of obstructed birth did bring up questions about women's purity or a relinquishing of control by midwives, as women increasingly preferred to go to clinics in 'danger' situations.

According to my respondents at Taljai, it was the (sexual) impurity of women that created obstructions in their labour as their 'tubes closed' during birth, due to the impurity of a woman in labour (a condition known as *nad-bandh*). In such a situation, drinking water from the hands of a pure man (who had retained his sexual power and virginity) was supposed to have the potential to release the woman from this obstacle and ease her suffering (this had been a common practice in rural 'times', before their migration to Pune, I was told) that would finally lead to the delivery of both the child and the placenta. Other women in such a situation formed a chain, touching this 'pure' man, who in turn was to stand, touching the source of water that would be passed back to the stuck or *adhleli* woman the drinking of which would release her. This ritual relegated sexuality to the masculine body and fertility and motherhood to the female, instituting a moral hygiene between the both, while dividing and segregating the two: sexual men and fertile women by constructing their position essentially to the two opposites. These could be related only through marriage and the ownership of women and children that the goddess presided over. This process was helped by those agents of the boundary between the upper and lower caste sections of the village, who were especially dedicated to goddesses as healers. They were considered androgynous in the sense that they had no traditional property rights in the village and inherited only the servitude duty presided upon by the goddess. They blessed couples and new-born children traditionally, even as they remained associated to the goddess cult and shrine as the lowest castes of Maharashtra (I will discuss dedicated castes in further detail in the chapters that follow).

Poor women themselves saw no other alternatives but the improvement of medical services provided by the state, where they would be treated better for cheaper fares. Help from other women during emergencies and 'absorption' of birth impurity during reproduction was provided/enforced through the caste system by clans in any case and did not need to be institutionalised any further, unless one was conceptualising a hyper-nationalist modernity. As pointed out by Kaviraj (2010), postcolonial society in India suffers from an illness of institutionalisation, which becomes the pretext for abolishing real injustice. Justice cannot be wrought through institutionalism, since the latter breeds the same injustice and corruption that it seeks to redress. In what has been described by A. Sen (2009) when commenting on the nature of transcendental institutionalism: institutionalism, even while seeking to bring about reform, remains divested from the very processes of justice provision that needs to include consensus within democracy. Instead, it supports the manner in which the mystic of institutionalisation is imagined to act as a panacea for justice provision of all kinds.

Finally, my respondents also chose medical practitioners with as much ease with which they chose non-clinical practitioners, such as midwives or personnel who were a mixture of midwives trained later on as community health workers or nurses or simply outright doctors (if they could at all exercise individual choice), on the basis of interpersonal rapport and trust building, if they could also mediate this with their clans. They did not choose practitioners based on the fields of medicine or disciplines these practitioners followed or represented in any exclusive manner to reflect their principles about it, unlike what health researchers and bureaucrats assumed, who required women to comply with their agenda of taking sides with either medical professionals or traditional practitioners. Since these are primarily policy battles and did not concern my respondents; it was only rapport building that remained more important for the latter. They accessed many sorts of health services all at once in order to get the best results, without feeling interested in entering epistemic battles, since it is the practitioners they had built relationships of comfort with.

Practice and service delivery is therefore of the greatest importance while planning health services for the underprivileged, which cannot be pre-decided to be culturally closer based on their emanation from religious or caste or clan bodies and such traditional sources; that would simply be an orientalist bias. Neither can it be assumed to emanate from cheap public health service. This may not be of good quality. Private and expensive clinical services might be unaffordable; these might not be good relationships for women to justify to their clans. That women already mix all these or none of the above and undertake a new option when suddenly available is already prevalent, even though it might not constitute a solution to their personal difficulties. What may constitute a solution is the presence of multiple and non-merged body/health options along with the presence of multiple practitioners (relationship and help possibilities) in their vicinity that could help women negotiate with oppressive clan relationships that controlled their body choices.

It was best for health and body services to remain non-institutionalised and decentralised in order for women to enjoy maximum health and body-related benefits, while negotiating for space and the possibility for building stronger interpersonal relationships with practitioners that they could manoeuvre and manipulate when negotiating with their families. Van Hollen's ethnography (2003) similarly demonstrates the acceptance of community health workers and service providers as traditional midwives in her ethnography about childbirth in Tamil Nadu as non-differentiated in terms of their epistemic frameworks, since they operate more on the basis of their rapport and relationship with women.

Continuity and Change

When explaining my research to people, who viewed goddess cults from a culturalist and nationalist angle and also after basing my research formally in an Archaeology department for a doctorate, it is also pertinent to describe some of the larger debates and biases about caste that are inherent within disciplines such as ancient history and archaeology and its interpretations in India that takes on the more recognizable discursive forms of marking the 'aboriginal' from the 'Aryan'.

Writing history about 'folk goddesses' (village goddesses have generally been considered 'folk goddesses' of the 'lesser tradition' by historians) has often involved their association with Sanskritic goddesses of the Hindu texts, whose residual forms they are often been considered to represent, when continuing into modernity as a subaltern stratum worshipped in rural India. Writings about such subjects as found in research conducted by authors like Coburn (1984), Kinsley (1986), Panikkar (1997) or White (2003) continue to exhibit this discourse of duality between Sanskritic and folk goddess cults that has either assumed the latter (folk goddesses) to assimilate into the former (Sanskritic deities) or the former to have left residual traces in diverse neighbouring regions in the form of the latter. Archaeological and historical discourses on folk goddesses claim the residual nature of her cult to be born out of an intermixture between the Brahmin and those who are considered the autochthonous (SCs and STs), resulting sometimes in the formation of the fifth caste of untouchables below the Shudras, associated with 'Shakta' or representative of goddess beliefs (Sharma 2003). Archaeologists, bolstering intellectual debates about the question of goddess origins and their antiquity, continue to employ the dualist terminology of 'high' and 'folk' religion, despite the commonly known interrelationship between these goddesses as sisters or adversaries encountered in their *vrata-katha* or stories that are read during rituals held for the wish fulfilment or vow of the performer, such as in the case of Jivati–Shashthi (the Satvai is often linked with Goddess Shashthi[19]) for example, that reinforces the caste status of ritual performers (Brahmins/the Brahminical worship Jivati, whereas the Marathas and other landed castes worship the Satvai). The interest in designating ferocious goddesses to the 'folk' remains invested in identifying autochthonous rural communities by dividing them racially from those recognised within the caste system as Brahminical and the

[19] Goddess Shashthi finds description in the *Brahma Vaivarta Purana*(Part of the Prakriti Khanda) as a deity, who resurrects children (see Sen 1974).

landed dominant castes, who worship Puranic goddesses and deities in temples inside the village; only lower castes are known to have 'superstitions' like the Satvai as clan goddesses. Current childbirth ritual practices among the rural dominant castes of the goddess are similarly conflated with the Vedic Sanskara rituals described in Brahminical texts in order to accord both power and authority to both sorts of rituals (goddess rituals and Sanskara rituals). This academic practice in turn produces Puranic goddesses as a residual aspect of Vedic rituals and constructs important power relationships for both forms of rituals that extends itself to include the Satvai's cult as 'folk' that then is pronounced the younger and malign residual aspect of Puranic goddess at the bottom rung. This thereby constructs an entire caste structure of ritual practice within academic understanding as well, starting with Vedic and Sanskritic Brahmin rituals at the top, conflating these with Puranic deities in the dominant caste middle level, which is joined by the malign goddesses bringing up the rear.

Writing the religious history of goddess Satvai's worship through archaeological evidence therefore, reads and writes the current ritual practice of the goddess into an interpretation of the past that is replete with the biases of the present. Models of ethno-archaeology or processual archaeology popularised by Lewis Binford during the 1960s and 1970s for example, looked towards anthropological traditions as continuities of the past and popularized research methods that compared modern scales of development with civilizational stages of cultural evolution. Goddess research followed a similar trajectory as the study of communities and castes in India (in terms of the census understanding of it) that was steeped in colonial bias (as suggested by Dirks 2001) dictated influential scholars such as Kinsley (1986), among others to label the early Matrika traditions and the description of these goddesses to have non-Aryan and aboriginal similarities without noticeable qualms. Even though the Satvai's cult resembles the goddess complex of 'Sapta-Matrika' (evidenced within Sanskrit texts and older sculptural traditions of the Deccan), my village respondents often traced the etymology of the goddess's name: Satvai to *Saat-aai* (seven mothers) or *Satva-aai* (mother of valour), since the Satvai and Maulya were also multiple death-repressing goddesses, and Maulya to simply mothers or *Asra* to *apsara* (heavenly damsels/ witches) that had probable origins in the Natha texts

Archaeologists have variously associated Satvai shrines with memorial, Sati or Hero stones, dating the development of shrine worship associated with hero-heroine stones to pre-modern ages, with its antecedents lying in the megalithic cultures of south India.[20] The Rashtrakuta kings built huge temple complexes and extolled the Sapta/Ashta-Matrikaas part of sculptures at Ellora, producing the tradition of the multiple goddesses henceforth as that of regional importance. Puranic myths about the goddess, meanwhile, came to play a large role in explaining the narrative of these sculptures and the reason for their existence within temples as protector deities.[21] These sculptural and Puranic traditions removed the Matrika from the personal context of women's worship during childbirth entirely (even though they were depicted with children), producing them instead as champions of kingship and militaristic or feudal power associated for the first time with Rashtrakuta[22] political and militaristic dominion. It is not difficult to imagine their role as protectors of kingship and childbirth at the same time however, since the goddesses came to embody the political perpetuation and necessary reproduction of social order that women's political role compulsorily entailed.

Even though the associated reflection between the sculptural

[20] D.D. Kosambi (1962) was the first to connect megalithic monuments of south India to the Satvai shrine of Theur near Pune (that he also considered a megalithic site) and more generally to the phenomena of Sati and Hero stones. Rajan (2000), following in the footsteps of Kosambi, traced memorial and Sati stones in south India to Sangam literature, corroborating it further with megalithic remains and monuments of the Deccan.

[21] It is common to find sculptural lintels of the Sapta/Ashta-Matrika, accompanied by Ganesha, above temple entrances, built in the traditional premodern styles found in the Deccan.

[22] Kinsley (1986) designates the origin of the Matrika cult to the first centuries of the Christian era, even as he dates their consolidation into the Sapta-Matrika pantheon to Puranic literature. He describes them in their initial phase as ferocious and aboriginal deities, who were later 'assimilated' into Brahminical Hinduism.

and Puranic Sapta/Ashta-Matrika and the current day Satvai or Maulya cult may provide us with valuable insights due to their mutual similarities, their convenient inter-connection as the 'same' or residual may also become problematic, due to the time difference between their cults. In that case, we could also use similarities as the only research method to prove diffusion and residual relationships between deities across lands, regional histories and cultures as well, if we can consider enormous time differences between cults to also be conveniently insignificant, since pushing back the antiquity of present-day cults assumes such nationalistic importance! It is important to remember how relationships between goddess dyads if they are worshipped together (like Jivati – Shashthi) can constitute regional relationships and rural-urban continuums within groups as ritual expressions of administrative and caste stratifications within understandings of what can constitute a political region, just as it is important to note how tenuous it is to pronounce cross century links between goddess cults in the absence of demonstrable historical linkage between their worship.

The similarities between cults within the same larger region of the Deccan across time can only be marked and enumerated to gain general insight, such as how the association between the Sati and Satvai cults (venerated on the sixth night after childbirth) finds its first reference in the thirteenth-century texts of the Dnyaneshwari (Panse 1952), as part of a night prayer for child survival. Even though Sati worship has traditionally never been part of child survival and childbirth rituals, such documentation demonstrates a less-researched example of how 'guardian deities' of villages and female ancestors of clans could have more personal meanings for the rural dominant castes, who worshipped them. They have for example never been included within Puranic textual and associated sculptural cults that are sought to be matched with texts, that are further linked with the political history of instituting local kingships that were sought to be made into one mono-tradition by archaeologists and Sanskritists.

The theory of 'residual' deities and practices for autochthonous communities has also percolated deep among those who are administratively designated as SC and ST today. Most of the Mahadev Koli in interviews with me described themselves as the 'original' inhabitants of the region, even as others pointed towards them as possessing some of the oldest traditions surrounding goddess cults. The reality in terms of the data I collected was actually quite the opposite: it was among the dominant castes that I discovered the most elaborate and detailed boundary rituals and motherhood taboos on separating sexuality from motherhood that were understood to protect women and babies from Satvai affliction. The Mahadev Kolior, the so-called 'original inhabitants' or autochthons on the other hand, simply treated the goddess as a clan deity without performing any special rituals to appease her at all. To point at the Koli as autochthonous with 'original complex data' on goddess was simply a pervasive colonial discourse that had strengthened caste and tribe as 'different' categories in my field area.

Meanwhile, there is also some brilliant supporting archaeological evidence that deconstructs myths about moribund caste-tribe segregations within ancient Deccan. Dhavalikar (2002), for example, demonstrates the way in which the same ethnic group in antiquity exploited different ecological niches of resource base as the climatic need for it arose, as agriculturists did, [23] rendering the politico-ethnic difference between pastoralists and agriculturalists null and void. Carrying out different occupations or being invested in different subsistence patterns did not necessarily require separate tribe and caste-based occupations with different ethnic indices attached to it, that had come to acquire deeper political resonance within modernist preoccupations of delineating 'communities' and postmodern nationalist politics of voting lobbies.

Returning to biases, archaeology and history as disciplines or subject matters are attached through their methodology to concepts of dating, stratigraphy and chronology. This has resulted in their attaching ideas of chronology to the 'folk' that, apart from connecting it (the folk) with the rural and the autochthonous,

[23] Personal communication with Professor S.R. Walimbe (retired, Department of Anthropology, University of Pune).

associates it with varying degrees of primitiveness. Consequently, the 'folk' is accorded a lower position in hierarchy with regard to the urban, upper-caste, Sanskritic, educated and technologically advanced. Archaeologists have traditionally followed certain materialist criteria for understanding and marking development that produces urbanism as a civilizational apex based on theories of technological materialism and societal evolution that have been outlined by some of the most influential Marxist archaeologists of the century such as Gordon Childe in *Man Makes Himself* (reprinted in 2003). Such theories of technological determinism and materialism have unfortunately also become biased lenses in terms of forming a world-view about societal development and modernity, applied to the present and the future. Such hyper-materialist approaches, more than anything else, lack a micro approach of how urban conglomerates often came together through the union of many hitherto disconnected neighbourhoods and the possibility of building central urban structures and bulwarks surrounded by rural but equally modern peripheries, with many other subsidiary and decentralised suburbia that did not have to be deemed 'primitive' or 'hunter-gatherer' the moment they were non-urban. A hyper-Marxist framework proves stilted in its continuous hierarchical approach to technology that leaves no space for plural and co-existing technological exchange networks.

I end this section with a discussion of one of the more obscure archaeological discussions concerning goddesses that is associated with the debates about social evolution, associated with the concept of 'primitive matriarchy' (Bhattacharyya 1988) and mother goddess worship. According to this theory, women were the first agriculturists and leaders within ancient Indian society, evidenced through the supposed antiquity of fertility cults that openly depict the sexual features of the female body in primitive sculptures and art, described by archaeologists as 'mother goddesses'. This theory is the result of a certain form of academic reification that interprets every female figurine found outside the 'purity' discourse (within which archaeologists as members of a caste society themselves are invested) as being powerfully reproductive, ritually important, associated with agriculture, and of goddess-like import, so that their interpretations may avoid realms of the sexual, mundane, banal, pornographic, threatening or even monstrous. Interpretations then fixate on other interpretations of these sculptures as forms of ancient fertility cults such as the Lajja Gauri that are explored within Brahminical and Tantric frameworks. Such cults are considered 'assimilative' of either lower sexualized 'folk' cults, lesser traditions, and magical and primitive exotic practice that can be found in residual form in lower caste religious practices or then directly representative of Vedic deities. These theories seek to control the female body, female reproduction and sexuality through imagined interpretive locations and paradigms of matriarchy, even while producing it as spectacular and exotic in an impossible political imaginaire that ultimately replaces ideas about women's power by the worship of motherhood and the hermeneutical control of birthing that is imposed over women's images that depicts their sexual body.

Images of the goddess, especially explicit birthing images in the squatting position such as the Lajja Gauri and their worship may act as powerful anti-witchcraft emblems that represent the control of potential witches through the enforcing of child-birthing and ownership functions over women's bodies that would have purifying agency over the exercise of their own will over it. The Lajja Gauri has been discussed as an example in endless classroom discussions as well as secondary literature. Almost all debates on 'goddess' or fertility cults that are not sure about whether to locate the exposed and explicit female sexual body in the divine and fertile category or whether to place it in the demonic and sexual, always converge on this topic. Verghese (2000) discusses the Lajja Gauri and her possible cult implications in detail in her perusal of 'fertility cults' in the Deccan and the Vijayanagara Empire. She explores the two groups of scholarship on the subject that have either viewed Lajja Gauri worship within contexts of childlessness (viewing the goddess then as a woman in child-birthing position) or then in the context of mitigating droughts (viewing the goddess in Tantric frameworks). Her research points to the predictable theories according to which the Lajja Gauri is viewed in a bipolar manner: either residual/folk that is later assimilated into the Brahminical or then Vedic in origin and later diffused and dispersed into the folk. Both theories perpetuate certain fixed views, whether it be about aboriginals, who are hyper sexual from where the cult purportedly originated or then the diffused Central Asian background of the ancient Vedic Aryans, who brought unknown concepts into the Gangetic plain from outside.

The Lajja Gauri cult has interesting similarities with the Satvai cult, since the Satvai is imagined to be headless and without specific personal identity by many of her healers in my field area as well. She is associated more with the function of childbirth and the inhabitation of boundaries, where her shrine is set up. Dhavalikar's (1977) excavation of the headless figurine (and bull) from Inamagaon that he identified with a Matrika known as Vishira, locates similar figurines (with exaggerated sexual features) from other excavations in Maharashtra such as Navdatoli, within the archaeological interpretation of being associated with childbirth, child-loss or the usual Tantric concept of mitigating droughts, since these evidences are sought to be heavily corroborated by Sanskrit texts. But archaeologists have failed to ask operative questions in their goddess research (even if using ethno-archaeology) about how idols such as that of the Lajja Gauri or the cult of the Satvai are in continuous use in order to control modern witchcraft and its hermeneutic association with those creating obstacles to childlessness (rather than childlessness itself), within present-day contexts, wherein the birth and death of children per se or drought for that matter, is comparatively speaking, under technological control.

Finally, I summarise some of the more theoretical aspects of this book that I have discussed above and will continue to assume as the basis for my further chapters:

1. Female sexuality, because it is considered impure, is divested from female reproduction with the help of Satvai rituals that locates this (impure sexuality) at goddess shrines outside the village boundary. Goddesses become repositories of female sexuality as divine creatures, capable of encompassing both biological attachment to new-borns and female sexuality

dedicated to them by women through ritual food, enjoining the labour of social and feudal motherhood on women as owned members of marital clans at village boundaries/ margins through rituals.

2. Goddess cults further enjoin the labour of 'absorbing' sexuality and its associated impurity from upper-caste members of society on lower-caste mediums, midwives and traditional healers, who are often dedicated to the goddess's service as ritual agents and service providers. They are considered 'immune' to illness and affliction, considered blessed, especially with fertility strong enough to encompass the goddess's sexuality, and ritually rewarded for their caste-based cleaning labour in the village, rendering them simultaneously unclean, sexually available and paradoxically auspicious. Goddess cults thus produce women as vulnerable labour both within and outside dominant caste clans; in the first case, as reproductive labour, and in the second, as sexual and absorbing labour for dominant castes in addition to reproductive labour for their own clans.
3. Goddesses are understood to punish both upper and lower-caste women with affliction for the non-fulfilment of their ritual duties on the basis of designated sexual and fertility roles. Women suffering childloss and widowhood suffer the ritual diagnosis of cannibalism, since all women are tacitly considered capable of witchcraft through the manipulation of their menstrual blood. Their refusal to purge themselves of their sexualised demands of possessing and owning their children or husbands is considered the main reason underlying the ritual diagnosis of the latters' demise. Redemption only lies in women's own deaths, as Sati (when dying to redeem the afterlife of their husbands) or as Satvai (when dying to save the lives of their new-born sons).
4. Similarly, goddesses send 'calls' to women who have forgotten their native village to remind them of their folly of having owned too many comforts and forgotten their own owned status, when their allegiance lies back home in the village, even as they send similar calls to lower-caste women through illness and trances to heal and answer illness-related questions posed to them by other women from upper castes, as they absorb the latter's maladies into their bodies as

feudal duty. If a medium were to refuse this 'divine call', the goddess is considered to afflict her as a reminder of her caste and gendered position of a labour provider and feudatory, her true roots.

5. The valorisation of dominant caste clans as units of nation building that also become associated with the strengthening of goddess cults and ascertaining their blessings for humans, especially amidst epidemics as protectors (as documented by Feldhaus in 2003 about the goddess Janai) constitute the main fulcrum of dharma, encompassing the extraction of labour from women as feudatories
6. Childbirth or childlessness goddesses, such as the Satvai and the Maulya, constitute a connecting string that links together many dissociated beads within a necklace of sorts: the pure fertility of women and their domestic agnatic roles of motherhood feudal labour inside village homes; sons who are dedicated to the goddess as the goddess's protégé henceforth for protection, who inherit property; women's split off sexuality considered afflicting for them and its connection with fallow lands full of garbage outside village boundaries near Satvai-Maulya shrines and, finally, the lower-castes inhabitations and bodies of the goddess's mediums considered unclean, auspicious, absorbent of sexuality and impure that are available for labour, also located outside the village boundary.
7. Exploring the subject of goddesses and their relationship with women, gender, caste, poverty and childbirth is not an innocuous exercise. It is ridden with an exploration of the political world of health policy, rationalism or other social movements and the historical and culturalist production of the same that differentiates and discriminates between dominant discourses, while projecting it as primary and silencing the shadow world that remains invisible, un-researched, unexplored, unsayable and obscene.

CHAPTER 3

Separating Good and Bad Motherhood

Various ambivalent, aggressive, angry or wild Hindu goddesses have been researched in India based on historical and anthropological analysis, as constituting mutual continuations or residual aspects of each other's cults, as has already been mentioned in the last chapter. The special significance within the worship of goddesses, however, lies in their various internal combinations (as dyads or arranged in what are considered to be auspicious conglomerates in odd numbers of five, seven, nine, eleven, thirteen and so on) that produce them either as sisters, groups (entourages) adversaries, or rivals of each other, often arranged in mutual hierarchy (when associated with Sanskritic goddesses). The effect that these combinations have come to acquire is a curious historical 'flatness' over region, as they project an image of 'sameness' or regularity in terms of their presence (only differentiated historically, when viewed as residual), as if these goddesses, put together in terms of their cult, have always and intrinsically belonged together and have always enjoyed a seamless engagement and contiguous trajectory that has remained unbroken till present times. This 'sameness' obliterates the historical journey of cult formation that has certain politics of unification, alliance and conflict in producing complex regional cultic phenomena, constitutive of multiple goddesses/dyads and so on, along with its fluid and changing ritual formats, coming together with rich explanative mythologies that expose political fault lines of hierarchy production and crisis management within it. The very static nature of its presentation belies its dynamic internal shifts and adjustments. These goddesses have not grown together naturally; they embody complex socio-historical processes to become the most powerful signifier of political organisation that has systemically extracted specific and thickly described forms of moralised labour.

While the worship of multiple goddesses (as groups) often signifies the presence and possibly the valorisation of an entire village as a political unit, consisting of different castes, since the goddesses themselves represent the stratified complex of souls of different castes of women, who have died during childbirth (demanding different forms of typical occupational products as ritual offerings), the dyad format among them often refers to the division of village castes between the upper and lower. Relationships of hierarchy between these goddesses and between village castes constituting the cult describe how this projected 'sameness' engages with a caste-specific and caste-based organisation of rural and land-centric relations of production and its reproduction that strengthens dominant caste demography. Their individual worship, similarly, glorifies clan-based traditions that come to embody feudal duties and property relationships within individual members of the clan, all laying claim to ownership and inheritance within a single region. The clan worship of single goddesses is often aimed at intra-clan and intra-caste cohesion, rather than of the inter-caste variety of worship that includes inter-relationships between more castes of a village or region. The popular worship of Goddess Gauri in Maharashtra can also be read as an example of dyad worship or caste disparity, though historians have linked it to residual Sanskritic traditions such as Lakshmi-A-Lakshmi or the worship of the Matrikas Jyeshtha and Kanishtha (Redij and Joglekar 2010–11).

It is of interest to note that the worship of a single Gauri (and not the dyad or multiple goddesses representing stratified castes) finds location in non-Brahmin families, who worship her as a clan deity providing them the blessing of cohesion, once worshipped. This varies from the celebratory stance of Brahminical families, who worship the goddess dyad-both the pure-impure combination along with their male counterpart Lord Ganpati to announce caste superiority. Similarly, the Satvai's worship as a single ambivalent deity finds its location only in the non-Brahmin rural families of Maharashtra, without accompaniment by the more positive Brahmin goddess Jivati, since it is the Satvai's worship that is supposed to keep children alive and provide clan ownership for non-Brahmins within the networked rural region. Brahmin families, on the other hand, mention the Satvai as a monster (the impure counterpart) of Goddess Jivati, when they worship the latter as the pure part of the dyad, while celebrating their superior status in the caste system based on dividing the lower and the impure from the upper that comes along with an entire gamut of feudal relationships based on a history of Brahmin land-ownership and kingship in Maharashtra. Ritual objects used for the goddess's worship come to be infused with both the purity and the impurity of caste, as these, like the bodies of the goddess's mediums or healers, are understood to have become 'absorbent' within the ritual context, divested or conjoined with power but possessing none of their own.

Goddess cults themselves undergo 'Sanskritisation', a process that was explained by Srinivas in 1987, as a particular form of caste mobility prevalent within Indian society (for people). Operative among goddesses as well, it serves to mobilise ambivalent and ferocious local goddess cults into the Brahminical, their shrines turning into large, pure and popular pilgrimage places as soon as their worship becomes associated with powerful upper-caste and dominant clans within the region. Many local goddess shrines have in this way gained *shakti-peetha* (recognised goddess temple city) status in the last decade, with smaller shrines in the neighbourhood attaching themselves to the primary shrine as a 'sister' shrine (shrine becoming the main goddess's sister) or an 'avatar' shrine that claims to be a diminished form or a lower aspect of the main *shakti-peetha* goddess. This process of Sanskritisation is more than evident within the formation of goddess dyads as one of them often starts representing a 'higher' form that also begins to reflect caste hierarchy against the lower, thus turning caste hierarchy between goddesses itself into a mechanism of allegiance and protective power networking provided by upper castes. This is understood as positive, since it depoliticises discrimination, labour extraction and the exploitation of lower castes, when converting an adherent community of the lower goddess in relation to the higher into subservient and feudal, service provider relationships.

Such dyads forming upper and lower castes between goddesses are often depicted as wives of divine kings, the rituals of whose double marriages harness all the communities the king rules over under his ritual and actual tutelage within his region or domain, such as in the case of the dyad wives of divine King Khandoba (with wives considered pure/high and impure/low in the forms of Mhalsa and Banai[1]), whose cult has been documented in some detail by Sontheimer (1989). The public ritual of marriage (just as rituals of childbirth) itself becomes an integrative medium for newcomers into the clan, designating them their role, labour, relationship and status within clan, caste and groups within politically recognised units such as village that are governed through stratified systems of caste that amalgamate ownership. The enlistment of groups within paradigms of relatedness and kinship also simultaneously mark its absence and elimination for others (when they are excommunicated), in order to concentrate ownership entitlements for those who produce discursive dominance within the same political unit and come to further perpetuate and reproduce its ideology. It is therefore the public ritual that often demarcates the extent of women's labour, which in turn decides the nature of relationships that women or goddesses mutually enjoy, without relationships ever being allowed to become disproportionate with the expected amount of labour that would go ritually unmarked; all that is ritually unmarked and outside designated labour and associated with embodied role and status is often under strict surveillance. Ritual enlistment of the body integrated within community (whether that of the goddess or the woman) is then what produces an embodied form of hierarchy

[1] Mhalsa belongs to the caste society of Lingayat Vani, which is quite common in Maharashtra, while Banai, also often referred to as Banu-*bai*, is Dhangar (considered Adivasi or Scheduled Tribe [ST] today).

and stratification among goddesses and women in terms of labour provision, status, their mutual relationships and their power.

Gatwood (1985) explored an important but incomplete concept of 'spousification' in her research, since she limited her analysis to how goddesses married off to Hindu gods became subservient to the latter from an earlier trajectory of fierce and independent existence. This analysis remains superficial because of the way in which it ignores how fiercer forms continue in low/impure dyads, complete with lower-caste adherents associated with their ascribed low, sexual and primitive nature that are 'civilised' through additional mythologies of subservience with upper-caste goddesses in dyad formations, even as these upper-caste and pure goddesses are married to Hindu Puranic deities themselves, simultaneously. Gatwood's theory, though essentially clever, as it marks off a process of subservience through marriage, ignores how large the implication of 'spousification' really is, when it can actually be read as a process of caste, viewed as prescriptive and idolised when the lower caste is made subservient by the so-called protection provided them by the upper caste, even at the cost of violence, exploitation and discrimination. According to pejorative upper-caste premises reflected in dyad formation, this discrimination just comes as a price for being included, protected, represented and enlisted within political units, headed by dominant castes. Spousification, further, is only one way of civilising. In Maharashtra, caste subservience between lower-caste women, who serve upper-caste women and conjoin with them to become goddesses take the form of unequal sisterhoods that turn into dyads across regions and are reflected in ritual performances to please the superior component of the cult. So many goddess rituals in *shakti-peetha* shrines mark the civilising mission of the lower deities and the populations associated with their worship, such as their healers/reformed witches or *yoginis*, who conjoin the higher cult.

I have dedicated the next section to exploring the obvious linkages between caste politics and the formation of ambivalent impurity and what are considered 'low' goddesses, to representations of 'bad' motherhood that have not received much discussion till now. Through this, I have tried to understand the way in which concepts of bad motherhood and impurity have in turn been historically and systemically deployed to develop a thick understanding of what really constitutes an impure woman and her basal, sexual and inauspicious, violent, epidemic spreading and lower-caste nature that is juxtaposed to the unmarked and naturalised body of an upper-caste woman, who is considered good and pure and is celebrated.

In the last section of this chapter, I have provided detailed descriptions of rituals that entitle women in return for distancing themselves from what is considered 'bad motherhood' that lies outside their village boundary, I have also detailed all those simultaneous ways in which they are rewarded for this distancing through celebrations, as those considered afflicted by attacks of bad motherhood (the monster-goddess) are also kept away from such celebrations. Rituals that celebrate their good motherhood and auspicious fertility, typically through the presentation of grain or *oti* and other ritual items, mark those who are successful as citizens of a community or a political unit, who are entitled to its agricultural or land-based produce, since women in my field area do not own means of production or land and are owned themselves like grain or land. This ritual celebration marks their labour (of motherhood) and their embodied roles, duties and prized status as women, and their relationships with the goddesses and the rest of their clan/caste/other political units.

To provide some details about the latter part of the chapter, almost all women's relationships outside labour, ritual and caste within the village where I worked were usually considered to be under strict surveillance by goddesses or were at least rigorously questioned by clan members; just as its opposite was equally true. The power of the goddess seemed to diminish only for those, whose gradually increasing class and education afforded them rationalism and freedom from surveillance. They were usually the ones who responded to interview questions about the importance of goddesses such as the Satvai and her rituals with answers about the importance of clan togetherness, about how it provided opportunities to meet everybody in the family and an opportunity of favouring the pregnant woman.

Others offered explanations such as wanting to conceive pregnancies and being able to undergo natural deliveries, wanting healthy and normal children, wanting their children to live safely, wanting sons; wanting to gain feminine fertility and normal menstruation or adequate breast milk, repulsing witches and the evil eye of other evil-intentioned women, purifying themselves so that they do not join the band of the Satvai, averting death at childbirth and freeing themselves from witchcraft attacks along with gaining status in their families as pure women, wives and mothers. All this was at least temporarily deemed heralded by the public Satvai ritual, where performing women would at least gain peace at home if everything at the ritual event went off well without any untoward mishaps. The list of their aims were really quite long and not many women revealed their personal motivations, especially if they already had traditional affliction diagnosis running in the family.

Conceptualising Bad Motherhood

According to the ideology of goddess worship inherent within Brahminical literature, goddesses enlist worshippers in the cause of establishing world order, universal morality, bringing about civilisation and dharma through the fighting of wars. These involve re-establishing caste duty and clan cohesion, protecting physical regions and their boundaries over which the goddess institutes protective tutelage and the protection of patriarchal institutions such as marriage, women's roles of wifehood and motherhood and feudal structures that perpetuate and reproduce social stratification and hierarchy, while facilitating labour extraction[2]

[2] McKean (1996) has written about associations between goddess cults and nationalism in the present times, just as Sukumari Bhattacharji (1970) wrote years ago about the rise of important Puranic deities, such as Vishnu and Shiva, out of a conglomerate of many small deities appended together out of complex socio-political exigencies over time, rather than looking at it the other way round, which is more usual and misleading: smaller cults as residual matter left behind from bigger cults as non-integrated traces.

that continues till today as a political process of 'region' formation and its attachment through Sanskritisation with greater goddesses through dyad formation. Greater goddesses then go on to form the imaginaire of the mainstream, cultural dominance, the 'heartland' and the nation. The role of minor ambivalent goddesses, such as the Matrika, was imagined in texts such as the *Devi Mahatmya* (compositions dated to approximately the sixth century C.E.) as a deadly and feral bloodsucking army, enlisted in the moral cause of the warrior goddess, identified as the great Devi. She fought dangerous and hyper-masculine demonic enemies such as Shumbha and Nishumbha, Raktabeeja and Mahishasura by drinking their blood, as she assumed her own warrior attributes and weapons from all the other hyper-masculine divine kings such as Vishnu, Shiva, Indra and so on, which became expressed in her female form. She became the quintessential Laclau-ian (2005) example of an empty signifier that had populist demand, since according to the logic of the *Mahatmya* narrative, she was only an 'absorbent' and fragmented entity, with no existence or power of her own, enlisted to complete a warrior assignment, used in a series of feudal decentralisations of duties and tasks, which was also passed down to the Matrika from her in a similar process.

The actual battle between the divine king and the malign demon was decentralised to the Devi and further down to the Matrika. It was their 'absorbing' nature of power from divine kings that produced and converted this power into violence, since they were lower in feudal hierarchy to divine kings and could not legitimately have access to wielding divine male kingly power of benevolence in the first place and could convert it only to violence as the lower form of this kingship. Since power is far more than violence, essentially including benevolence as its central aspect when it is deployed against enemies with the help of 'absorbing' mercenaries who are lower in hierarchy with no power of their own, it only translates into the production of violent mercenaries-scapegoats that produce pure and impure dyads between the pure wives of gods and their impure sisters—imagined between the entrenched and support-providing upper caste and lower caste constructed as potentially violent and absorbent. Those that are upper and higher have traditionally enjoyed systemic power that has always sought to manifest itself in benevolent forms. This has been counterbalanced by the production of absorbent and violent mercenaries, through ritual and mythology that has in-built the dis-entitlement of the lower castes to real sources of power within these structures simultaneously, even while compensating them through rewards of protection, in return for violent feudal duties. It is this which has always created the body of the woman and the lower caste as violent, prone to witchcraft deeds and cannibalism and as base, sexual, absorbent, immune and valorous, while also auspicious and fertile at the same time; an empty category to perpetuate the masculine and upper caste and a potent signifier of his status that could absorb and fulfil whatever populist demand was made out of his domain, since she represented his materiality. The Matrika arose from the different parts of the great goddess's body and eyebrows in war, as an expression of her rage and frustration, as she lost concentration and became increasingly agitated. Neither the great goddess nor the Matrika had access to real power, since they were themselves expressions of 'absorptions' of higher power and symptoms of anger, but they expressed and only could express the compensation to real power: extreme violence against their master's enemy, for which they were produced as servants.

When I happened to relate these stories and my interpretation of it during my fieldwork, my respondents always told me of how these stories exemplified the duties of women to protect their own chastity, without needing men to protect it especially for them. They told me of how the morality of their marriages had given them the power to repulse the sexual attentions of other men and fight it off, like the goddess did, even if they were personally unhappy or abused in their marriages. It was a lesson of moral servitude that they took from these stories and they loved listening to such stories of the goddess winning the war.

The fierce developments among goddesses pertains to what has been identified by historians and archaeologists as the different phases of the pre-'Aryan', the Matrika interlude, the later-Matrika or Sapta-Matrika interlude and the epidemic village goddess interlude that finds reference in texts such as the Bengali *Mangal-Kavya*, written during the medieval period. These four interludes work at two political levels: (a) their regional-level and caste-centred *shakti-peetha* worship base with local meanings, rituals, taboos and mythology that suffer internal conflicts, despite remaining ambivalently associated; (b) their Sanskritisation associations with the mythological mainstream of Puranic Brahminism that exerts hegemony on the construction of its regional and local history and transformation (a process already pointed out by Bell 1992). References and descriptions about what appear to be seamless continuities (that hint at the notion of regions being residual of heartland rather than the opposite understanding of regions constructing notions of heartland) between regional *shakti-peetha* and mythological Puranic goddesses are replete in influential historical, textual and archaeological literature about goddesses.[3] Very few of these theories however allude to caste-based transferences of Sanskritisation operative within the cult formation of ambivalent dyads or goddesses that have turned composite or increasingly mark only the lower-caste body of what politically straddles spatial boundary based on dominant caste with Puranic goddesses and their worship.

Bad Motherhood and the Matrika Continuum

The story of the original conversion of a bad and cannibal mother into a good and compassionate one, finally fit to be part of civilisation, is first encountered within Buddhist texts, dated to approximately the sixth century B.C. (according to Kinsley 1986: 153). The Buddha, hiding Hariti's children under his begging bowl, taught her empathy for mothers suffering childloss, whom Hariti was hitherto robbing (of children), when she was hunting them for feeding herself and her family. By teaching her empathy therefore, he civilised her! In the writing of the story however, though the Buddha simply diverts attention to Hariti's evil and

[3] Cf. Coburn (1984), Kinsley (1986), Tiwari (2002), Panikkar (1997), and Hawley and Wulff (1982) among many other authors.

non-acceptable nature, converting and civilising Hariti to become a child protector, he actually leaves the healing of actual childloss and its pain quite untouched (for those Hariti had already robbed). The story has been popularly read as signifying the pre-Aryan phase of Matrika development, when what has been viewed as the first 'Aryan' population, who spoke the Indo-European group of languages began making inroads into the Gangetic valley, where they encountered primitive and aboriginal communities that 'hunted', ate other human beings, lived on the wild and forested fringes and peripheries of their cities and settlements, looked different and spoke foreign languages, apart from being bloodthirsty, war-like and violent.

The story of God Skanda Kartikeya (also appearing in the Mahabharata) goes a little further, as the Matrikas or 'mothers', by now considered a great band of horrific child-eaters and blood-drinkers, described as ugly, dark, the speakers of different languages and living in caves, crossroads and cremation grounds and on the other peripheries of civilisations, had won a protagonist for themselves in his form: the divine King Skanda Kartikeya. It was only after coming in contact with him that the Matrika were known to have temporarily lost their fierce nature as they began oozing milk from their breasts and found a way of linking themselves, as an entire band of fierce goddesses, with the mainstream of other Hindu goddesses, by acquiescing to becoming enlisted to his civilising mission through motherhood. As a divine king, he gifted them with rights of ritual propitiation in return. They requested Skanda to reserve their rights to harass all children with diseases till these children reached maturity and puberty, so that they would have their primary right over each child, rather than its own biological mother. This was a boon that he was to grant them. This was supposed to be in reparation of an injustice they had faced as seven sister goddesses (Krittika),[4] wives of seven sages, who were unjustly divorced by their husbands, when accidentally

[4] Referred to by Ghurye (1977) as the Pleiades or a seven-star conglomerate that, according to him, must have demonstrated an astrological phenomenon in antiquity and become mythologically associated with beliefs about goddesses.

impregnated through Shiva's semen floating in the water, while they were washing, innocent of this knowledge about the floating semen. They were later to give birth to Skanda Kartikeya in secret and tell him their misfortunes and express their anger at this unjust abandonment, at which he would redeem them with the right to harass children (since once abandoned they wouldn't have any more of their own). Skanda would later win the hand of Devayani, who is variously interpreted as Indra's daughter or army and also a Matrika called Shashthi, since their marriage or Skanda's own Sanskritisation or ritual initiation into the world of gods' takes place on the sixth day after his birth through his marriage with Devayani. Thus, this equates marriage with childbirth rituals on the sixth day as a form of ritual initiation into the social world or a civilising ritual. It is after this that Skanda becomes a divine king and kills the demon Tarakasura. The Matrika through various roles and relationships remain his staunch supporters throughout as they help each other into the world of accepted social relationships.

Thereafter, in accordance with Skanda's conferred boon, the texts describe the Matrika as lurking in confinement chambers of women in labour and afflicting pregnant women and new-borns with different kinds of illnesses. According to Kinsley (ibid.: 154–55), Skanda Kartikeya's reverence for his wronged mothers mirrors the untimely death of women in childbirth that has led to their reverence as goddesses today. He also views these goddesses as an existent aboriginal substratum of society that conflicted with the Aryan. Even as these theories are interesting, there are few ways to match the two (of grieving and jealous childless women and aboriginal people in conflict with Aryan society) when trying to understand the nature of Matrika origins. On trying to combine his two theories, however, one may come to interpret his concept as that of a demographical crisis or shift, either within aboriginal or Aryan community (or both) approximately during the sixth century B.C. that was believed to be effected by a violently civilising Aryan invasion and an equally violent reaction to it. This was the basis for the emergence of local and divine kingships from obscure origins, such as that of Skanda, supported by the Matrika. What such a theory fails to appreciate is the implication of the manner in which it (the theory itself) also creates modern notions of caste as it divides Aryan and aboriginal groups into proto-castes, even as goddesses considered originating from the Matrika today, along with groups associated with worshipping them and their rituals, are associated with dirt, impurity, illness and affliction and what lies on the peripheries, outside boundaries and outside the heartland.

The urgency of converting bad mothers into civilised-reformed-child-protectors or of fearing victims-turned-demonic out of the pain of childloss are, after all, both familiar tropes of imagining the former as the lower-caste healer and the latter as the victimised and afflicted upper caste. These relationships (as is evident) exist both at the goddess level as well as between women and healers, who are mutually and internally linked through feudal duties that dictate absorption. In the form of Jyeshtha or A-Lakshmi (Leslie 1991), the Matrika were said to be of a base and sexual nature and their sculptures depicted them as having animal heads (such as Matrika sculptures dating back to the Kushana period, from the first centuries of the Christian era) with exaggerated sexual features.

In modern times, Goddess Renuka from the *shakti-peetha* of Mahurgarh (Maharashtra), Goddess Yellamma from Saundatti (Karnataka) and Goddess Mari-*aai* (found across the Deccan) or Mari-*amman* (all considered to be forms of Matrikas or Kali or other violent forms) are 'composite' or goddesses who have undergone a further process of conjoining, wherein their dyad form has conjoined into one body, dismembering the goddess into halves and in the process making her more terrible in her afflicting form. The goddess is considered to have become increasingly violent because of the mixture of what is considered to be the more base and violent and malign lower-caste body into hers, as her mythologies mostly describe the way in which the lower-caste attendant is murdered to put both dismembered bodies together to form a composite goddess and to redeem the Brahmin woman's sexual or caste rule-breaking sin. Such goddesses don't just represent the inside and the outside of the village, but the boundary of the village itself. She also embodies the sharp divide between castes and marriage rules (perpetuation of pure reproduction) based on caste as a village deity presiding over epidemics and infant mortality, in her bid to uphold dharma.

Servitude to such Brahmin goddesses or to the upper caste by the lower caste always entails cleaning for the upper caste and the village interiors, while their own inhabitation areas become the dumping grounds for village interiors or constitute areas near cremation grounds. Traditional lower caste duties include absorbing the maladies of the upper caste (healing), absorbing excessive male sexuality and heat (a form of cleaning) or mitigating real or epidemic attacks that come from outside the village so that its pressure does not reach the upper castes living inside the core of the village. Ritual dedication of children among many castes such as the Matang towards clan and village goddess cults and the reproduction and perpetuation of lower caste service provision in return for rewards and temporary or context-based upper caste protection becomes a form of cultic morality associated with village goddesses.

The Sapta-Matrika, the Shashthi and the Jivati Continuum

The 'Great War' against demons such as Shumbha, Nishumbha and Mahishasura fought by Goddess Durga foregrounds her as a divine queen, or an agent of divine kings, who created her to fight the great war that they were unable to win against the demon Mahishasura, since the latter had a boon from Lord Shiva that made him immune to death meted out to him at the hands of a man. This boon of Mahishasura is the most interesting explanatory framework for enlisting women as celebrated feudatories within kingship, through the aggressive upholding of duties surrounding wifehood and motherhood. They are to protect their role of being reproducers of dominant caste clans and of feudal class and its demographical strength, even at the cost of violence. Reproduction as a powerful feudatory role has hitherto been unrecognised in the study of perpetuator modes for hierarchical dominant caste agrarian relationships and values.

The goddess, after erupting from the divine kings, was made in seven or eight forms as part of a reflection of the warrior aspect of major divine kings, unified together into one feminine form, with the various Matrika erupting out of her later. Therefore, not only were the Matrika her fragments, but she herself was constituted out of fragmented counterparts, upholding the necessities of a dictated war agenda. According to scholars such as Kinsley (1986), however, the Matrika multitudes with myriad names and characteristics mentioned in the Mahabharata gradually became reduced and 'standardised' to seven or eight within the Puranas, composed in the medieval period, that further became associated with important Puranic gods of the time, during the composition of the *Devi Mahatmya*, approximately during the sixth C.E, wherein the Sapta-Matrika have been described as taking up war cudgels on behalf of the great goddess, as they emerge out of her in war against Mahishasura. Even as the Sapta-Matrika participated in the army of the great goddess as her generals and warlords in the story of the war against Mahishasura, their worship remains associated at the same time with the production of regional cults and *shakti-peetha*, [5] as the latter come to be viewed as forms of prominent Sapta-Matrika such as Chamunda or Kali. Alternately, these spots are also considered to be holy places, where the pieces of Goddess Sati's dismembered body are known to have fallen during Lord Shiva's enraged *Tandav* dance, after goddess Sati died from jumping into her father, Daksha's, sacrificial fire, which had been aimed to insult her husband, thereby upholding her pure wifely duty for her husband for all to behold, only to be reborn as Parvati, Shiva's wife, in her next birth. All goddesses below this Puranic mythological status enter into Sanskritisation relationships with the greater goddesses of the *shakti-peetha* (far more numerous by now than the original places designated as Goddess Sati's body

[5] Jansen (1995) has written about the interrelationship between King Shivaji and his clan goddess, Tulja-Bhavani (her shrine is an important *shakti-peetha* in Maharashtra today), whose worship became one of the major discursive reasons for Shivaji's war campaigns, as he ascribed his valour to her sword, presented to him by her, when he was in a trance.

parts from Lord Shiva's *Tandav* dance), forming either dyad or composite relationships with the latter, resulting in the enlisting of their region and adherent community through the integration of the boundary between them into feudatory relationships that would introduce civilisation within their regions.

Matrika, such as the Jivantika or Shashthi in Puranic literature, are already associated quite closely with epidemics and childloss. While the worship of the goddess Jivati/Jivantika can be traced to the *Skanda Purana*, the worship of her lower and more ferocious sister, Shashthi, who causes the death of children, is linked within oral narratives of Brahminical contexts surrounding Jivati worship in Maharashtra to a monster-like entity named Satvai, even as the goddess Shashthi finds reference in the *Skanda Purana* and the *Brahma Vaivarta Purana* (*Prakriti Khanda*). Even though the worship of Jivati takes place independently of the Satvai among urban Brahmin families, just as the Satvai is worshipped independently in rural Maratha and other *Balutedar* families, Jivati and Satvai form an important dyad of pure Brahmin and impure non-Brahmin castes, as indicated by their oral narrative and their mythology in the *Skanda Purana* (where they are referred to as Jivantika and Shashthi). The goddess Jivati (also described as a Matrika in the Mahabharata[6]) and her negative counterpart Shashthi (also a Matrika, with an alternative name of Devayani, when she is identified as the wife of Skanda) can be considered part of a stabilised Matrika-dyad continuum, representing caste distinction and the rural-urban divide between Brahmins and non-Brahmins in Maharashtra. Their story that I recount here is extrapolated from grey literature that is used by women for private religious practice in their homes as part of *vrata*[7] traditions.

The story of Jivati-Satvai recounts the manner in which King Priyamvrat was originally stolen from his Brahmin mother as a baby and replaced with a stone pestle by a midwife for gaining riches from the childless royal couple, King Sushil Singh and

[6] See Tiwari (2002: 148).

[7] Nicholas (2003:17) points to how *vrata* traditions receive inadequate study because they are mostly practised by women inside their homes.

Queen Sukeshibala. The story describes his battles with the inauspicious monster-goddess Satvai, who brought death to new-born babies, when writing their fates on the sixth night after childbirth, while he is on pilgrimage to Gaya, with the help of Goddess Jivati, who repels the Satvai and protects the baby. His real Brahmin mother, never having originally believed that she gave birth to a stone pestle, had undertaken the ritual fasts and worship (*vrata*) of the goddess Jivati and had taken to praying to her for protecting her son's life. Goddess Jivati therefore comes to his rescue in his battle against the Satvai as he tries to safeguard new-borns. Saving new-born children from the inauspicious monster-goddess Satvai, with Goddess Jivati constantly by his side, King Priyamvrat fulfils his duties at Gaya, where he has spiritual experiences about his ancestry and comes to understand the importance of Goddess Jivati and her worship for his own biography. He institutes her worship in his empire on his return from Gaya, only to realise his foster parents to be imposters, swindled into believing they had a son by the midwife. He is then, finally reunited with his real Brahmin mother, who had been faithfully following the Jivati *vrata* for many years, never believing in the birth of a stone pestle. The Brahmin woman then automatically becomes the queen (since her son is king) and the Jivati *vrata* for this reason is therefore a divine-kingship *vrata* followed by Brahmin women, or women from clans aspiring to be considered Brahminical, on every Friday of the months of the *Chaturmasa* or the Indian lunar calendar months of Shravan, Bhadrapad, Ashvin and Kartik.

The monster-goddess Satvai is relegated to areas considered to be 'rural' Maharashtra, or the outlying regions surrounding what is understood to be the Brahmin seat/heartland of political power and culture or administrative urban centres, where the maximum number of Brahmins from rural Maharashtra gradually migrated from their rural land grants throughout the eighteenth and twentieth century (characterised by Peshwa centres such as Pune, Nasik, Satara and so on). The rural peripheries, where the Satvai still presides as part of an impure dyad with Jivati, have come to embody the 'boundary' of Brahmin zones (even if these remain

Brahminical, because the Satvai is still connected to the Jivati as an adversary) and hence become the Satvai zone.

Shashthi, the adversarial Matrika to Jivantika (in the *Skanda Purana*), is considered to be a cat-faced, feral goddess, representing the sixth digit. She is appeased on the sixth night after childbirth (even though my respondents perform the Satvai ritual on the fifth night, going on to the sixth day, expecting the cat to visit their house to eat ritual food offerings made to the goddess) and is considered an inauspicious goddess of childloss presiding over the cremation grounds of children. She is also often mentioned in conjunction with the god Kartik, his worship and cult referred to variously as Champa-Shashthi, through this conjunction. Her references in the *Mangal-Kavya* texts of Bengal are dated to a much later period and though her *vrata* in these texts are numerous, few women apart from those who may lose all their children would follow all her numerous rituals throughout the year (Nicholas 2003: 17), since she presides over childloss.

According to one of her independent stories (where she does not form a dyad with Goddess Jivantika), recounted in the *Brahma Vaivarta Purana* (*Prakriti Khanda*), she appeared to King Manu at the cremation ground of his child, in a grand celestial chariot covered in white cloth, when he is mourning the horrific death of his only son, whom he has had with great difficulty, after performing a ritual sacrifice. As a result of this sacrifice, a holy saint offers the king's wife a bowl of magical milk and rice. After eating this, she gives birth to a handsome child who is unfortunately stillborn. After the goddess restores the child's life at the cremation grounds, where the king is found mourning, the king celebrates her worship throughout his empire. This last story from the *Brahma Vaivarta Purana* is typical of the *Mangal-Kavya* genre, since this text was mostly also composed in Bengal, approximately during the tenth century, by which time most composers of mythologies were more interested in issuing threats to their readers, forcing them to worship the religious *vrata* they espoused. The absence of dyad descriptions in the *Mangal-Kavya* hints therefore at not their absence per se, but the predominance of a certain 'converting' aim of this genre, as these texts describe all sorts of disasters befalling those, who fail to worship the goddess, even as she miraculously forgives them and confers them with boons the moment they follow her.

Epidemic Goddesses, Shitala and the Mari-aai Continuum

Village goddesses, by approximately the sixteenth century (when they found mention in many texts of the *Mangal-Kavya* from Bengal), were intimately associated with agriculture and the consolidation of agrarian castes, caste systems as we recognise them today, and rural famines that made this caste system increasingly rigid—introducing poverty and systemic disinheritance within caste hierarchy, and epidemics, with contagious pustules held akin to grain/pulses. The *Mangal-Kavya* texts are replete with affliction-related village goddesses presiding over poxes, fevers, illness and death, so that they could convert people to their worship. Many of these goddesses mentioned in the *Mangal-Kavya* are also important village goddesses in Maharashtra, presiding over similar types of agrarian afflictions, such as Shitala-*devi* (presiding over pox). Their characters remain the same even if their local names have undergone change: Jari-Mari-*aai* (pox and cholera), Khoklu-*aai* (coughs and cold/whooping cough), Vaghzai (tiger attacks) and many snake deities associated with anthills and snake burrows such as Sateri-*devi*. These goddesses continue to preside over rural spaces in Maharashtra as important village goddesses.

While on the one hand these form discursive frameworks that explain rural disasters associated with wilderness/forested boundaries of farmlands, infection and contagion within close-knit rural inhabitations and their networks with patterns of resource distribution and redistribution, on the other hand they stop marking the upper-caste body as part of a dyad altogether. The upper-caste body is now naturalised and left unmarked, while these cults mark only the lower caste, producing it as animalistic, basal, monstrous, vindictive, epidemic-spreading, impure and coercive that is deployed into civilization, to enlist women into following discipline, to follow *vrata* and to keep the effects of disaster away so that they can distance themselves from the chaos of violence and absence of protection from an empire and king and heal themselves. This marking or branding of the lower-caste body or production of bad motherhood is the beginning of what one recognises as the origin of the Satvai/Maulya tradition as a village goddess-monster tradition presiding over infant mortality that is based on caste and the inclusion of the peripheral into what is considered Brahminical: the upper caste land grant and the dominant caste village. But before transiting to the rituals of good motherhood that is invested in distancing bad motherhood, the peripheral and the impure lower-caste that becomes emblematic of the uncivilized, it would be important to explore the *Mangal-Kavya* and their exposition on epidemic monster-goddesses a little further.

Goddess Shitala-*devi*, the village goddess of Ghodegaon (my primary fieldwork location), also finds her most detailed textual reference in the *Mangal-Kavya* texts, in a rendition known as the *Shitala Mangal*, [8] even though there are references to incantations of her used for the prevention of disease in texts such as the *Skanda Purana* and the *Picchila Tantra*. Shitala-*devi*, according to the text of *Shitala Mangal*, is known to be of snow-white complexion and of a cooling nature (as known by her name, accorded to her by Lord Brahma), who was born from the cooled ashes of the sacrificial fire that King Nahusha had made in order to have a son. She carries a winnowing fan (to separate husk from grain), a short broom (to dust away impurities such as husk), and a pot containing different kinds of pulses and grains (that decide on the dharma of those who accept these from her) and rides side-saddle on a horse/ass. She is dressed either in a red sari or is naked and accompanied by demons (propitiated along with her) such as Jvarasur (fever demon), Oladevi/Olabibi (Olabibi being the Muslim version of her name),[9] Goddess Raktabati (goddess of blood infections) and

[8] According to Nicholas (2003:199), this text was published in 1878–79, though he writes that it was printed a century after it was written. Moreover, there is no doubt that many versions of Shitala-*devi*'s story may have been orally prevalent much before the story was ever written.

[9] Oladevi is a cholera goddess; in a manner that is similar to Jari-*aai*, the cholera goddess, who accompanies the pox goddess Mari-*aai* in most parts of Maharashtra.

Ghentu-debota (deity of skin disease). The adventures of Shitala progress from the heavenly to the this-worldly, spreading and selling her fatal grain-cereal/pustules to all unbelievers, who as a consequence fall ill and die of pox till they realise their folly and convert to the dharma of the goddess. She then brings them back to life in return for allegiance and worship, after which her dominance over various celestial and earthly kingdoms is established.

In rural areas of Maharashtra, Mari-*aai* is often considered to be the 'mobile' or younger sister of Shitala. By this it is meant that while Shitala usually has a temple in the village and is a 'stable' goddess with a Puranic mythology, it is Mari-*aai* whose shrine lies outside the village, within lower-caste areas. The Mari-*aai* shrine in most cases is also made into a box and carried over the head or shoulder from village to village by the Matang caste, a *potraaj*, ritually dedicated to her service by his family. The Mari-*aai* as a younger sister of Shitala is her lower dyad with her own entourage of Jari-*aai*, presiding over childloss, even as Mari-*aai* and Mari-*amman* have a separate trajectory of existence in Tamil Nadu and the Deccan as an independent deity presiding over epidemics. It becomes a classic case of the two levels mentioned at the beginning of this chapter: the regional existence of deities interacting with mythological deities through a Sanskritisation process.

My respondents explained how winnowing fans, often used in Mari-*aai* ritual dedications, are ways in which worshippers demonstrate allegiance to her cult through the acceptance and donation of grain. Her fan is known to separate believers from non-believers, just as easily as grain from husk, wherein the flying and impure husk becomes emblematic of scabs from drying skin infection, that in the case of diseases such as pox (and chicken pox in contemporary times) represent its most contagious stage. Her broom is considered to sweep away such husk from the doorstep of believers, even as her pot of pulses is reserved for those whom she enlists into her ambit by passing them her illness. Once they have the illness, or 'have her in them', they accept it as her love (the Mari-*amman*'s pustule being known even in Tamil as her flower or '*pu*' of love), enlisting themselves within her discipline and love, performing her rituals (and enlisting within civilization and morality) in order to escape death, just as the *vrata* story suggests.

Many theories about the origin of goddess cults within the context of epidemics fall into the functionalist trap of implicitly, suggesting how goddess cults developed within societies beleaguered by epidemics.[10] It becomes assumed in these theories that goddess cults represent a deliberate social consensus that would mitigate disease, without actual religious belief in them, viewing these only as countering techniques and mechanisms to illness. This propagates a theory of 'ritual as technique' rather than those that ritualise a belief in prevalent power relationships that involve the fear of or belief in a spiritual world.[11] Functionalism presupposes many social formations and principles of ritual and social action, when it inserts a naturalised and unmarked mentality into an understanding of what it produces and presupposes as universal, since theories of technique, even if they may come to include a belief in spiritual power that effects this technique, may also be based equally in negating this spiritual power or in rationality. It cannot be stated, for example, that it has been only the technique or strategy of healing and not belief in God that has goaded religious conversion to evangelical Christianity among Marathi Dalits. It would be an act of discrimination to 'other' a spiritual and psychological capacity for belief and the emancipatory potential for it, before reducing experiences of healing too quickly to a prior 'traditional' knowledge of alternative science that deploys it towards technique. If my women respondents indeed needed to ritually appease Mari-*aai* and Shitala-*devi* for chicken pox as residual technique in modern Ghodegaon, their belief in medicines and doctors in the village must have after all been misplaced.

[10] Chawla (1994) has pointed to how time gaps between performances of different post-partum rituals could represent 'tetanus periods' for demarcating the safety of children. It is a thought-provoking observation, even though it depoliticises religion, reducing it to science, which runs the danger of producing caste and gender discrimination/ notions of impurity that are implicit within these rituals to medical rationality.

[11] Bell (1992) has explored how ritualisation is a far more apt category to understand structural power than the binaries of belief and practice.

Finally, to provide a brief summary of this section: I have explored the formation of group goddesses and dyad formations between goddesses, their composite forms as these dyads combined into one body and the emergence of a single ambivalent goddess, even as the pure and upper-caste goddess body became increasingly naturalised, non-depicted and unmarked. This formation of the presiding goddess also came to construct and divide village and regional spaces into the outside and inside of boundaries, heartland and region that demarcated their margins as important locations invested with the power of establishing hierarchy and stratification.

The next section is dedicated to exploring all those rituals that 'insider' and upper-caste women perform to keep the impure boundaries and the impure body of the goddess and lower castes at bay (unless healers and midwives are ritually summoned to absorb away their impurity that is considered to obstruct their fertility). They perform these rituals for a large number of personal reasons that are seldom shared (as already mentioned above). The primary objective of the ritual, however, remains 'separating' sexuality from fertility, impurity from purity, the Satvai and her entourage of witches' who are dead in childbirth from the moral and living women (and their agnates) along with their babies, the outside from the inside, the lower caste from the upper caste, and illness/death from health/longevity, so as to avoid a merging between them that is understood as attack and affliction. I also describe celebrations that take place, marking a reward for women, which herald successful separation and purity (as everything negative is left at the boundary shrine). I describe how women are gifted with land-based entitlements (grain) for being able to successfully become good insiders and civilise themselves by being able to perpetuate 'inside' spaces and institutions through its reproduction as marital-clan owned feudatories.

Producing Good Motherhood

My respondents carried out preventive rituals to keep away the inauspicious attentions of impurity and the monster-goddess

Satvai from their pregnancies and children. The Satvai and the Maulya were multiple in number (as they were believed to derive from the souls of different castes of women, who had died in childbirth or after having achieved puberty) and were typically organised under a dyad. Examples from among the multiple villages of castes who turned into the Satvai or Maulya typically included *Bamnin* (Brahmin), *Malin* (gardener caste), *Chambharin* (from the leather-worker caste), *Mangin* (Matang caste) and so on. They also stood for different kinds of diseases among women and children and demanded different kinds of ritual goods that typically defined these castes within public imagination: a *Bamnin* demanded a piece of white cloth; a *Malin*, fruits and vegetables; a *Chambharin*, a pair of slippers; a *Kolin* (a fisher woman), a piece of fish; a *Mangin*, a broom, etc. They were known to afflict women and children in different ways and had different colours of their own; a blouse piece in specific colours had to be ritually dedicated to each of them, when ritually propitiating them, if any one of them had especially afflicted a woman or her child.

Though these goddesses were multiple, they were often organised under a dyad known commonly as Ranu-*bai* and Santu-*bai* in my field area (in the case of the Satvai) that then had their entourage of two, four, six or eight minions to add up together into a total conglomerate of four, six, eight, twelve or sixteen goddesses. Both the Satvai and the Maulya also had one brother or male minion accompanying them, who was the soul of a dead post-pubertal boy, who functioned as the gatekeeper for their shrine. For the Satvai, this brother was often the *Munjoba* (the post-pubertal Brahmin boy), or the *Chedoba* (a lower caste boy), a *Mangir-baba* (a Matang man, who was sacrificed to the village boundary) or *Mhasoba* (a Dhangar man), whose inclusion makes the numbering of the whole group to an odd digit: to either five, seven, nine, thirteen, or seventeen. He is offered different ritual dedications that includes a little curd rice (since the offering has to be vegetarian and Brahminical) or then in the case of the *Chedoba* or *Mhasoba*, animal sacrifice or eggs or a small stick with a bell tied to it's end and a piece of blanket (since *Mhasoba* is considered Dhangar).

When I asked some of my male field informants about these 'brothers' and gatekeepers of the Satvai and Maulya (*dvaar-paal*), they told me of how in earlier times all communities like the Dhangars, the Brahmins and everyone else lived together in closer proximity in and around the village and how what is considered the actual village today was a large and urban city in the past. They told me of how archaeologists had come to the neighbouring town of Junnar for fact-finding and scientific excavations, since there were many ancient trade routes passing through the mountain passes of this region. And it was this fact that was reflected in the 'brothers' of the village goddesses, such as the Satvai and Maulya, which hinted at the proximity of many communities living together in the past suggesting the prevalence of cosmopolitanism. It was only later (in their estimation) due to famines, ecological problems, increasing droughts, aridity and the drying up of trade that urban centres moved away to other places, leaving what were earlier cosmopolitan centres to diminish into villages. These only had archaeological sites today, since agriculture had become the main economy. All those who were poor had gone to other cities and forest and pastoral activities had grown distant from the village. According to them, it was only the tradition of the goddess that still revealed the history of urbanism through her brothers. Although I could not see how the distancing of what seemed like many stratified feudal lower castes and Brahmins from village settlements could herald the demise of cosmopolitanism and urban centres, it definitely seemed to herald the demise of a complex land grant-based agrarian economy.

Satvai or Maulya rituals had to be performed by each and every woman and every single instance of ritual appeasement would then allow the goddess to transit between malevolent (close to mother and child, inside the village boundary, hot and wet in terms of effecting bleeding for mothers and diarrhoea/vomiting for children) and benevolent (distant and retreating, outside the village boundary, cooled and dry, signifying ceasing of bleeding/discharge and formed stool/no vomiting for the child) forms. There was no way of pleasing her permanently, since every single instance and mistake mattered adversely.

Women who had died in childbirth were understood to have become cannibalistic witches, on their way to joining the Satvai. They were also considered to have become enraged and unhappy because of their incomplete transition into social motherhood and its associated rewards that would have accorded them status due to their untimely death. While rituals dedicating 'motherhood' attachments to the baby were part of the offerings made to the Satvai in order to distance the latter from the child and push her across the boundary, equal care was also taken to distance the soul of the actual mother (if she had died in childbirth) from the child till both the mother's death impurity period and the child's birth impurity periods were both over, i.e. till such a time that the dead mother's transition to the Satvai realm was not complete and till the child's transition to the social world of relationships was not complete on the other side.

My respondents told me of how the whole neighbourhood of the new baby's house and the roads leading to it would be strewn over with mustard seeds, which was believed to be a powerful anti-witchcraft agent, in order to ward off the dead mother, still 'wet' and non-transited to the Satvai world. According to this status she still had access to the child, which had itself as yet not completed its transition to the social world. When the dead mother (still considered a witch, till she joined the goddess) came to breast feed the child in the night, since she was cannibalistic and attached to her own motherhood desires simultaneously, she would have to pick up every one of those strewn mustard seeds first to clear her path in order to reach the baby. Some of my respondents, who had witnessed cases of maternal death, recounted how they could hear the spirit of the dead mother-turned-witch moaning and crying in the nights outside the streets of her hitherto home, while the new-born slept inside, also troubled and crying for its mother. It filled them with dread for themselves, terrible grief for the dead mother and the lonely baby, and fear for the witch at the same time, who despite all her pain was a dreadful cannibal.

Visiting any new-born as a childless woman was a matter of the greatest caution as each guest had to wash their hands and feet very meticulously. It was believed that the witches/dead mothers/

Satvai, waiting outside the locality, could turn into grains of sand and stick to the feet of those women who also had witchcraft potential, so that they could enter the homes of the new-born. These grains of sand were known as *pai-rava*.

Experiencing the Satvai Shrine

In order to avoid all kinds of dread and grief in their own lives women performed Satvai rituals to dedicate their motherhood, their attachments, and their impurity, 'dirt' and cannibalism to the Satvai in 'preventive' rituals at her shrine. The shrine thus became a cultural repository of all that became defined as 'dirt', since other women before them had left this dirt behind over here, which was a part of the shrine's location and environment. Accompanying women on this ritual journey of dedication, I was privy to some of their emotional reactions and transformations that this internal effort at separation and establishing civilisation entailed.

The Satvai shrines were not everyday shrines, where priests or others came to clean the premises, taking trouble to imbue the shrine with a sanctified atmosphere. Most of them were crumbling, open air places, where those performing rituals were meant to leave 'offerings' or the impurity inside them behind. These shrines were often located near lower-caste or poor inhabitations, garbage dumps, village gutters, outside village boundaries and inside thickets and tangles that were once considered groves and close to the wilderness being infested with small predators subsisting on garbage, apart from dogs, pigs, snakes and other more uncomfortable spectres for village women. Many of these shrines were also near cremation grounds. Mothers sat amidst areas strewn with the ritual remnants of other women's dedicated impurity that impressed them with the heavy collective weight of divesting themselves of it, all the while the alienating boundary at which they did this suggesting the possibility of their own excommunication and even more ultimately, death in childbirth and the death of their own children. The shrines itself were usually covered with the remains of stale and old food, once dedicated to the goddess and other ritual items such as: bangles; clumps of hair and clothes belonging to new-borns; plastic packets of turmeric (*haldi*) and vermillion (*kunku*); small cradles, bells and toys (known as *khelna-palna*), indicating childbirth wish fulfilment (known as *navas*) and small earthen pots of milk indicating the absence of natural milk in mothers (known as *sugad*).

The shrine dissociated women from 'real' life back in the village, as they came to associate something that was within themselves to the fear-inducing and impure things that they beheld at the shrine. They had to moreover dedicate what was within them to the monster-goddess and head back home as pure women; only then would they be able to become successful mothers. That which was within them was very difficult to articulate and often caused them shame and pain. This was because it was deemed dirty and it became constructed and associated with the dirt of the shrine and something that was immoral because of the separation effected upon it. When they spoke of the Satvai, to whom they made their ritual dedications, they described her in two ways: (a) as a monster-goddess, who was part cannibal when not appeased and not distanced enough from themselves and their children and part a goddess, when adequately distanced and appeased, 'cooled' and 'dried' through ritual to be pushed beyond the village boundary; (b) as the real mother of the village children henceforth, as they as biological mothers would have to dedicate their children to the Satvai, after which the latter would automatically protect them and their children. If they did not dedicate their children to the Satvai, this would insult the Satvai, who had died unjustly and this would lead her to punish them and their children with illness and death.

The debacle at the shrine therefore, marked a scene of transfer between the motherhood of women and the motherhood of the Satvai, located on either side of the boundary, where the gates situated at the shrine were temporarily opened by ritual in full public display. This bridge would have to close immediately after this transfer of motherhood between women and the Satvai, as dedication through ritual items and food (considered to be absorbent materials) was over, unless motherhood was to be capriciously retained by disbelieving women. The Satvai then afflicted her and her child, as punishment for this. The ritual food (motherhood) dedicated by women is thought to be absorbed by the Satvai through the eating of ritual dedications, and women were not allowed to look behind their shoulders as they returned from the shrine after laying out the food for the monster-goddess, since this would anger the Satvai and open the closed door. Many of the women described goose pimples and a prickling sensation on their skins, while recounting the ritual, saying that they could almost sense the Satvai pouncing on the food as soon as their backs were turned. From that moment on the Satvai became the real protectors of the children; their real mothers, who had absorbed the motherhood attachment of biological mothers away. The latter on the other hand become produced as the children's feudatories, milk relatives and nurturers, who had to constantly avoid the impurity and affliction of attachment.

Accompanying women did not always make things any easier for those performing rituals at shrines, as they (the former) walked around the shrine, trying to identify their own ritual dedications tied to the shrine body, while chatting affably about their own Satvai 'times'.This sometimes heightened the new mother's dissociation from the ritual at the shrine, as she remained apart from those women, who had already been socially confirmed and integrated as pure. She, on the other hand, was still stuck with the spectre of 'danger', since the floodgates between herself and the much feared Satvai had been suddenly opened.

There are limitations to how ritual spaces for women in India can be typically viewed, at least at a popular level, as collective, friendly and shared spaces, since it is also their prescribed nature that dictates experiential quality and produces all, which does not fit into its prescribed devotional and bhakti nature (such as being deeply inarticulate, lonely and invisible) as marginal. Most women I accompanied performed their first rituals at the shrine in a trance or a sort of haze, not remembering much of the ritual later. Some giggled and some cried in interviews or just stopped midway and sat in silence. Some remembered fragments and some grew angry with me and asked me to perform my own ritual if I had so much unholy curiosity or *chombdepana* about their experiences of it. Most of them remembered other people's rituals better, where they had accompanied, while others recounted their second- or third-time round rituals more lucidly and with bravado (since they recounted the mistakes other women had committed, unlike themselves, alongside).

The transformative and fear-filled process of surrendering one's own motherhood to the goddess (since the new-born child had to be laid in front of the shrine and dedicated to the goddess) and the larger collective of agnatic clan women is marked and produced through a sequence of rituals that begin in the seventh month of pregnancy itself. This is the time the child starts showing definitive signs of movement inside the womb, heralding the mother's time for 'giving it up', i.e. impure attachments and all, soldering the child's attachment with the help of the midwife (who soaks up the birth impurity) to the marital clan, whose interests are represented by the goddess instead. The birth impurity period lasts approximately till six months post-partum and ends with the *jaawal* ritual. In the following section, I begin first by describing the *paach-pauli* that is common to all Satvai rituals (in terms of structure and format).

The Paach-pauli Ritual

No fertility celebrations can take place before the affliction-preventing *paach-pauli* ritual is first performed in the afternoon of any one day of the first week of the last trimester.[12] The Satvai rituals are known as *paach-pauli* because they are necessarily performed at boundaries (five steps away) away from spaces considered to be internal or the 'inside' of the core inhabitation space. Spaces imagined five steps away from the 'inside' constitute boundaries at many structural levels or junctures that are then chosen as ritual locations. These begin with marking domestic margins for the homestead/clan at the first rung and travelling

[12] Satvai rituals always take place in the afternoon (as mentioned in earlier chapters) as it is in the afternoon heat that the goddess is considered to become mobile (*phiristi*) from her shrine.

outwards in concentric circles to the locality at the next rung (that in many cases also formulate caste boundaries). The village boundary as an important political unit acts as the third rung and this finally ends at the goddess shrine that represents regions, such as pastoral/forest/wilderness and their important characteristic vis-à-vis the imaginaire of the agrarian heartland that enlists the Satvai as a lower dyad as the final rung.[13] Masselos (1999) has already described purity in terms of the outward concentric circles, starting from the inside of the clan and moving towards the outside, the locality and the village, while describing the plague epidemic in Pune and Mumbai and its associated concepts of impurity, when British officers invaded upper-caste homes in order to clean them of infested rats. It is at the juncture of these very concentric circles (in the bathroom or at the exit point of the home, where the waste water from the bathroom exits the home) of clans of the same caste living together (crossroads outside a neighbourhood of relatives and agnatic households) and of village and region that the Satvai's *paach-pauli*[14] is performed.

When I asked my respondents the logic behind choosing these specific ritual locations for *paach-pauli*, they explained that these areas consequently 'cleared' the places inside their perimeters as safe spaces for the mother and child, where the Satvai's cannibalistic powers would no longer pose any threat (or areas up to which the child's initiation and mother's transformation had been established). The bathroom ritual, therefore, established safety for the child inside the home; the locality ritual ensured safety of the child inside the various clan homes of similar caste purity levels and as the ritual area expanded to encompass village and region at the third rung, the child became safe in the whole area (where its mother became accepted as a pure mother of high status). It was the final public visit to the Satvai shrine at the village

[13] I have demonstrated the various rungs within Satvai ritual spaces as possible administrative structures within medieval settlement patterns (Dandekar and Dandekar 2011).

[14] I have also provided a detailed description of the *paach-pauli* ritual in Dandekar (2009, 2015).

or regional level (that also took place right at the very beginning, at the seventh-month ritual) that was considered to interconnect mother and child to a network of Satvai shrines across the region, which then also had the effect of creating the entire area of inhabitation as a rural 'region' in relation to the Brahmin urban heartland that worshipped the Jivati.

The *paach-pauli* ritual constituted an attempt at reflecting the shrine of the Satvai in an impromptu arrangement at these various local boundaries that secured the ownership and inheritance of spaces inside these boundaries for the new-born, while simultaneously producing it's mother as an owned and esteemed feudatory, who traditionally did not have ownership rights within these areas but had rights to consume in return for duty. A place for the *paach-pauli* was first cleared at the designated corner of the chosen location and smoothened over with cow dung paste to clean it. A lump of dry cow dung (usually used for fuel) was arranged in its corner as a vigil watcher over the ritual (it is sometimes set on fire to purify it). Next, eleven or thirteen pebbles, roughly of the same size, are washed and arranged in a line next to each other on this smoothened surface. The eleven or thirteen pebbles embody the two Satvai sisters with their further entourage of numerous sisters each, in addition to the last pebble that embodies the *Munjoba*, which as my informants suggested could have reflected a history of Brahmin land ownership of the past and indicate to the other half of Satvai's dyad, the Brahmin Jivati. Sometimes women substitute the *Munja*'s pebble with a betel nut or a rupee coin to signify Lord Ganesha. A black thread (*nada*) is laid along the length of the pebbles to form the hair of the goddesses and a yellow thread added alongside it to make up her clothes (*vastra*). The ritual actor brushes the deities so arranged in a line in this impromptu shrine with the tail end of her hair, as this is known to establish ritual contact (of the absorbing kind) between the goddess and the woman as she goes on to sprinkle the deities with *haldi*, *kunku*, red and black powder (*gulal* and *bukka*) and raw rice (*akshata*) as a form of her veneration. Incense sticks are lit in front of the goddess (often stuck into the burning cake of cow dung) and food and other ritual offerings (also known as the goddess's *oti*) are made in front of the shrine, that include a coconut, dry fruits, puffed rice, sugar, *haldi-kunku-gulal-bukka*, a piece of cloth (a blouse piece known as *khan*) and flowers. Food offerings usually contain *roti*/leavened bread, cooked rice, lentils, sprouts, green vegetables (fenugreek) [15] and stuffed sweets that are emblematic of the 'filled' pregnant body (known as *kanole*) and a small portion of curd rice for the *Munjoba*.

These impromptu shrines of *paach-pauli* made to reflect the structure of the Satvai shrine also always faces her main village temple, in order to facilitate a ritual mirroring. As a result, the ritual reconstituting of the shrine actually becomes an act of reflecting it at local boundary places in ways that simultaneously created these local spaces as parts of a larger region presided over by the Satvai at the main shrine. The actual ritual of the *paach-pauli* further reflects the funerary rite of the *pinda-daan* ceremony among Hindus, [16] which necessitates the distancing of dead ancestors to the next world and the inheritance of their social position and property by their descendants, once their transition to the next world, marked by death impurity is over. It was as if biological mothers were passing a painful obstacle of trading motherhood for gaining social individuation by performing an ancestor worship ritual for mothers in order to achieve status as feudatories and not die like the Satvai, who was malign, somehow un-dead and outside the village boundary.

The social persona of the child is created through ritual as a living and owning member of clan, caste and society with an identity that commands inheritance and demands labour as well. In the initial period of my fieldwork, I believed only women and mothers to be ritual actors. It was only later that I realised how babies were significant ritual actors too, in addition to their

[15] Food offerings to the goddess always include the herb fenugreek, locally known as *methi* in Maharashtra, as part of green vegetables. It has been mentioned as the goddess's special food offering by Feldhaus (2003) as well.

[16] Parry (1994) has provided detailed descriptions of the *pinda-daan* ceremony in Banaras.

mothers, as rituals such as *paach-pauli* produced them as those who had souls, those who could dress in different kinds of materials and jewellery as life grew increasingly safer for them. They began eating cooked food in combination with milk as their days spent in safety grew more interesting. Those who could get used to proper names and increased social contact, developing an identity and friendships of their own, alongside their mothers and enjoyed newly found family life.

Returning from *paach-pauli*, ritual actors are still considered to be 'possessed' by the Satvai, since the brief channel of communication between them is still new. The ritual ends with the woman/mother feeding a group of premenstrual virgin girls at home, known as *kori-savashne* (also described by Feldhaus 1995) or the 'unmarked auspicious', who are considered to be the protégés of the goddess and like her in nature—a band of females without menstruation and marriage. Although sometimes a midwife is called for food. The *kori-savashne* are supposed to mimic human impurity and yet herald the auspicious nature of the goddess, since to be without menstruation, marriage and be a virgin and as yet female is a mark of androgyny, impurity, sexuality and asceticism, a theme that is implicit within the Matrika tradition for goddesses. The food fed to the *kori-savashne* is specially cooked for the ritual. It consists of the same leavened bread (*roti*), rice, lentils, fenugreek, sprouts, and sweets as the offerings during the ritual. In the absence of *kori-savashne*, the ritual food is offered to lines of turmeric and vermillion drawn on the wall. Menstruating or other pregnant women in the village are asked to steer clear of women returning from *paach-pauli*, since they can become afflicted, being outside ritual contact themselves, if they are accidentally caught in the path of the woman returning from the *paach-pauli*, who is still considered to be possessed of the Satvai's afflicting essence. They are not supposed to eat the ritual food cooked for the *kori-savashne* either, since outside ritual context it would cause them affliction as well. Some clans have the tradition of feeding *adich-savashne* after *paach-pauli* that are constituted, literally (since *adich* translates to 'two and a half'), by 'two and a half auspicious women': a midwife, a married woman from the family,[17] and the usual young virgin making up the third half-part of the triad.

The Seventh-Month Ritual

The sequence of the Satvai ritual usually begins in the seventh month of pregnancy. As the seventh-month (*saatva mahina*) ritual constitutes the first Satvai ritual for a pregnant woman, it is considered to be particularly 'serious' and is mostly conducted at the main shrine of the goddess (unless the woman is not in good health, in which case it is done just outside the locality boundary) that will 'register' (*nondni*), her pregnancy, her baby and her family with the goddess of the area, like a government office. The ritual consists of performing the *paach-pauli* usually followed by a ritual feast (known as the *dohale jevan*) at home which celebrates that the mother's purity has been established. The food prepared for the *dohale jevan* feast usually includes all those delicacies that the pregnant woman has expressed 'cravings' (or *dohale*) for, as the nature of this *dohale* is also considered to indicate and publicly announce the sex of the embryo. Embryos of certain sexes are known to create specific food cravings or tastes in pregnant women and hence the expected babies are already classified according to their sex through the *dohale* of their mothers, prior to their birth. The ceremony includes traditional songs and celebrations, marking the pregnant woman as pure, as her *oti* (lap) is filled with grains, fruits and many foods that she is provided with an entitlement to enjoy. Depending on the amount the clan wants to spend or whether it is the first pregnancy for the woman, expectant mothers are dressed in new clothes of auspicious and favourite colours that are *dharjin* or allowed in the clan along with jewellery made of flowers. The mother is seated on a swing and holds a bow and

[17] I have often observed this second woman to be a younger widow, though none of my respondents really answered questions about whether this triad necessarily included a widow, since widows were otherwise not represented in Satvai rituals. The usual answer I received was that the widow was included to replace an ordinary *savashne,* only so that affliction could be avoided.

arrow in her hand, also decorated with flowers (to signify the birth of a son), while traditional games are played that include her and other women, identifying the gender of the child through tell-tale items that are hidden within sweetmeats.

The *dohale jevan* is the first public celebration of an expectant marital clan childbirth, whereas there do exist other smaller celebrations of pregnancy that are more private among women, their childhood girlfriends and their parents, that do not involve the public, their marital clans, the Satvai and the establishment of purity. The *chor-choli* is a small and more tender and domestic celebration in comparison to the *dohale jevan,* as a new blouse or some new clothes are stitched and presented to the newly pregnant woman in the first trimester of her pregnancy by her mother and her girlfriends (this is usually the time when a woman discovers that she is pregnant herself) in a small party, where pleasurable seasonal snacks of a cooling nature are eaten or an outing is organised. This is a deliberately non-public celebration, demonstrated in its name '*chor-choli*', which means a 'blouse presented in secret'. Some women recounted how the *chor-choli* is sometimes celebrated in a moonlit boat ride.

The Paachi Ritual

After the *dohale jevan* and the seventh-month *paach-pauli* is over, the first post-partum ritual is known as the *paachi* or the fifth-day ritual. This is performed on the day when the Satvai is believed to become mobile from her shrine outside the village and enter its interior in order to write the child's fate. This ritual is usually performed in the evening between the fifth and the sixth day post-partum, associating the Satvai with the Matrika Shashthi, who represents the sixth digit. Women from both natal and marital clans and associated clans of the new mother's village neighbourhood attend the *paachi*, after which the big celebration is repeated to establish the mother's purity that is linked to the child's survival to mark which women share black sprouted gram amongst themselves (*ghugrya*). This sharing also relates them together as agnatic women and therefore as the baby's milk-mothers and caretakers, responsible for his well-being and as his seniors.[18] Any act of insolence from the child henceforth would have women answering him with reprimands of: '*Tujhya paachi chya ghugrya khallyat!*' (I have eaten the *ghugrya* from your *paachi* ritual). The sprouts are said to resemble the dry and healthy excreta of the baby, which in Karnataka is known as *helu-ghugrya* and according to Abbot (1984) connote the goddess's non-afflicting distance from the mother and child, achieved through adequate ritual propitiation. The eating of this distanced goddess (her indirect blessing) symbolises the sharing of positive fertility among agnatic women.

The women constitute a 'pure' community of fertile women (*savashne*) who will transfer and share their purity and fertility with the new mother and borrow hers, once her purity is established, so that they can have more sons like her. *Oti* or lap-filling celebrations take place as these women gift the new mother grain and take back a fist full of it home with them, tied at the ends of their sari *pallu* or in kerchiefs, in order to share in the goddess's distanced, cooled and dry fertility. *Savashne* share their fertility with each other in many ways; a pregnant woman can delegate some of her closest friends (among *savashne*) as her *helkarni*. This means that they will water her doorstep every day during her pregnancy (these are usually return favours) as this trickle of water (known as *hel*) would bring the pregnant woman fertility and through it an easy childbirth. The word *hel* or *helu*, according to my respondents, connotes auspicious powers contained within women and goddesses and is originally a word from Karnataka, used in the same way as *helu-ghugrya*.[19]

[18] Kurtz (1992) has demonstrated how multiple goddesses reflect agnatic women in the psychological development of a male child.

[19] The possible etymology of the term is rather interesting. In the early nineteenth century, Molesworth's Marathi dictionary defined the meaning of the term '*hel*' as 'the business of carrying burdens' and 'the supplying for a few days (with water, milk &c.) of a family in which a child is born. Usually performed by Shudra females, and viewed as a sort of tribute or as an acknowledgment of respect' (Molesworth 1996: 909). In addition to demonstrating again the feudal nature of labour provided to the child, the understanding of the term among my respondents may be connected to two Kannada verbs: *heru* (with long 'e'), meaning 'to lift up, to load', and *heru* (with short 'e'), meaning 'to give birth to' (Bucher 1994: 533).

Savashne and *helkarni* worship sources of water once the birth impurity of the mother is over along with her in rituals known as *panavtha-pujan,* wherein they fill the *oti* for the tap/water source laying out ritual items in front of it. The ritual also sees them grow grains into saplings in areas nearby to these water sources as each *savashne* regularly waters each other's *panavtha*, while filling water for the household, just as agnatic women are supposed to look after each other's children.

For the first five days post-partum, mother and child are bathed in the corner of the birthing room or in an enclosure where an outlet for water is prepared beforehand that exits right outside the house, from a 'bathroom' dug especially for women during childbirth. This however, has become impossible in bigger villages with permanent houses that have to make do with women, who have given birth, bathing in the corner of the kitchenette bathroom, as the entire kitchen shifts outdoors to the next room and the courtyard tap. The placenta (*vur*) of the child is kept in one corner of this bathroom covered under a basket, since it is considered auspicious for the *vur* to share a common space with the mother and the child during the first five days, when it is as yet considered to be 'alive'. The water falling on it from the mother's own bath, flowing in turn on to the child during the latter's ablutions in the first five days, is considered life-giving for the child, since the *vur* is considered to represent the motherliness of the child's first and real mother in the womb, now separated from it by the midwife. This falling and flowing of water from the *vur*, the mother and the placenta is considered to help the child emotionally stabilise after birth, so that its soul is able to settle in its body, even as it misses its first mother. These traditional beliefs about the *vur* being the original mother of the new-born and ritual practices around the placenta have in fact led to its scientific documentation and medicalisation within recent childbirth and midwifery research.[20]

The *paachi* ritual is known as the *pata-pujan* ritual, since the *paach-pauli* in this case is performed on a grinding stone (*pata*). On

[20] Chawla (2002) and Sadgopal (2009) have claimed that heating of the placenta can resuscitate a stillborn baby.

the evening of the *paachi*, a hole is dug in the special bathroom and the *vur* is buried inside it, in a small earthen pot, along with some oblations of *haldi-kunku*, *akshata* and an iron object (such as a nail) so that it could not be henceforth deployed for witchcraft, after which the *pata* is ritually placed on top of this grave. Some of my respondents disposed the *vur* in the floor of garbage dumps outside the village boundary or in rivers, since these constituted conduits to goddess zones and shrines outside boundaries as well.[21] Care was however taken to dig the grave deep enough so that the *vur* would not be violated, desecrated or eaten by a dog or wild animals, since it formed the child's alter ego and controlled its emotional well-being. A cranky child would often be reprimanded with comments such as: '*Tujhi vur kutryane khallya-gat radu nakos!*' (Don't cry as if your placenta has been eaten by a dog!). After the *pata* is instituted on top of the *vur*'s grave, pebbles representing the goddess are placed on its surface with the usual *nada-vastra* lining its length and the usual *paach-pauli* commences thereafter.

Some respondents drew the two goddess sisters with cowdung on two yellow pieces of cloth in front of the *pata*, while others made two anthropomorphic figurines of the sisters with raw rice on the *pata*. The Satvai is also represented by a large stone lamp that is lit at the head of the *pata*, the lamp being shared between women of the same clan after their rituals are over. Small lamps representing the goddess's entourage made of cooked dough, known as *divte*, are kept at the five corners of the *pata*. The pestle (called the *gopa*), [22] dressed attractively in the clothes presented to the new-born, is also kept in the corner of the *pata*, so that the Satvai, visiting the house in order to accept the ritual offerings made to her, may mistake the pestle for the child instead, if the avarice of taking the child may strike her capriciously, despite ritual propitiation. Many kinds of special offerings are made to the *pata* during the *paachi*, in addition to the usual food offerings and *oti* materials that are a constant

[21] Feldhaus (1995b) has written about riverine routes as mobile female fertility.

[22] Duvvury's work (1991) on childbirth rituals among Brahmin women in Tamil Nadu explores many such similarities with Satvai rituals such as dressing up the pestle as a child.

feature in all *paach-pauli* rituals. Many herbs, plants and special foods and concoctions along with cosmetic and comfort-giving items that are prepared and considered especially important for women and children in the post-partum period are first presented to the Satvai, so that she may not feel 'left out' and subsequently curse these items. Among the other special offerings, the stump of the umbilical cord (known as *naal*) is also offered to the Satvai at the *pata*, since it is considered to mitigate against pneumonia and rickets (known as *potatla* and *mudadoos*, respectively). Lastly, a pencil and a notebook are laid on the *pata* for the Satvai to write the child's fate, even as some of my respondents believed that the Satvai wrote a child's fate on his/her forehead. Five different kinds of plants including cactus, pomegranate leaves, acacia leaves and leaves from other local plants, such as *neem* (these leaves differed from clan to clan) are offered to the *pata* along with river sand.

Abbot (1984) has provided great details about the various combinations of five sacred plants or *paach-palavi* that act as totems (*devak*) for Maratha clans evidenced during his anthropological research in Bombay Presidency, that find use in all sorts of auspicious occasions such as weddings and childbirth. The mother and child pay obeisance to the deity thereafter as incense sticks are lit and the baby is laid in front of the *pata*. Care is however taken to keep the baby's face averted from the flame of the Satvai lamp, since its power is supposed to turn the child cross-eyed.

On the evening of the *paachi*, twelve small anthropomorphic figures (called *bali-rana*) are drawn on the walls of the birthing chamber, the bathroom and the house (including the outside walls).Ritual and food offerings are made to them to 'enliven' them each day, even as one of them is daily wiped away and considered 'taken' by the Satvai as a sacrifice instead of the child, since she still hovers around the house during the days of the mother's birth impurity, not entirely distanced from motherhood and cannibalistic attachments with the baby till the rituals are completed herself.

During the night of the *paachi*, the door is kept open for the Satvai, who is understood to come as a cat (like the cat-faced Shashthi) and accept the ritual offerings from the *pata*. My respondents from Ghodegaon often recounted a humorous story of wilder times from the past, when a small leopard (*bibtya*) from a nearby forest (that pressed in on village boundaries at the time) in search of food had accidentally sneaked into a house in order to polish off food left for the cat on the *pata*, much to the family's consternation and fright. The boy whose *paachi* it had been was often teased in the village for having a 'special' Satvai.

The next morning the dough lamps are offered to a group of *kori-savashne*, who are especially invited to visit the family to remove the *pata* from its ritual position near the bathroom and to bless the child with incantations of '*Kapsa sarkha mhatara ho, harali evdha veli ja!*' (Grow as old as the white cotton wool and grow as fertile and spread as widely as wild vegetation/grass!), while stroking the mother and child's brow with oil. The *kori-savashne* receive some gifts such as coconut and dry fruits in return, just as the midwife receives a blouse piece (*khan*), a coconut and some bangles as a ritual gift for being part of the *adich-savashne* and for having absorbed the new mother's birth impurity.

Great efforts are made during the period of birth impurity to misguide the Satvai and mislead her away from identifying the real baby. In the initial days, mother and child are sought to be protected by laying their mattress on dry wheat and millet stalks so that it constantly crackles, indicating to the Satvai that the mother or other family members are always awake with every one of their movements. The mother sleeps with an iron knife next to her pillow in order to ward off witchcraft (iron is supposed to work against witchcraft), with a paste of *hing* (asafoetida) applied to her and the child, since asafoetida is a mark of belonging to the civilized world, through trade and being under the goddess's tutelage in Maharashtra.[23] Leather footwear is also hung over the main door to ward off the evil eye along with a horseshoe nailed to the door jamb; these are different ways in which the clan demonstrates its location within accepted and recognised castes (such as cobblers or ironsmiths) of the village who are already protected by the Satvai

[23] One of my respondents told me how Tulja-Bhavani's real name was Hingulja Bhavani (*hing* is asafoetida in Marathi).

and who are protected against witchcraft simultaneously. The child's position on the cot is also changed frequently, and is even covered by a woman's dress so that the Satvai would mistake it for someone else. The eating of food 'allowed' to mothers only after its dedication to the Satvai on the *pata*, is considered to prevent post-partum abdominal cramps or *vayu-gola* (referred to by Chawla 2002 as *hawa-gola*), since the first 'respect' or right over the food has been provided to the Satvai. Care is taken to not offend the goddess in any way during the period of ritual impurity and not wear colours or eat things (such as betel leaves) that constitute a part of the goddess's privilege.

When I asked my respondents what the *pata* signified, many among the upper castes told me that it signified Lord Shiva-Parvati's union and the Shiva-linga. The marriage ritual of Lord Kartik with Champa Shashthi had also taken place on the sixth day after Skanda Kartikeya's birth (since the *pata* is also used as an agent of fertility and indoctrination/family initiation within marriage rituals). However, scanning through my photos of the *pata-pujan* ritual later, I came to see how the entire arrangement of the *paachi* ritual resembled the plinth of the Satvai shrine, assembled on top of the *pata* that transfers motherhood attachment from women to the goddess, with the buried *vur* of the real biological mother below the *pata* in the earth under the shrine. The pictures of the *pata* shrine showed the way in which the *paach-palavi* resembled the sacred grove or thicket around the goddess's shrine, while the sand from the river came to symbolise the presence of a nearby river (stream or gutter) that was also almost always near a shrine.

The Mahadev Koli in my field region, on the other hand, who worship the local Satvai as a clan goddess and not a goddess presiding over childloss at all, follow none of these rituals of ancestor and boundary worship involving motherhood attachment transfer. They have none of these rituals of *pata-pujan* and other such complex rituals, even though many of late have started copying people of the caste villages by tying the hair of their children to sticks and hoisting these sticks on top of their houses in order to show the village that their baby is alive (this practice, according to other respondents, had not existed earlier). The placenta of their children is buried inside their huts and when I asked them whether these spaces were once bathrooms built for childbirth, my Koli respondents looked blank and nonplussed. Most of these placenta burials were covered by heavy round stones as many proud children showed me 'their' placentas.

According to one of my respondents from the Ghisadi caste (considered nomadic ironsmiths), the morning of the *paachi* ritual sees the new mother wearing yellow clothes, walking around a thorn twig planted in the courtyard amidst the singing of insulting songs about the goddess, who is imagined as an old hag. Till the day of the *paachi*, the mother would be bathed along with the baby every day on the birthing cot itself, and the placenta would be buried in a hole under the cot. There was, however, no ritual of *paach-pauli*. Later in the day, the families on both sides would begin to arrive for a feast cooked by the newborn's grandmother, which included an animal sacrifice made to the goddess. The families would then use the opportunity to settle property disputes that may have arisen since the marriage of the child's parents and also settle the child's inheritance. According to my Ghisadi respondent, many of these meetings ended in drunken brawls but had nothing to do with geographical boundaries, since they were nomadic.

The Baaravi Ritual

The twelfth-day *paach-pauli* or the *baaravi* ritual, as it is called, takes place during the afternoon of the twelfth day and is followed by the *baarsa* celebration the same evening. It moves the concentric circle of boundaries around the new-born another notch away from the homestead, distancing the Satvai another step away from the latter by bringing all interrelated clans of the same caste within the purity ambit of the mother and child. During this ritual, the participants go to the crossroads outside the neighbourhood to perform the *baaravi*, the mother covered in a blanket and holding an iron knife in order to ward off lurking witches, with the child held by relatives following close behind. I often observed clans effecting continuity between their Satvai rituals, as ritual objects retrieved and tied into a bundle from the *pata* ritual were offered once again along with fresh ritual offerings prepared for the new ritual were presented all over again at the *baaravi paach-pauli*.

The *baaravi* also marked the end of the larger part of the Satvai's 'death impurity' along with all the dead mothers in her retinue, since the *Shraddha* ritual that marked the transition of the ancestor after death into the next world also required between twelve and thirteen days to get over, after which death impurity was also considered finished. This childbirth ritual of *baaravi* therefore freed the mother and the baby from the clutches of the dead ancestor mothers while associating all life cycle rituals together: the *pata* with marriage and the *baaravi* with death and all of them together with the birth of children, their initiation into the social world and the social production of women into mothers.

The evening celebration sees the laying of the child in a cradle (*palna*) for the first time (but the *gopa* or the dressed up pestle is put into the *palna* first) and its naming ceremony commences, as it is believed to have developed a soul after the first twelve days of healthy life when it is considered to be mostly out of danger. The edges of the cradle are decorated with betel leaf, sweets and *ghugrya* during the function as women make the new mother (who can engage in household chores henceforth) sit in a square (*chowk*) made of raw grain, commencing with filling her *oti* and the exchange of gifts. She is supposed to first hold the *gopa* in her lap, while the women rain down grain on her lap and only thereafter replace the *gopa* with the real baby. This is done because the *gopa* is considered to belong to the goddess and women want to pay the Satvai their first respects and not offend her childlessness or absence of motherhood, which would be at their own peril. While respecting the goddess's childlessness, however, they take care to keep away all real childless women and widows from such celebrations, since such women are feared for being witches.

Many *baarsa* songs are sung on this occasion as the child's maternal and paternal aunts play with the baby. Finally, the child's paternal aunt is designated the responsibility of communicating the child's pre-decided name to it, which she whispers into the baby's ears for the first time and she is playfully slapped on her back by the others for giving it its first identity and robbing it of its infancy and for initiating it into the world of social relationships. Many women begin to take the baby for small outings to close by neighbours or a nearby temple thereafter, as the baby is brought to meet many new people and wear normal clothes and starts becoming slowly introduced to different faces while being moved from lap to lap as mothers start doing small household activities.

The Jaawal Ritual

The newborn, however, is not considered to be completely out of danger till the *jaawal* ritual is completed and the whole village and region are made safe for its inhabitation by distancing the Satvai from it altogether. Women are also instructed to continue with breastfeeding and remain concentrated on the child till the *jaawal* ritual is not over, remaining outside what is considered polluting sexual contact for the first three or four months post-partum, till which time it is considered sinful for a husband to even touch his wife's clothes. Sexual contact before the *jaawal* is considered to lead to the ceasing of mother's milk and result in her shame and public humiliation, since this affliction will necessitate the ritual dedication of small earthen pots (called *sugad*) full of milk to the Satvai at her shrine with a ritual request of releasing milk (*dudha sodne*) that first makes it imperative for the concerned woman to accept her mistake. The corollary is also held automatically true; women unable to breastfeed are viewed as sexually impure. Sexuality and breastfeeding were commonly viewed in my field area as two opposite sorts of functioning valves; the exercise of one seemed to shut down the other and this myth seemed to be more of a conundrum between women's impurity/sexuality and purity/motherhood than have any biological basis to it.

The child's infancy clothes (known as *balote*) and *jaawal* (hair grown on the head while in the womb) are considered to be absorbent of the child's vulnerability to witchcraft, since they are extensions of its body and take on great sensitivity till the time the *jaawal* ritual is not completed. It is believed that the *balote* absorb the child's life force, just as the *jaawal*. Till the time of the *jaawal* ritual, a new-born's *balote* are closely guarded, since it is believed that if a childless woman engaging in witchcraft were to find a new-born's *balote* before the ritual, she could burn it, ingesting a daily pinch of its ash, until she herself became pregnant with the same child, while the actual new-born whose *balote* it was would waste away and die. I have known of village women who have swum for miles in order to retrieve *balote* that had accidentally flowed away in the stream, while being washed, even as they spoke of the witchcraft of *balote* more as crimes against clans and their heirs than against babies.

The *jaawal* ritual consists of offering some strands of the child's hair (that has grown from the time he was within the womb) placed within two halves of a coconut, wrapped in the *balote*, along with food offerings to the Satvai during her last *paach-pauli* performed at the Satvai shrine. The *jaawal* ritual ends the pregnancy calendar for both mother and child, after which the mother returns to her normal life and the child can subsist on an increasing amount of cooked food as it becomes a citizen and develops a soul.

The *jaawal paach-pauli* (taking place most often at the shrine of the goddess) is usually witnessed by members of both natal and marital clans (the maternal uncle and the paternal aunt holding the child and its cut hair, respectively), and introduces the child to extended clan, caste difference (as the barber and midwife attend as ritual agents) and the region of action. Some clans have a big celebration after the *jaawal* ritual, making an animal sacrifice to the Satvai, wherein its liver is especially offered to the goddess along with the food and other ritual offerings in addition to the *jaawal* and *balote*, which are tied to a part of the shrine or outside to a tree with other such dedications. Many families for whom clan Satvai shrines are located too far away for travel perform their *jaawal paach-pauli* at a nearby forest or grove, facing the direction of their shrine. The hair and clothes are packed away, kept for a journey to the family Satvai shrine, to be taken at a later time for several clan children all together.

Even though there are many different caste groups and clans in Maharashtra recounting their own kind of post-partum rituals (that I have tried to group together to the best of my ability), I would like to end this section with a small note on Western research on childbirth rituals per se (just to contextualise an understanding of it in the wider arena) that views these as supportive for mothers, in contrast to what is considered to be Western women's 'baby blues', brought about through the latter's independence from the child's father and marital clan. Studies in transcultural psychiatry (such as Zelkowitz 1996) have traced the way in which post-partum care can be reflected through the clan and the family's preparedness to host childbirth rituals for the mother and child. It is exactly this rationalist approach (that some of my upper-caste respondents shared) which is ridden with dualisms between 'the East' and 'the West', that stop short of probing deeper into the labour-inducing meanings of what Satvai rituals for women could constitute, when an understanding of its oppression would fall outside an awareness of local history, religion, local texts, local languages, and local caste or poverty politics. The transformation at the end of the *jaawal* rituals that separate biological mothers from their children in rural Maharashtra results in as much of dissociation for many mothers, since it essentially produces their sons as owning members and masters of society like the goddess herself, who champions their cause as their 'real' mother, while producing daughters and women's bodies as owned.

I would finally conclude this chapter by pointing to an understanding of how bad motherhood conceived systemically and historically through time is arranged in complex manners through the formation of caste groups, purity-impurity dyads and complex/composite forms that reflects caste stratification and the demarcation of rural spatial boundaries based on this. Women, moreover, attempt to achieve pure motherhood by mirroring the dyad between monster-goddesses by internalising caste distinctions against the lower caste that push and extend pure spaces from inside, from within their own body towards the outside, to result in the creation of the pure inside. Thereby they become feudatories of high castes linked to the inside, who receive rewards and celebration from the subsequently purified and reproduced internal structure as owned members.

The third group—the Mahadev Koli, the Ghisadi and the Adivasi, and their clan goddesses, whose rituals I have also briefly described in this chapter—fit into the lower counterpart of dyad formations with more established village goddesses such as Shitala Devi. They have been traditionally nomadic or migrant and are still considered to be outside caste organisation that are imagined to be fixed within political units such as villages, even though they have begun to be 'settled' artificially and appended to caste-like villages only recently. Their villages are mostly made out of clans or even consist of the same extended clan, or if it is a very big village, two or three clans. They have begun to make relationships with caste villages and since the Satvai and Maulya organise labour only through caste and the propagation of caste through reproduction/childbirth and marital alliance associated with land, Mahadev Kolis, who have entirely different meanings attached to the worship of clan goddess have come to form the lower counterpart of dyads with caste villages.

CHAPTER 4

Region, Community and Political Demarcation

Scholars such as White (2003) and Feldhaus (2003) have argued that rivers and associated fertility goddesses within it, act as embodiments of the region and as signifiers of kingship. Feldhaus, in her book *Connected Places: Region, Pilgrimage and Geographical Imagination of India* (2003), describes the way in which goddesses in Maharashtra act as the fertile physical signifiers of natural aspects such as rivers flowing through regions that interconnect worshippers and pilgrims across its boundaries. These construct paradigms of different kinds of possible cross-regional kingship relationships within a patchwork of interconnected regions that are presided over by a vast network of linked goddesses (as sisters or dyads). Feldhaus describes various stories of travelling goddesses scattered across neighbouring and therefore related regions, in various relationships with their worshippers, travelling in different contexts. She also recounts stories of pilgrimages in which worshippers retrace the goddess's path as they journey back towards her and attempt to integrate a larger, segmented region with her cult. According to Feldhaus, goddesses facilitate connectivity across region as sister rivers flowing through each other's territories or as response providers to the plea of old pilgrims as they climb down from the hills and their shrines towards the latter.

I would, however, like to add a further dimension to this theory of regional and cultic connectivity. The networks of alliance and marriage between clans presided over by goddesses primarily take place between dominant castes of the region, who are almost always of an agrarian or the pure and village-interior inhabitation variety. These don't (in most cases) include the lower castes of the cleaning-absorbing kind, who traditionally neither own agrarian property and only inherit the servitude of a feudal class, having the duty of reproducing this servitude of impurity absorption. It is important to note that the demarcations and boundaries between these sought-to-be-unified and interconnected regions presided over by interlinked goddesses are still important and kept intact, despite the travelling back and forth and pilgrimages across and between them and the close affinity and the sisterhood between the goddesses presiding over them. What this assumption of univocal affinity between goddesses effects is the simultaneous obliteration and underlining of the lower-caste boundary between them that at the same time produces the region as 'natural' and unmarked like the dominant castes within them, along with their alliance with other dominant castes in other 'naturalised' regions. This marks the dualism: a creation of a dark boundary, despite the happy connectivity beyond boundary as what is unmentionable and obscene within its charmed circle. It is this boundary, despite the connectivity beyond all that is not boundary, that remains invisible, obliterated and yet extremely obvious and politically produced as discriminated against and darkened, impure, gendered and lower caste. Now the interesting factor is that although most goddesses originate at boundaries, they don't face these boundaries; they only civilize all those peripheral and marginal at the lower rungs of caste and unify those dominant at the upper extremes common to all regions in alliances that remain unmarked. They face away from boundaries and embody all the dreads and exits for what comes to represent 'downfall' within dominant caste imagination.

White (2003: 32–35) has written about how the flowing of rivers in Maharashtra is compared to goddesses such as the Sati-*asra* (seven nymphs) because they represent the flowing of female fertility, menstrual blood and vaginal liquids that in turn represent motherhood. These rivers, goddesses and their fertility flow hologramatically through India to mimic relationships between goddess worship, the river Ganga and its deification as it waters so many agrarian regions. He writes about how regions become linked together with natural resources such as rivers flowing through them, religious values such as goddess worship that become linked in turn with clan fertility and specific tantric rituals that mimic this symbology through the usage of menstrual and vaginal fluids that flow. Even as White remains sensitive to a gender perspective, it would still be important to point to the 'utilisation' aspect of women's liquid flows within tantric rituals, as women's bodies become conduits to clan fertility and is likened to the agrarian community's use of water from a river that flows through its farms. As for the question of reproductive liquids being essentialised to clan fertility, there is also the question of sexual fluids within tantric rituals that are differently related to *yogini* worship and exploit women as equally as fertile fluids yoked to the cause of gaining divine powers or *siddhi*. That women's consumption and usage becomes invisible and obliterated, even as women's sexual body becomes its most obvious object is its obvious paradox. Tantrism, while extolling the power of the female sexual body, when comparing it in terms of how a river conjoins clans with their own fertility, used women's bodies to associate goddesses with clan reproduction.

Boundary Politics

Only caste-based villages perform Satvai rituals, in terms of demarcating their boundaries against various other neighbouring ecological zones that lie adjacent to them, while imagining the communities that live there as 'wilderness' and 'other' communities, on the basis of which they establish unequal or hierarchical relationships with them, reflected in the Satvai cult. Most villagers from village Ghodegaon, for example, worship the Satvai from the neighbouring region/village of Koldhawde, whom many told me was a Van-Satvai (especially now because her shrine was located in a forest) as she is a clan goddess for the Mahadev Koli. Earlier she was the Satvai of Ambegaon village but Ambegaon was now under water, under the reservoir of Dimbhe dam that was built in the year 2000 on the river Ghod. The Mahadev Koli of the region, living in the nearby forests don't have a boundary relationship with her, even though they use her name 'Satvai' as a proper noun and not as a name that signifies a boundary association. It is partly through the Van-Satvai of Koldhawde that the caste village of Ghodegaon and erstwhile Ambegaon views the Mahadev Koli and their own hierarchical relationships (trade in forest produce and so on) with the latter.

Satvai rituals, therefore also integrate ecological resource sectors and communities that exploit land/resources in sectors outside the boundary of caste villages in relationships that are hierarchically lower to themselves. The conversion of clan goddesses from neighbouring ecological zones and clans that live outside caste structures into boundary goddesses for caste-based villages, therefore, effect their 'Satvai-fication' or boundary-fication, for the utilisation and benefit of caste-based villages. Adherent clan groups, who consider the goddess a clan deity are further related to additionally, as lower castes of the region living outside the caste village boundary, even as women from these 'lower' clans became integrated within caste villages as 'healers' and mediums. Since the goddess is in any case linked with worship in their clan, they become co-opted within caste society as agents of the boundary, healers on behalf of the Satvai and boundary markers, who receive patronage from the village (the current healer and medium for the Koldhawdya-*chi-aai*, for example, is a lady from the Mahadev Koli tribe from the Dimbhe resettlement colony) [1]. Many villagers and Kolis themselves cite this as a historic process, wherein they initially began receiving dominant caste patronage from local kings in return for healing duties.

[1] Kusum Karnik, founder of Shashwat Sansthan in Manchar (Ambegaon taluka), has been agitating for the Maharashtra government to grant the Mahadev Koli traditional land and land-resource rights in the Ahupe and Bhimashankar areas that have been taken over by the forest departments (especially after the Dimbhe dam was built in the year 2000). Even so, many Koli clans have voluntarily converted to state rehabilitation and agrarianism, thereby rejecting her claims (personal communication with Neema Pathak Broome, Kalpavriksh Environment Action Group, Pune).

Satvayya (plural) were either called by place names (such as Koldhawdya-*chi-aai* or the mother from village Koldhawde), by the ecological types they represented (such as Van-devi) or by the two names of the dyads (Ranu-*bai* and Santu-*bai*). Sometimes Santu-*bai* was replaced by Mes-*aai*. Sometimes there were descriptive epithets such as lady of the village inhabitation or *pandhri-varli aai*, since *pandhri* or white soil always signifies inhabitation juxtaposed to *kali* or black soil that signifies agricultural land. The boundary between ecological zones and their associated clan groups, that were organised into hierarchically lower castes living outside the caste village boundary, then represented politically produced demarcations that became grey zones to the regions inside them. On the other hand, the regions inside them that criss-crossed beyond them hardly ever intermixed with them.[2]

My respondents often explained the difference in community relationships with the Satvai, who was a clan goddess for the Mahadev Koli and worshipped as the Satvai by caste villagers, as reflections of different relationships in the lives of real women and their natal and marital relationships: the Satvai was a loving mother for the Mahadev Koli of Bhimashankar and Ahupe but for the caste women from agrarian villages such as Ghodegaon, the same goddess was no less than an exacting and punishing mother-in-law in the form of a boundary goddess. In their responses about how their relationships with their goddess-mothers-in-law changed with marriage, once they became daughters-in-law, I detected reversals of power as the Satvai became constructed as more punishing for upper-caste women from inside the village, than those other women from among the Koli who were actually from among the 'enlisted' within the rule of the agrarian village, considered as living outside its boundaries and margins. These 'punished' women belonged to dominant caste groups and were at the apex of political demarcations of boundary-marking with other 'communities' considered 'lower', but instead viewed themselves at the receiving end of Satvai afflictions, while they

2 The Dhangar goddess Bhivai (described by Feldhaus 1995a) is also constructed and worshipped as the Maulya in my field area.

viewed Koli women as 'free' from punishment, enjoying greater liberty from affliction as daughters of the Satvai. Here lay the seeming paradox that separated women within upper castes and classes from a view of their own privilege of safety and comforts that in turn imprisoned their bodies within morality, even as this separated their lack of experience of real hardship, labour and poverty that turned their conception of the lower-caste woman's body into a fantasy of freedom, magic and adventure. My Koli respondents, on the other hand, imagined village women to be free of labour, safe and privileged, since they could not appreciate the burden of clan morality and labour that the upper-caste woman's body had to constantly uphold.

The 'seemingly' natural boundaries that the Satvai controlled made spaces outside 'boundaries' seem completely unnatural and full of affliction possibilities and danger for my upper-caste respondents in experiential terms. The fear of danger from 'outside' made them imbue the women they considered 'lower' from 'other' regions and communities from beyond boundaries with attributes of unrecognisable immorality that were akin to affliction diagnosis for their 'own' women, whom they considered betrayers (if the latter somehow were to divulge boundaries) and whom they hoped the Satvai would punish. This in turn led to the production of further marginality, stigma and rivalry for women to prove even higher moral grounds for others, who took it upon themselves to discriminate against them.

Even as my respondents craved the liberty of being without afflicting boundaries, they coped with the existence of these in their lives by dreaming about fearful failures in sleeping hours and competing with women who lived or tried to live without boundaries, or struggled against these during their waking hours. They feared of what would happen to their social status and protection outside boundaries and fantasised about its liberty quite simultaneously, even as they continued to be contemptuous about the immorality of living a boundary-less life at the same time. Travelling alone for women across ritual boundaries was difficult in my field area as the possibility of individual attacks on women was presented to me as being omnipresent outside village, locality and home boundaries. Paradoxically so, even within the narratives of those women who suffered the maximum amounts of domestic violence and humiliation at home and within so-called safe boundaries;[3] women almost always travelled in clan groups or with female companionship and children.

Boundaries, therefore, became political agents of the social stratification encapsulated by them, as has already been suggested by Douglas (2002). They constituted central and fundamental parts of a larger structural hierarchy that did not just demarcate the outside from the inside but themselves become central zones of power that controlled the interaction of many 'outsides', tying them to an inside through a shared margin that defined exchange and hierarchy and the politics of mobility. The boundary became that potent space of power from where periphery-enlisting stratification emanated, which in turn produced politicised domains of differential labour and rights that were reflected as innocuous and naturalised and valourised aspects of space and environment. Boundaries presided over by goddesses supporting kingships and dominant castes therefore became the central focus of statecraft, defence, politics and war (as also noted by Zbavitel in connection with goddesses in 1976).

A Case Study of the Mahalakshmi from Chivri

The shrine and cult of the Mahalakshmi of Chivri from Osmanabad district[4] constitutes a good example of the way in which larger *shakti-peetha* shrines in the region of Marathwada, like the Tulja-Bhavani (from Tuljapur, also in district Osmanabad), come to 'acquire' the older sister-goddess status, in which goddess cults such as the Mahalakshmi's fulfil the boundary-

[3] Women told me how they wore a lot of vermillion (*kunku*) while going out so that they could eat it if they were attacked. According to them, *kunku* remained an effective poison (since it consisted of mercury [*paara*]) that would protect their chastity in case they were attacked outside their village.

[4] My examples from fieldwork at the shrine of the Mahalakshmi of Chivri are not just limited to this section.

keeping mechanism of region production, through a process of Sanskritisation and dyad formation (already theorised in the last chapter). I suggest that similar processes can be observed with regard to the territories of other predominantly benevolent *shakti-peetha* goddesses, who incorporate different territories as elder sister goddesses, with their boundaries being presided over by subsidiary goddess cults. Small *shakti-peetha* or village goddess cults growing regionally important take on the younger sister goddess position in relation to larger and more benevolent cults, that then carry on in a continuous processes of interaction and regional incorporation through boundaries with the help of local goddess mythologies. Even as benevolent and pure goddesses of a region acquire smaller and fiercer boundary-protecting goddesses, associating with them in dyads (and ultimately linking all goddesses together as sisters of each other), the latter simultaneously travel towards benevolence themselves, acquiring other smaller local fierce goddesses below them in a process that reflects upward caste mobility within worshipping groups. The Mahalakshmi of Chivri forms a good example of this process of region formation, since she is one such village goddess of Marathwada, turned into a small *shakti-peetha* (this is purportedly because of her potent *Shakta* rituals that are in turn denounced by the Maharashtra Andhashradhha Nirmulan Samiti or ANIS and the state). She is now considered a lower and fierce sister of the Tulja-Bhavani, in upward transit towards benevolence, developing many lower sister forms of herself in neighbouring regions as well. She has many male and female healers dedicated to her service.

The Mahalakshmi from village Chivri (or 'of Chivri', since she is also considered to belong to Chivri) is originally understood to be a clan goddess of the local Pardhi community, just like the 'Satvai' of Ghodegaon was originally considered to be the clan goddess of the Mahadev Koli. The local dominant castes of Chivri moreover believe the Pardhi community to be extremely violent and traditional thieves and dacoits, forest hunters and criminals (a myth that has also been perpetuated to a large extent by the Maharashtra state). The Pardhis are one of the largest minorities of the Osmanabad region today.[5] Apart from some of the better off families in the region around Solapur that have been rehabilitated by the government, the Pardhi (or Phaase-Pardhi/'noose-making Pardhi', as they are sometimes called) suffer from acrimonious and distrustful relationships with the caste society in Chivri which often results in state and social violence against them. At every *jatra* or annual festival of the Mahalakshmi the place is teeming with the local police who keep a vigilant watch on every Pardhi, since the latter are expected to act violently during rituals. Furthermore, hardly any villages in the immediate areas around Chivri, according to my village-to-village survey in 2010, yielded another village goddess; all the villagers in the immediate vicinity of Chivri considered the Mahalakshmi to be their village goddess and spoke of how the goddess had travelled to their region behind devotees returning after worship at Chivri (a sort of goddess mythology I analyse below, and one already sited by Feldhaus 2003). Also, they linked the annual worship festival of the Mahalakshmi with the Tulja-Bhavani (the latter being the greater benevolent *shakti-peetha* in Marathwada), timing the *jatra* of the Mahalakshmi with spring (conflating the smaller spring harvest with the onset of summer, childbirths and epidemics), while they located the larger goddess festival of *Navaratri* to coincide with that of the Tulja-Bhavani (conflating the onset of planting in agriculture with conception of children, fertility and pregnancy). It was only after a certain distance beyond Chivri that other fierce village goddesses emerged that linked themselves to the Mahalakshmi and Tulja-Bhavani in

[5] The colonial or modern documents about Phaase-Pardhi confirm their 'origins' to lie in the Marathwada regions of Maharashtra (mostly Beed district). They were popularly considered to be a tribe with a criminal mentality during the British period and jailed pre-emptively for it, along with their families. They are presently declared a denotified or ex-criminal tribe of India but are still criminalised by the Indian police/state and stigmatised by society, besides suffering terrible poverty and absence of education, since they have lost all forms of caste profession that still define rural forms of agrarian entitlement. They are understood to consist of violent bands of roaming, hunting and drinking criminals, who perpetuate all sorts of crimes on 'settled life' in popular and bureaucratic imagination (Gaikwad 1998).

independent, complex and parallel ways as the younger sister. It is important to note that the village Chivri did not have a Satvai either; the women offered their *jaawal-balote* at the shrine of the Mahalakshmi.

The enlistment of the Pardhi clan goddess in a way that appended a 'dacoit region' to agrarian civilization, as a low and fierce sister in a dyad-like relationship with the neighbouring Tulja-Bhavani represents the incorporation of the Pardhi tribe at the lowest rung of caste society, in which settled agriculture takes place at the core and heartland. It also enables the introduction of a state and social machinery to marginalize Pardhis, who are situated lowest within caste hierarchy within these appended peripheries, even as the Pardhi clan goddess becomes utilized within the Shakta worship format to connect regions through dyad relationships with the heartland that link boundaries and produce mainstreams. Further, the potently *shakta* ritual sacrifices of the Mahalakshmi that is condemned by the ANIS creates the mainstream of the greater sister as unmarked, whose cult is actually as much of a co-producer in the dyad.

It is the ritual sacrifice demanded by the Mahalakshmi that consists of an embryo removed from a pregnant ewe, that further produces the Pardhi community as inhumanly violent and cruel within the village of Chivri, since this sacrifice is compared with *their* private practices, without the caste society at Chivri ever having asked themselves the reasons for having incorporated these so-called violent sacrifices as part of their own village goddess rituals, if they despised the Pardhis so much. One of my respondents from Chivri grew angry, when I idly speculated about whether the caste villagers of Chivri and villages around Chivri were historically all Pardhi in origin; he retaliated by saying that then they should all have been in jails till fifty years back. They were also very angry with me when I pointed out that the goddess's sacrifice should have actually embodied the Pardhi (the ewe and the sheep), since sacrifices always embodied the condemned, according to goddess lore, where the sacrificed always represented evil (making out the caste villagers to be the cruel ones and the Pardhis the condemned victims). But they were adamant that the Pardhi clan goddess demanded a violent Pardhi-type ritual, since they were the original sacrifice makers of innocent farmers to their clan goddess in wild pre-colonial times. It was the take-over of the goddess cult by the agrarian villages and the replacement of the farmer/ pastoralist with the ewe that had finally satisfied the goddess in current times; she however still remained especially benevolent to the Pardhi. The agrarian adoption of the Mahalakshmi as a village goddess at its boundary then, reflected the opinion of what I had witnessed at Ghodegaon: competition between Koli daughters enjoying freedom and liberty at the cost of a lower caste status and poverty versus dominant caste daughters-in-law bearing the brunt of moral affliction at the cost of village protection, economic stability and comparative luxury.

But did the Mahalakshmi take her sacrifice of the ewe? Each year, since 1990 ANIS crackdown on her shrine (that denounced the rituals over here as especially superstitious), she had turned increasingly benevolent, even as some of her other lower boundary sisters in faraway villages (such as the Mes-*aai* in Mangrul, also in Osmanabad) were said to take on her fiercer boundary roles. Her own temple was painted, became larger; she acquired a new silver mask, a Brahmin priest, and began accepting sweets as ritual offerings as Brahminical rituals are performed for her today. She had also been regularly rejecting animal sacrifice, with the help of state intervention, as I was told by the village headman, who was walking about the temple precincts with an enormous, rusted and blunt sword on the *jatra* night. When I asked him why he had the sword, he told me proudly that he was ready for the sacrifice in case the Mahalakshmi suddenly expressed a desire for it. At the last moment, however, she gave her *kaul*, a divine sign, rejecting the sacrifice and the *Patil* wistfully put the enormous, rusted and blunt sword away. He however allowed me to take many photos of it and of him with it, since according to him it demonstrated Maratha grandeur and the caste's traditional relationship with goddess worship. I asked him when the goddess had last taken her sacrifice of a pregnant ewe but he could not remember ever having witnessed this. However, when I asked him, whether it was just part of the goddess's story, he re-emphasized on how it was most definitely a Pardhi-type ritual sacrifice and so it must be true and refused to believe that it was a stereotype.

Along with the Pardhi, the Matang caste from Chivri, who are now considered to inhabit a grey zone between tribe and caste categories, popularly undertake the Mahalakshmi's ritual agentship or '*potraaj-ki*' at Chivri.[6] The Matang are however, considered to be more integrated into the lower rungs of caste society, as a settled community in Chivri, in comparison to the Pardhi, since they are ritually dedicated to the Mahalakshmi in a marriage ritual (as the goddess's wife) and believe themselves to be a caste (more than a tribe) based on traditional clan goddess rituals that they increasingly undertake as part of *Balutedari* feudal duties. These rituals of dedication produce them into a feminine gender and into the servants, absorbers and cleaners of the upper-caste villagers and their afflictions. They do however recount a history of being considered akin to a separate *samaj* in Maharashtra (of associated clans) such as Madiga or Telang in other states such as Telangana, when they recount their forefathers referring to themselves as Mang-garudi, who were imprisoned in colonial jails. Another reference to Matang is associated with the Matang Rishi from the Ramayana text, even as the Mangs are documented in colonial records as a changeless, aboriginal and depressed community (Guha 1999:10).

There have, however, been various musings among my respondents about how the word *potraaj* came into existence (when discussing the ritual dedication of Matang men to the Mahalakshmi as wives and through this to the village as subservient) from the etymological point of view, beginning with whether the word *pot* refers to the wearing of the goddess's *cowrie* shells (sea shells) or auspicious beads of marriage and feudal duty.[7]

[6] The Matang are also known as Mang-garudi in regions around Osmanabad and Solapur and were originally also considered an ex-criminal community or a *maji-gunegaar samaj* like the Pardhi. They are however considered a caste today, unlike the Pardhi.

[7] A more likely explanation is that the word derives from a Dravidian word denoting the male of an animal, specifically the male buffalo, connecting the *potraaj* to the buffalo demon (Burrow and Emeneau 1998: 302, entry 3747).

Potraaj-ki is undertaken by those Matang and lower-caste men (never women) dedicated to the goddess, who take up the duty of healing the upper castes of afflictions sent by the goddess. This ritual of dedication and marriage debars them from inheriting and owning property or land and makes them perpetuate *potraaj-ki* as a feudal duty among other male members of their caste. It is a process of creating lower-caste men as the goddess's wives through ritual dedication, the undertaking of which is a feudal duty that has certain historic continuity in the Deccan, extending to goddess cults and their lower, male demonic protectors-cum-servants, who also embody the goddess's vanquished enemies and take on the role of her vehicle. These serving demons or vanquished enemies have subsidiary shrines outside the gates of goddess temples and act as her protectors or gatekeepers like the Satvai's Munjoba/Chedoba or Mhasoba. Goddess shrines and mythology in South India (mostly Tamil Nadu and Andhra Pradesh) are typically replete with these servants, who are referred to as Pottu Raja. In Maharashtra, the *potraaj* is a feudal title and *potraaj-ki* is a feudal duty actually carried out by lower-caste men in ritual servitude of the goddess, whose gender (not sex) is changed for the purpose of effecting this servitude. The pain and humiliation of *potraaj-ki* has been written about in powerful Dalit literature such as Polke's 'Abhraan' (1984). Hiltebeitel (1988) has documented and described in detail the outcaste Pottu Raja's association with the goddess, both as her protector and as the buffalo demon in South India in his explorations of the cult of Draupadi as does Biardeau (2004) when she associates the Pottu Raja's cult in the Deccan and South India with ancient traditions of Vedic sacrifice in India.

Becoming a *potraaj* of the Mahalakshmi (a male healer/medium, her lion/vehicle, her protector and sometimes doubling up as the buffalo demon) entails taking up the ritual labour of *potraaj-ki* in the village as a mark of honour and incorporation at the lowest rung of hierarchy. A *potraaj* performing the duty of 'absorption' for dominant caste afflictions that is reserved for 'low' and feminised bodies as *Balutedari* in exchange for village protection, is a deeply gendered subjectivity for him. He becomes a wife and agent to the goddess and like an absorbent and lower sexual partner for the village's impurity without personal inheritance and ownership, when performing this feudatory task as he becomes owned by her cult and the village. Many *potraaj* find this humiliating as men but try to overcome their personal emotions as part of their economic choices and family decisions.

These men are dedicated in marriage ceremonies to the goddess by their clans (ceremonies mostly officiated over by a Telang or a chief *potraaj* from another region, who would then initiate the novice) to ward off poverty, personal crisis in their families or gain more support from the village and blessings from the Mahalakshmi. The undertaking of *potraaj-ki* increases their clan's status in the village, as they preside in their ritual roles at village functions, even if this is at the status of impurity and a lower-caste role. After dedication, many of them accept caste hierarchy, since it imbues their caste function with power and valour, despite gendered humiliation. The goddesses afflict the *potraaj* only if he refused ritual dedication and marriage enjoined upon him by the goddess and his clan, sometimes being accused of bringing calamity upon his entire clan and village. Once he is married to the goddess, keeping to his caste labour and gendered duties to the village, upholding the very institution of marriage and undertaking caste absorption, he became her agent, even as members of the dominant castes complain of the Mahalakshmi loving the Pardhi and the Matang too much by not afflicting them enough. It is the usual fragmentation that social stratification effects, creating opacity and valour among its fragments that facilitate labour extraction without acknowledging the pain and imprisonment of living within this caste hierarchy.

Undertaking *potraaj-ki* for the first time is mostly very difficult for individual boys as they have to look like the goddess during her annual festivals and ritual days. They have to grow their hair (many of their mothers recount how they are teased by their peers from other castes for growing their hair and looking like girls, even while these women felt sure that one day the goddess would bless their boys and take away all this humiliation, in return for the long hair), wear a swirling skirt made of differently coloured *khan* or blouse pieces attached together in a belt on top of an army uniform (that one of them told me represented the goddess's army). They paint their faces red and smear their foreheads with *haldi* (turmeric) and *kunku* (vermillion) like the goddess. They wear the goddess's bangles around their arms, hands and neck, and wear anklets, playing a drum (called *halgi*) and dancing to its beat, swirling their skirts during rituals as they heal clients and hold lemons in their mouths to ritually play-act as lions holding the demon's head as sacrifice in their mouths. This is also to show how they absorb demonic affliction from society.[8] Nearly every Matang household in Chivri had dedicated a male member of their family as a *potraaj* to avert some or the other personal or collective crisis, so that they could remain safe in the village, while none of the individual *potraaj* had any say in their own ritual dedication. They had been married to the goddess and this was their primary feudal allegiance that was associated with clan and village welfare.

An important part of their public performance and display surrounding valour, caste status, impurity, the power of absorption of disease, and immunity from epidemics remained the constant self-flagellation with a loudly cracking whip during processions, as a ritual that demonstrated their immunity from pain. By whipping himself, the *potraaj*, absorbed skin infections from the rest of the society, taking disease upon himself, while the goddess in turn protected him from pain and disease as a reward. This whipping also acts as entertainment nowadays for dominant castes (as most *potraaj* whip themselves while dancing and begging on the streets) as its cracking heralds the arrival of the overdressed Matang, demonstrating the valour of caste duty and underlining a lower-caste man's inhuman strength at withstanding pain, with nothing being capable of hurting him because of the goddess's protection, as well as his own acceptance of caste duty, since it was he who whipped himself. I repeatedly asked my *potraaj* respondents the ritual meaning of the whip but all I was able to elicit was

[8] One can see a good number of *potraaj* begging on streets in big cities nowadays as the Matang constitute a large part of the urban poor.

that the whip, like the goddess's affliction, never hurt a real and truly dedicated *potraaj*. The whip constituted the noose of the goddess, the tail of her lion vehicle, and the buffalo demon's tail, all rolled into one. Each *potraaj* had his own oiled whip as a special instrument, its handle made out of a dry coconut, while his self-flagellation stood for his absorbing power that was supposed to be healing for others, since he belonged to the lower caste.

The small details of this section have elucidated the agency of the boundary as an active space forming dyads with more visible and auspicious goddesses, who are unmarked as malign because they receive patronage from dominant castes. Only lower goddesses are marked as malign and impure. Those, who are dedicated to this boundary are moreover not the ones, who demonstrably make associations across these boundaries, since they are at the lowest rung of appended regions and its society, creating its dark and shadowy outline.

Different 'Types' of Satvai

Returning from the subject of boundary politics and the Mahalakshmi's example that demonstrates how lower caste agents of boundary are deployed into gendered servitude, I continue with the concerns of how goddess cults turned into boundary goddesses themselves, undergo Satvai-fication and develop different ecological 'types' as attributes. This typology produces an ecological understanding of regions into political arenas, as various clan groups are produced as autochthonous and changeless 'communities' having ownership/inheritance rights to resource exploitation within these zones. The Satvai's types (and the various ritual dedications pertaining to this typological difference) are vitally concerned with how various communities on the margins of dominant castes are imagined and depicted through this ecological typology. The section analyses how these divisions and typology within the Satvai cult reflects modern vote lobby politics between clans imagined as autochthonous communities and how differences between these (as 'tribe' and 'caste', respectively), when created as 'others', produce hierarchy and competition in terms of resource allocation to political and economic zones.[9]

The different 'types' of Satvai or their subdivision into different ecological categories[10] actually demarcate traditional inhabitation zones for clans that are constructed as 'autochthonous' communities belonging to these areas. These zones are allocated on the basis of their traditional right to exploit various resources pertinent to what is considered their elemental nature, appropriate with the ecology of these zones (the Mahadev Koli and Pardhi become essentialised to forests or mountain lakes as fishermen or hunters and the Dhangar, as pastoralists, become stereotypically connected to migration routes and fallow farmlands, where they graze sheep). The idea that these communities might also be full-fledged and settled agriculturists within villages of their own becomes subsidiary or unimportant to the ritual imaginaire of Satvai boundary rituals. The Satvai ascribed to these inhabitation, resource-group, community, or Adivasi clan zones seem to mirror colonial notions of the connection between people and ecology, while simultaneously reflecting postcolonial electoral vote bank lobbies and caste-/community-based identity politics arising from interest groups that are simultaneously organised in relation to caste society.

In my fieldwork in Ambegaon taluka, I found that the Satvai was distinguished into different types such as Raan-Satvai (presiding over farm and fallow lands), Van-Satvai (presiding over forestlands), Jal-Satvai (presiding over water bodies) and Gaav-Satvai (presiding over lower-caste inhabitations just outside village boundaries). There was also a fifth type of Satvai known as the Ghod-Satvai, who was considered to be associated with the horse and the birth of a foal and was known to preside over migration routes and travel paths. I am sure that fieldwork about Satvayya (plural of

[9] Benjamin (2002) made a similar argument contesting the assertion of 'racial' differences between 'tribals' and agricultural populations in the Malay-speaking world. He favoured interlinked developments based on patterns of complementary exploitation of ecological niches and processes of state formation.

[10] I have attempted to describe these categories also in Dandekar and Dandekar (2011).

Satvai) in other parts of Maharashtra would accordingly yield other ecological/political micro-regions and other corresponding Satvai subdivisions. But in my field area, the Raan-Satvai is known to belong to farmlands and pastoral tracts. The *paach-pauli* rituals of a Raan-Satvai almost always include a twig of thorns among their *paach-palavi* ritual dedications, just as the Ghisadi ironsmiths circumambulating thorn twigs in their courtyard on their *paachi* are known to worship the Raan-Satvai. Clans whose Satvai shrine is located too far away to travel to, but are known to have a Raan-Satvai, often conduct their *jaawal paach-pauli* rituals in a little thicket on a farmland outside their villages facing the shrine. During my fieldwork, the Raan-Satvai was the commonest type to be found among worshippers, since most agriculturists, including the 'settled' tribes, have begun to worship the Raan-Satvai, who presides over farmlands and those lands left periodically fallow for grazing (pastoralism being a full-time agricultural activity in terms of the manure generated by it). The Van-Satvai (often referred to as Van-*devi* by the Mahadev Koli and considered a clan goddess among some Koli families) presides over forest tracts, even as respondents spoke of how the Van-Satvai and the Raan-Satvai had begun to merge because of deforestation and increasing number of villages. Van-Satvai shrines also appear in areas where the forest department has officially taken over spaces as state territory as if the Satvai had thereby developed a formal reason to be classified as Van-Satvai by worshippers. The Van-Satvai has also taken up dyad-like relationships (as the lower counterpart) with an important Koli clan goddess around Bhimashankar known as Goddess Kamaljaai, who has become Sanskritised now to be associated with Goddess Parvati and is considered a local *shakti-peetha* in the region. Many of my respondents told me that while Kamaljaai was the elder sister, Van-*devi* was the younger, while many on the other hand treated Van-*devi* as the Van-Satvai as well, just as many people at Chivri performed Satvai rituals at the Mahalakshmi shrine. The third type of Satvai whose shrine is considered to emerge from near or within a water body (even if amidst a forest or a farmland) is the Jal-Satvai. I was to find an old Vishnu sculpture dating to the medieval period from the village of Pargaon (district Pune) that had been worshipped as the Jal-Satvai, since it had been rescued from the backwaters of the local dam. The Raan-, Van- and Jal-Satvai have now begun to merge in my field region, where water bodies have begun to emerge near shrines that are in thorn thickets or in forests.

The category of the Gaav-Satvai or village Satvai has often confused me, since she has been referred in overlapping terms by my respondents as the 'boundary goddess', with names such as Mukta-*aai* or Lakshmi-*aai* (*veshi-varchi-Mukta-aai/Lakshmi-aai*), who fulfils the same functions as the Satvai, but is closer to the descriptive imaginaire of the lower-caste woman (with basket and broom held under one arm to collect and absorb dirt and affliction from the village and a child held in the other arm to denote their anti-witchcraft and healing aspect), viewed from the upper-caste angle. Village boundary goddesses such as Lakshmi-*aai* or Mukta-*aai* are considered less ferocious, more stable and the higher and more benevolent aspect of epidemic goddesses, such as Mari-*aai*, who form the lower part of the dyad with them, even as they fulfil the role of the Gaav-Satvai[11] simultaneously. Even as goddesses merged and took on different ecological personalities with changing regional developments, my respondents hardly worried about changing shrines. They kept going to the shrines everyone visited without worrying about its true identity, since it was worship and belief that mattered more. They simply performed the *paach-pauli* facing in the correct direction and travelled outside boundaries in groups and followed taboos or rules.

The ease in assigning labels to ecologically different zones and their associated inhabitants as autochthonous communities, and their presiding goddesses as boundary markers of agrarian caste villages as timeless phenomena, casts doubt on the usefulness of some other concepts that have been employed by scholars to understand social formation in Maharashtra. An example would be Sontheimer's (1989) application of the *tinnai* idea found in Old Tamil Sangam literature to Maharashtra. The idea of the *tinnai* associates different landscapes and the people inhabiting them

[11] Personal communication with Professor Anne Feldhaus, Arizona.

with particular emotions and poetic genres, superficially similar to the connection between Satvai 'types', ecologies and communities from these regions. These ideas of society and state formation that are subject to certain forms of ecological determinism, essentialise human and cultural type of interaction, reducing them to ecological and communal stereotypes that are subsequently produced as aesthetically typical and mutually different. Such theories about stratified human society, borrowed from ancient courtly cultures in India accept typologies and systems of classification that are outside the politics of caste, even while remaining entrenched within literary tropes of aesthetic stratification. The ecological and aesthetic classification of the Satvai can similarly be imagined to be outside their relationship of production, if one were to ignore the actual politics of caste stratification, agrarian land and reproduction/person-ownership and childbirth and domestic labour that they were an essential part of it. The Satvai's cult that perpetuated the inheritance of caste could create ecological type as aesthetic experiences, but these could only be read as euphemistic accounts that depoliticized discrimination, stratification and difference in the present context, having had their roots in literary tropes that were remnants from past courtly culture.

The fifth and last kind of Satvai, the Ghod-Satvai, was considered by my respondents to be of the most virulent and dangerous variety, as any accidental contact with her was immediately supposed to lead to affliction (abortion if a woman was pregnant and childloss if the child was new born). In fact, the ritual propitiation of the Ghod-Satvai introduced her worship permanently into clans, after which preventive rituals had to be performed for her throughout the following generations during pregnancy and childbirth. Great efforts were taken by women to not encounter the Ghod-Satvai at all if her worship wasn't already a clan tradition. The birth of a foal was supposed to herald the arrival of a Ghod-Satvai within a region as a guest (*pahuni*) and all those inheriting her worship in their clans thereafter (because an ancestor had sustained accidental contact and affliction) had to worship her first as a mark of respect before they turned to their own clan Satvai, so that they did not offend her. The Ghod-

Satvai ritual demanded ritual worship on a separate *pata* than the ordinary clan Satvai's and her stone lamp was also different, which could not be lent out to other women not sharing in the same clan traditions. The Ghod-Satvai had to be compulsorily given an animal sacrifice at the *pata*, since she did not accept vegetarian food and her ritual item of dedication included a small horse bridle and harness (*tan-tobra*) made of metal during her *paachi* and other *paach-pauli*.

Women who did not have clan traditions of the Ghod-Satvai did not attend the rituals and functions of those who had these traditions and neither did they send their daughters to such homes as *kori-savashne* to eat meals after the *paach-pauli*. Such women with Ghod-Satvai traditions offered ritual food to lines of *haldi-kunku* drawn on the wall. Only those from within the same clan, who had the same Ghod-Satvai attended the ritual because even families with Ghod-Satvai from different locations differed in terms of their individual worship pattern and one did not want the affliction tradition of more than one Ghod-Satvai in one's clan. Women with small children living in the neighbourhood of those who had a Ghod-Satvai affliction tradition temporarily left the locality when a ritual was being arranged so that their children may not be attacked by the goddess. Even though the Satvai is generally associated with the horse as her vehicle, since she may be associated with the Dhangar wife of the divine King Khandoba,[12] who is also on horseback (as told to me by one of my respondents), the horse was specially associated with the Ghod-Satvai. My respondents also told me of how the wedding mare with a girl child sitting on it, carrying the groom behind her to the wedding in a marriage retinue, also represented the Satvai as a war goddess, as it was similar to Khandoba's war retinue against the demons Mani and Malla.

The cult of the Ghod-Satvai and its inexplicable dread of horses seems to be an association with the history of militarism and military raids in the region that once were part of Maratha

[12] The Dhangar are associated with horses, since they migrate across regions of Western Maharashtra on the way to the Konkan, on horseback.

administration that was linked to the goddess (like epidemics were). Militaristic raids and taxation based on the pillage of villagers were a staple method of sustaining standing armies of local chieftains and rulers with their forts atop the flat mountains found in the *desh* region of Maharashtra, as has already been pointed out by Gordon (1993) and Guha (1999) alike. In this context, these local kings in Sultanate records came to be largely identified as the *Deshmukh*. The goddess of war, atop a horse, arriving to collect her ritual dues, appears to be emblematic of a hyper-violent tax collector, especially as Satvai rituals are already associated with kingship, war and roadways leading to and from villages. Respondents told me of how an old horse shoe was nailed to the door of a new-born as a preventive measure against affliction, to demonstrate to a roaming Satvai that ritual dedications (or taxes) from that house had already been made to her by the mother and clan. Respondents also told me of how the mare was not *dharjin* for villagers to keep, since the mare could prove especially dangerous for pregnant women, to the extent of causing them abortions, even if the woman just stepped across a horse's harnesses lying on the floor during pregnancy. Women with younger children fled the village when a clan with Ghod-Satvai tradition had an impending *Paachi* ritual, just like villages were known to flee when Maratha marauders pillaged villages for tax, in the absence of loot and tax (Gordon 1994). In reminiscence of Doniger's claim (2009) of how the mare in Hindu mythological texts is an object of unbridled female sexuality, her presence can be considered an agent introducing sexuality within an arena of fertility for pregnant women, which is considered to disturb boundaries between purity and impurity.

I asked a lot of questions, pestering my respondents about the reasons for worshipping the Ghod-Satvai and made copious notes about her cult, her special worship and her shrines all through my field area. I felt intrigued by her mobility in public spaces (roads) in comparison to the other Satvai types that politicised concepts of static and owned spaces and enjoyed such overwhelming association with boundaries, even though these were being altered and modified constantly. Gradually, I came to understand how the Ghod-Satvai entered clans generationally only through parameters of affliction that resulted from encounters between her (the place where a foal was born, where the shrine for her was made to receive ritual offerings) and pregnant women on the road, while they both travelled (her rituals were inherited as only preventive thereafter in the clan). She, as a guest or *pahuni* to the region, was essentially different from the other Satvayya, who were clan goddesses of marginal communities, since she belonged to a horse (perhaps symbolising an imagination of the state) and entered clans through affliction alone.

The women who 'acquired' the affliction-preventive rituals of the Ghod-Satvai were therefore usually poorer women, who had to travel during their pregnancy and could not afford to have stationary lives that were safely ensconced within village boundaries (like richer agrarian clans) even if they belonged to the middle-level of castes from an artisan background.[13] Since they were not lower in caste, enough to be immune to Satvai affliction and not rich/upper caste enough to afford not travelling and working during their pregnancy, retaining their purity during vulnerable menstrual and reproductive phases became a subject of maintaining and demonstrating even greater purity for them. This led to a greater preponderance of Satvai affliction among poorer but non-Dalit castes, who came to inhabit a new margin or grey zone between the upper and lower caste, as they had to prove their purity with more emphasis, even as they struggled the maximum with modern means of earning their livelihoods. The existence of the Ghod-Satvai preventive rituals in their clans thereafter structurally demarcated them as pure, modern but poor because they were susceptible to both impurity and impoverishment but also the fastest learners of professions and trade. The price for this was being located in the 'middle zone' of being afflicted the maximum (as if they were asked to pay the highest amount

[13] I have noticed women from the ironsmith (*lohar*), potter (*kumbhar*), weaver (*sutar*), tailor (*shimpi*), water filler (*chumli*), bangle maker (*kasar*) and such 'middle' castes to practice the maximum amount of Ghod-Satvai rituals in their clans during childbirth.

of Ghod-Satval ritual taxes for the changes in society that they brought about by splitting it through the middle).

The Ghod-Satvai thus sought to mark and consolidate an artisanal rung of the caste system, even as her virulence reflected an equalization of caste status compared to Maratha standards. The high preponderance of these afflictions associated the artisanal group in the village with lower class privileges. However, they became marked as those, who were not landed enough but had to travel for their professional sustenance to various villages, seeking employment, networks, consignments and projects. Even if these families no longer travelled themselves, the evidence of Ghod-Satvai childbirth ritual traditions in their family publicly displayed their traditional but dichotomous caste and class status.

The Ghod-Satvai ritual tradition in such families therefore formed a ferocious lower sister dyad with the comparatively benevolent Satvayya (Gaav/Van/Jal/Raan) that the family had before one of their women contracted the affliction. These were one rung lower than the ecological Satvai type, since they represented the soul of animals that were considered more basal and sexual than the lower caste clan goddesses.

Internal Administration

According to the various stories I collected about the Satvai, the goddess was known to have appeared to various local kings in antiquity in their dreams and visions, exhorting them to follow her worship or requesting them to shift her shrine to new and more important locales or asking them for newer, more embellished and better shrines. Each of these requests were, however, laced with threats of male heir loss and childloss and the consequent loss of empire and kingship, producing the maintenance of the kingship institution itself as divine feudal dharma. Some of these stories went on to relate the manner in which the goddess killed the king's children in gruesome ways, in case the king forgot his dream promises to her, till he completed her requests. The narrative of child death concerning Goddess Shashti in the *Brahma Vaivarta Purana* for example, does not leave out details of the child's eyes hanging out of its sockets (Sen 1974: chapter 43, verses 9–11) in a macabre description of its death. The violence of retribution is deliberate and intentional in these stories and an important part of the goddess's narrative and it's ritualised telling. The initiation of horror is vital to the power it generates, since it supersedes the king's and leads to his submission and the submission of his entire kingdom to her worship. These child deaths in the stories were however also always reversible, revocable and redeemable unlike in real life, since bringing the child back to life counterbalanced the destruction of a-dharma (absence of dharma). In real life, however, although dharma was signified by the safe birth and longevity of children, their mythological resurrection was now considered impossible by respondents because of what they considered to be the omnipotence and omnipresence of evil among young and modern women in *kali-yuga*, causing an impurity that could hardly ever be destroyed by bringing their children back to life.[14]

The Satvai, in some stories, spoke to kings or devotees from inside anthills or from within dilapidated shrines inside forests or from roadsides, where her injunctions were overheard by wandering and lost princes and pastoral herders, who instituted her worship after they in turn were reinstituted to positions of power. She appeared to each of them in these stories with a promise to make them kings of their territory or put them back on their thrones, once they promised to establish her worship in their empires. Sometimes she appeared in the dream of a king, calling upon him to undertake a ritual journey to attend to her neglected and forgotten shrine in an unknown territory and wage war for the right to her worship and build her a new shrine. She asked a king in one dream (according to my informant at the Satvai shrine at village Valan, district Pune) to cross the river Mina so that she could be instituted as a sister in the shrine of the Satvai from village Lauki, so that both the villages could be unified (the earlier inhabitation of village Valan, according to my informant,

[14] There was great similarity between the blackmailing epidemic goddess cults of the *Mangal-Kavya* texts from Bengal (Curley 2008) and the stories about Goddess Satvai that I heard from my field area.

had been separated from village Lauki by the river Mina). After the Satvayya became sisters, the villages and the kings had to come together as well. The Satvayya in this way were supposed to have made many micro-political decisions.

Both the birth of a son and the 'finding' of the goddess by a Matang woman within her stories constituted an epiphany for women beholding kingship and the leadership of sons as paragons of fertility[15] among dominant castes. My informants told me archetypal stories of how a queen first gave birth to seven inert dolls/daughters, who were immediately transformed or activated into seven pretty maidens, princesses, protective goddesses (in one case, seven snakes) the moment the queen mother gave birth to the eighth son, who was to become the future king of the country and found an empire (*desh* and *rajya*). Thereafter, they remained in his service as his protectors (like the Matrika goddesses have been pointed out to be the protectors of royal kingship by scholars such as White 2003).

The story of a lower-caste woman 'finding' the goddess in order to provide loving services to the latter is equally important, since it indirectly helps the goddess to provide the king with divine blessings and services and produces the lower castes as enlisted service providers and healers of the feudal state. In such stories, the Satvai is sometimes found in a dilapidated shrine by a Matang or Koli woman as a result of the goddess calling out to her. She receives her duty and power of 'healing' from the goddess, after loving (bathing, clothing and feeding) and worshipping the goddess with incense sticks and putting her on a pedestal after rescuing her from where she was lying discarded, blinded, diseased and wounded.[16] It is a common motif marshalled by goddess mythology, when the goddess, in disguise to test the faith of her devotees, blesses them for tending to her and looking after her. There is further decentralisation in this story type that allows mothers epiphany

[15] The king was supposed to be an intensely fertile being, as also demonstrated by Apffel-Marglin (1982).

[16] This story is recounted in another form by Feldhaus (2003: 92–100), while relating the mythology of Goddess Janai that, however, does not describe caste.

as service providers of male healers/mediums/ritual agents of goddesses, as this becomes a further indirect method of serving kingship.

A Pardhi woman, who had dedicated her child to the Mahalakshmi of Chivri as *potraaj*, told me of how he (the child) had been in her womb (and was refusing to be born) for six years before she promised to dedicate him to the ritual services of Goddess Mahalakshmi first. She undertook a ritual dedication for him as a *potraaj*, while still pregnant with him, promising to make the actual marriage ceremony with the goddess (*paat-lavane*) after he reached puberty. She had grown sick of the unending pregnancy. It was only thereafter that she could finally rid herself of her six-year pregnancy and give birth; everyone in her clan considered the child special and holy. She had dedicated/married him formally only a year earlier and she expected him to become a famous *potraaj* in the region some day because of this spiritual experience during her pregnancy. If he, on the other hand, grew too modern, heeded the teasing of the other boys too much and cut his long hair because everyone said he looked like a girl, great calamity would befall him and his clan; all the sacrifices made to the goddess would be wasted with one act of misjudgement. The house was searched at the end of this interview and the eleven-year-old *potraaj*, playing with a mobile phone, was soon produced for a photograph.

Finally, the most important part of dharma within the schema of Goddess Satvai's 'internal administration' concerned the necessary labour of childbirth that each woman had to undertake in order to gain social status even as queens. The story of the Koldhawdya-*chi-aai* or the Satvai of Ambegaon ratified this duty of childbirth for queens (and therefore for all subject women as well). According to this story, when the king of the region was childless, despite having two wives, he sought the Satvai's help. The Satvai's healer/medium, a Mahadev Koli, lit the goddess's lamp and gave two magical oil-soaked burning wicks from the same lamp to the king's two wives to swallow at once. This was considered to result in conception and pregnancy. When the first wife dutifully proceeded to swallow the burning wick, it turned into a lump of sugar in her mouth (*battasa*); the other wife, feeling afraid and repulsed, secretly hid the burning wick under a nearby stone. Soon, the elder wife gave birth to a son, while the younger wife cried foul at first, blaming the Koli healer of sabotage and favouritism. But later, when an investigation exposed how a stone near the Satvai shrine covered a crushed body of a male embryo, she confessed to having hidden the magical burning wick under there. So grief-stricken and enraged was the king that he banished his younger wife from his kingdom and repented at having married a second time and for having doubted the virtue and purity of his first wife. In another version, the banished younger wife is forgiven after the dead son is resurrected by the Satvai. But before that the younger queen has to accept her mistake and the Satvai's worship and performs the *paach-pauli* ritual at the shrine.

The duty of reproduction and caste (in terms of perpetuation and maintenance of social order) for women in stories such as these are obvious, even as their role as formal feudatories has not received much importance in research that has studied agrarian relationships. Their duties as reproducers of social structure and stratification are pivotal for its demographic and physical power, making the question of female morality central to agrarian politics.

External Administration

It was the ethnography and documentation of Bindumadhav Joshi's family shrine near the mountain passes (Khed Ghat) of Rajgurunagar (Pune district) that finally helped me consolidate an understanding of feudal alliances surrounding female ancestor worship that turned clan goddesses into village goddess and Satvai cults and back again into clan ancestors in a circular way. Marxist theoreticians of Indian history have developed a theory of a unidirectional co-option of 'tribal' goddess cults within tantrism as part of theories of medieval state formation based on the prevalence of land grants in central India from the fourth century C.E that continued as a political practice in the Deccan to much later times (Sharma 2003). My fieldwork, however, suggests that this process is more circular or can work in the opposite direction as well. Female clan ancestors of land lords presiding over land grants could also turn into Satvayya for their subjects within these areas. The distancing of upper castes from the memorial stones of their female ancestors then reflects a relationship of fear and punishment between these ancestors and the lower in caste subjects of the land lord, in what becomes a discourse of impurity surrounding women and witches, who have died in childbirth. I will explain this with the help of an example from my field area near Ghodegaon.

The shrine of Khed-*chi*-Satvai was understood by my respondents and informants to be an ancient Ghod-Satvai of great aggression, whose cult was considered very afflicting for pregnant women travelling through the Avasari Ghat between the cities of Manchar and Rajgurunagar (Pune district). The mountain pass between Chakan and Junnar on the Pune-Nasik highway, near where the shrine was located (in the valley), was full of sacred groves and a large reservoir that was watered by a semi-perennial stream. The shrine itself could be architecturally identified as dating to the Peshwa period, with remnants of wall paintings inside, in architectural style that had a typical Peshwa period tradition. Some archival exploration around the land of the shrine soon led me to its owners: the Brahmin family of Bindumadhav Joshi, who was himself a renowned lawyer, now settled in Pune. It was Bindumadhav Joshi who finally told me the story of what was originally a family shrine belonging to the Joshis in village Khed (now renamed Rajgurunagar).

Village Khed was once an *inam* territory or land grant of the Joshi family during the Peshwa period (land grants during the Brahmin Peshwa rule were typically given to other Brahmins). The shrine, according to Bindumadhav Joshi, was a memorial stone commemorating an important Sati from their clan, who had immolated herself when her husband, another important Joshi clan member, had died fighting in the battle of Panipat in 1761.[17]

[17] Though Bindumadhav Joshi showed me the ancient swords used by his ancestor in the Panipat battle, he failed to remember his name or the name of the Sati who had died for her husband. We henceforth referred to her as 'the Sati' (*tya Sati-bai*) in our conversations.

There was a small shrine inside the big Satvai temple where the stone commemorating the Sati was housed; the larger temple had been built surrounding it. She was subsequently worshipped in the region as a Satvai and that too the most violent type of the travelling Ghod-Satvai and this was something Bindumadhav Joshi already knew. According to him, these were remnants of the past; it was common and for subjects of the land grant territory in older times to take over the worship of those, who were ancestors in the families of their liege lords as protector gods of their regions. These ancestor gods/goddesses that became the protectors of subjects in that region were different than actual *shakti-peetha* in that territory. According to him, Brahmin clans, on the other hand, only worshipped their own clan gods and goddesses of their territory (the *shakti-peetha*) like King Shivaji worshipped Tulja Bhavani, whose cult was part of his (Shivaji's) land grant. Brahmins performed Vedic rituals and they did not dedicate *jaawal* or *balote* to Satvayya or believe in any monsters. They worshipped the Jivati as a protecting goddess of childbirth during the months of Shravan instead, who was a goddess from the Puranas; he told me how the Shashthi was similarly worshipped in Bengal. The kind of Satvai ritual that I was asking him about marked specific subject-hood within land grant economies, wherein those who lived within these regions were subservient to the protecting champions of the region generated by the dead ancestry of the liege lords as boundary protectors.

The more macabre a manner in which these ancestors appealed to popular imagination, such as women who had died in childbirth, as Sati or people in epidemics, the more their fear increased among subjects, when they began worshipping them as punishing and protective deities who upheld dharma. He reiterated that all this was however superstition but on the other hand also the expression of love of his erstwhile subjects for the landlord's family. He explained how the Joshi's own clan goddess was still of some importance in the central areas of Khed which they visited two or three times every year, where they owned their original ancestral home as yet. He told me of how worshipping the goddess at the *shakti-peetha* had helped to cure his grandson's ailments, though he remained adamant that the Satvai could not be a goddess, despite her temple and the way in which people worshipped at her shrine inside it, since he knew that she was his clans woman. He insisted that it was only something that his family subjects had once instituted and now carried on. At last he showed me the swords with which his ancestors had fought with in Panipat, although he regretted that he could not remember the name of either the ancestor who had died fighting or his Sati wife. It was only after repeated interaction with Mr Joshi and his excessively Brahminical and rationalist stance that references about the overlap between the Sati and the Satvai cults began to fall into place for me. The relationship between the Sati and the Satvai cults seemed to reflect a feudatory relationship between women of upper-caste land grant-holding clans (*Watandar/Inamdar* clans women) and *Balutedar* clans women, who were their feudal subjects within the estate, as subjects formed an allegiance with land lord's ancestry, through the Satvai-fication of female ancestors.

In the story that Mr. Joshi told me, his Sati-Satvai ancestor had formed the lower counterpart of a dyad with the living and married women of his family in a repetition of what could be read as a reflection of the Sapta-Matrika story, since the only difference between the ancestor clans woman and the living clans women of his present family was the distance established by death. The land lords and their married wives could only delegate their militaristic and boundary protecting powers to malign, dead and distanced, impure ancestors erupting out of them but malign due to their deaths. They like the Matrika represented the fragmented parts of the gods and their wives (who in this case was like the great goddess), who could only inherit the violent part of the masculine king's power, since they had no legitimate status of being benevolently powerful themselves. The land lords in this case held divine masculine position themselves, delegating power to their wives (like the stable and great goddess). The numerous and multiple dead ancestors were malign and distanced towards the boundaries and could form dyads and retinues with strong internal continuities with the central and stable Matrika, since they were simply continuities of her as dead clans women. They could form composite forms with the stable Matrika, the moment one of the latter fell from masculine Brahminical grace, such as in the case of goddess Renuka, Yellama or Mari-*aai*, who was made of two conjoint forms. The women among the lower in caste, subjects of the land grant dominion were thus civilized within the hegemony of the liege lord with the help of their dead/ alive clans women forming a dyad through metaphoric mythologies and ideologies of the Devi Mahatmya and Matrika formation, even without this relationship ever being explicitly mentioned to either them or me by Mr. Joshi.

The next logical question that I had to tackle was: how did these ancestors generated by land lord families come to be considered clan goddesses from 'lower' enlisted communities in their empires, when others considered them to be boundary goddesses or Satvayya of different ecological types, while even others considered them to be Ghod-Satvayya? What was the inter-relationship between dominant castes, artisan castes and those considered lower caste within erstwhile land grant regions ruled by land lord generating these Matrika-like malign ancestors? It was obvious that female ancestors from land lord clans underwent vital 'reinterpretation' as different kinds of goddesses who entered into different relationships (clan/village/Satvai/Ghod-Satvai) with the different castes of an erstwhile political region or estate as the very mode in which the stratification between the different castes came to be affected by the state. Pondering on this would only remain speculative.

On the other hand, there were many relational layers in this discussion that marked other conundrums that could be demystified first: these conundrums lay firstly in our assumptions that lower-caste clans would indeed have 'original' or autochthonous clan goddesses that would yield to Satvai-fication by dominant upper-caste agrarian villages, when the two engaged in boundary relationships. We were assuming that the assimilation of these autochthonous lower-caste goddesses took place smoothly into agrarian caste villages for purposes of labour extraction, as if paradigms of goddess assimilation for labour extraction was a tried-out formula that was simply waiting to be readily accepted and absorbed as a cultural implement/instrument used for stitching boundaries together. On the other hand, actual discrimination against the same lower-caste groups, whose clan goddesses were after all being readily adopted, continued unabated, splintering the same neatly stitched boundaries apart, on the other hand.

We had to reorient ourselves instead, to the understanding that the boundary rituals of these goddesses that reflected the *pinda-daan* or funerary Brahminical rituals of dead women from liege lord clans ruling over feudal estates were in effect Brahminical rituals and reflected the worship of Brahminical ancestors from the same Brahmin liege lord families, which hinted at remnants from a history of a Brahmin land grant system operative in rural Maharashtra. All rural castes, whether agrarian, artisanal or those clans living outside village boundaries, had taken on the worship of these female and impure ancestors from the liege lord of the estate, whether as clan goddesses or as various types of changing Satvayya.

Boundary goddesses or affliction cults with Matrika associations and animal sacrifice traditions were therefore not necessarily 'lower caste' cults in origin at all, even if in their imaginaire they were demarcated as so, with the ANIS cracking down on them. Their cult enjoyed differing relationships between all the stratified castes of the village and the very mechanism of caste stratification and its reproduction, even as many goddess cults such as the Sati and Satvai (that became associated with the Matrika) emerged from the female ancestry of dominant upper castes with land entitlements. The likening of the Satvai cult or affliction cults to the lower caste in terms of clan relationships then, marks their greater duty of compulsory servitude to the goddess that enjoins them to heal dominant and upper caste clan members of the village and clean the interior of the village inhabitation. The Satvai-fication rituals undertaken by the dominant castes on the other hand are an effort to keep impurity, witchcraft and obstacles to childbirth away and across the boundary so that it can become a way for purity to grow in demographic strength and power, represented by the live clans woman of the liege lord's family.

Forming 'Kingdoms' and Theories

There are also political or kingdom formation stories about the travelling Satvayya (it is a common enough story that is repeated for many other deities in Maharashtra, including its recounting by Feldhaus 2003) that demonstrate the manner in which the Satvai gradually builds a region of influence around her primary shrine and its village to include smaller neighbouring villages into its ritual and political ambit. According to this story, she agrees to follow a devotee from a neighbouring hamlet to his home because he can no longer keep visiting her shrine due to his old age as she is pleased with his devotion. The only promise he has to make to her in return is to not look back at her during this liminal journey. Although he knows that she is following him on this journey, he fails his ultimate test by breaking his promise to her and turns back to look at her, at which she turns into stone at the very spot, refusing to make the journey any further. This spot is explained as the reason for the location for her shrine outside every village boundary.

This story is most commonly used in my field area as an explanation to associate the village Satvai to her main and regionally important shrine, from where she is supposed to have travelled. The smaller village in this way becomes a ritual extension of the main goddess shrine and the larger village that lies at the heart of the 'empire', even as the shrine at the hamlet is known by the name of the main Satvai shrine and not by the name of the hamlet. The zone of the Satvai depends on where she has travelled from. However, these goddess regions cannot be imagined as contiguous and undisturbed circles of influence like well-regulated states either, since villages and hamlets are a cross-hatch of influences between Satvayya. Inhabitations, devotees and kings seemed to have been up for grabs for any Satvai, who could find devotees to follow and appear in their dreams in order to exert dominion and political control over their villages. Thereafter, they would exert a long-distance ritual relationship of *paach-pauli* 'reflection' with clans in these villages, linking them to the goddess's main 'empire' and trying simultaneously to spread to more villages as part of their civilising agenda, even as many Satvayya converged upon a single nodal point as sisters.

Apart from the way in which stories or rituals about the Satvayya could provide hints about manner in which regional interaction between communities was politically formed over time, there have been no pervasive theoretical narratives about state formation within political micro-regions in Maharashtra. Theories of Maratha and colonial state formation (in western India) and the importance of caste as a form of occupation/land right (*Balutedari*) has been explored by scholars such as Gordon (1993, 1994), Guha (1999) and Anand (2005) in contributions to historical debates about state formation in South Asia. These discussions have however not formed or adopted a clearly delineable theory of state formation in manners that may be similar to ideas such as 'feudal', 'segmentary' or 'integrative/processual' state formation.[18] Though I am aware that these historical debates pertain to state formation for earlier time periods (namely the early medieval) that predate the changes of the Maratha-colonial interaction witnessing the Rajputisation of the Koli into warriors within the caste systems of western India, we may be able to identify the nature of the early modern state in western India as one signified by 'absorption'.

The fragmented development of state formation, best chronicled by Guha (1999: 83–107), resulted from the way the Mawle clans or Mahadev Koli of the Western Ghats/Sahyadri ranges, as part of Shivaji's infantry negotiated with the declining Mughal control over the Deccan. Independent kings and chieftains of the Deccan, the recognised *Deshmukh* of the Sultanate period, who hitherto had standing armies, were brought together under the leadership of Shivaji and absorbed through a process of Rajputisation. The narrative further describes how this 'Rajputisation' resulted in the transformation of the Koli into recognised local rulers, kings and independent rulers under Shivaji and the inclusion of some of their clans within the Maratha or Kunbi castes and other occupational castes or herders. The colonial rulers seem to have further used the

[18] Singh (2011) has described the theories of early medieval state formation in India.

Koli armed forces (even as they used the Peshwai as an instrument of effecting this) to quell threatening Bhil uprisings in the western mountainous regions, in return for consolidating Koli status within the 'empire', establishing their identity simultaneously as Koli and settled agriculturists. This rather ambivalent story (full of reverses) of caste absorption/Rajputisation continues till today. It provides leadership for the absorption of 'lower communities' and what is vended to them as 'their autochthonous clan goddesses' as these become part of dyads to herald their entry into caste systems as violent Kshatriya warriors within paradigms of the 'empire' that generate these goddesses.[19]

Apart from the absorption of diverse caste groups, the basic mechanism of state formation for the Marathas was land grant administration, constituted through the administrative unit of the *pargana* or sub-district, which represented administration at the local level based on revenue (Gordon 1994: 124). *Watandars*, or those who had land grants or large gifts of *inam* or court land at the pargana level, were instituted as *Inamdar* in positions that were akin to minor kings themselves, along with other Brahminical bureaucrats with feudal titles to aid them in administration such as *Kulkarni* (accountant) or *Muzumdar* (record keeper). These sent only parts of the pargana revenue to the centre. The feudal mechanism at the top (that was largely Brahmin) did not fall within the ambit of *Balutedari* duties but probably established them among local artisans and peasants that constructed villages as caste-based units yielding tax and revenue for financing standing armies simultaneously as defence against internal rebellion, expansionist attacks from neighbours and as mechanisms of constant tussles with the centre for independence. The Maratha period, as pointed out by Gordon (ibid.), was characterised by almost constant local warfare.

[19] Militaristic activities among clan groups and castes, presided over by goddess cults, have obviously played a large role in keeping political segments within the state together. Laine (2003) describes Shivaji's relationship with the sword of Goddess Tulja-Bhavani and the way he was possessed by her clan rituals and the duty of kingship and war.

It was probably within this scenario that goddesses cults such as the Satvai came to preside over clan birth, social stratification, caste and gendered labour, production and inheritance of motherhood or witchcraft and the concepts of demographic power for dominant castes, boundary politics and kingship, war, taxation, resulting in droughts, and epidemics. The estate of land lords and warlords may have teemed with horses as a result of armies inhabiting rural areas. The Satvai and Maulya represented the moral power of the liege lord's ancestry that was adopted by their subjects and controlled and effected the reproduction of women as feudatories of the estate, whose duty it became as citizens to reproduce and perpetuate its ideology.

Changes within Modernity

The growth of villages into larger taluka-level towns with big roads interconnecting them has, however, changed many fixed values about the village's 'original boundary'.These erstwhile margins have now become transformed into new spaces for government offices, banks, educational institutions, government hospitals, post offices, a central bus depot, a few eateries/teastalls or a small marketplace selling modern merchandise such as torches and handbags (different from the traditional village markets in the centre square of the village). This change, according to my respondents, had resulted into two sorts of contradictory repercussions on the way afflictions took place for women nowadays. First, the afflictions increasingly took place only when in contact with the goddesses Satvai and Maulya and their specific rituals and shrines, and no longer at all village boundaries like earlier, since the extent of the latter was now indistinguishable. Second, the affliction now also took place increasingly within these government areas that have partially obliterated earlier boundaries. These afflictions commonly occurred during the goddess's time of the day (especially the afternoon), when these areas were largely isolated. This process reflects the observations of Clark-Deces (2008) concerning the bus stop as a prime site of spirit affliction in contemporary Tamil Nadu. My respondents also reported that affliction in both these cases (around shrines and government areas) had started becoming more 'strict' due to there restricted area and structured organisation of the spaces and the times that the incidents of affliction occurred. Modern or government spaces had somehow therefore added to the Satvai's role in creating an alien structural oppression in the lives of women that created a second afflicting boundary to it, in addition to what the 'outside' realms of danger beyond the Satvai's moral control for women originally held.

Women recounted many stories of how a sudden wind running through a concrete government building passage could be of an unknown afflicting nature, since the same corridor in a dilapidated zilla parishad (district headquarter) office could have been inhabited by so many castes and religions of people, who could be in stages of unmarked and afflicting *vitaal* that could lead to spontaneous afflictions and abortions in pregnant women visiting government offices. There were many implications of social resistance to modernity in the development of this double-boundary of affliction in women's lives that made the middle and 'safe zone' of pure and dominant caste inhabitation ever narrower and privileged in the imagination of my upper-caste inhabitants. The primary implication of resistance to modernity was invested in the equal intermixture of castes and religions within modernity and modern institutions that would lead to the impurity of the dominant caste women and hinder the perpetuation of the dominant castes as superior and pure. It was feared that these modern spaces would facilitate anonymous and potentially illegitimate meeting points that would disturb clan and caste purity and female chastity. These boundary spaces themselves acquired the agency of modernity within their own construction, that is aptly demonstrated by D.D. Kosambi's reference (1962) to offerings made to the Matrika goddesses at crossroads in the Sanskrit play *Mrichhakatikam*. 'Crossroads' increasingly is defined as an area seemingly belonging to no one, that act as a hub of interaction and invitation for unknown and unrecognisable outsiders that disturbs the purity of internal spaces.

Modern Satvai shrines have also transformed and assimilated

to more established forms of 'purity', resulting in the formation of the Satvai as a recognised benevolent goddess among local landed agrarian elites as a result of dominant castes from rural Maharashtra consolidating their privileged position as its discursive mouthpiece. While doing fieldwork at the shrine of Valan-*chi-aai* on the banks of the river Mina in the village of Valan, near Narayangaon (district Pune), I was startled to find an upper-caste shrine ritualist (not a healer or medium) who had composed a liturgy about the goddess on the lines of one that is usually sung in the Brahminical worship of Lord Ganesha. The idols of the two Satvai sisters in the shrine wore brocade saris and real gold necklaces in addition to gold *mangalsutras* to signify that they were wives of Lord Shiva and avatars of Goddess Parvati. Usually it is unheard of for Goddess Satvai to have a husband; she only has a minion (*Munjoba/Chedoba*). The inside of the shrine was decorated with shiny tiles and modern flooring. Iron railings were built inside the main hall to manage crowds, indicating that people did not just come here for their own rituals but for festivals too. It was far from an abandoned shrine and there was no horrifying ritual burden of collectively discarded motherhood settling in on each ritual actor.

The ritualist further told me that the goddesses no longer afflicted women and that women were not allowed to come close to the goddess's actual shrine (they had to stay behind the iron railing) as no one went into a trance here or sacrificed animals any longer. The goddess only blessed women with children and sons and many women came here for celebrations. After I coaxed her a little, she told me of how all these impure rituals (such as animal sacrifice) were carried out at a smaller scale at a proxy shrine of the goddess behind the temple at a distance. Going down just a little further near the river's edge, next to the garbage dump of the village, I found the 'other' shrine of the Satvai with aniconic multiple figurines under a tree marked with five lines (signifying five deities), flanked with the shrines of other usual minion deities, which she had said, were shrines of the Munja and other such spirits. It was here that I found the usual ritual dedications of *jaawal-balote* hung on the tree and other rituals remnants such as *khelna*, *palna*, *sugad*, *oti* materials, the stale food from offerings and so on. It was here that I found the burden of inherited motherhood.

Goddess Satvai at Valan had therefore divided against herself into a pure and impure form, wherein she was a married goddess, Sanskritised to take on the avatar of child-giving Parvati inside the temple but retained her impure boundary function of a child-eating demon outside her shrine. Only afflicted women or women needing to prevent affliction, who were performing her rituals, would have come to know about the 'other' real shrine hidden behind the new shrine. Newcomers would have only confronted her as a benevolent and powerful goddess and in turn accepted the arrival of the dominant caste in rural Maharashtra as natural and unmarked, unless searching deliberately for all the impoverished women even among the rich, whose clans were slowly abandoning them and turning hostile to them, due to their childlessness. The Sanskritised Goddess Satvai of modern times in rural Maharashtra, meanwhile, could become recognised as 'her pure self', with the rise in power of the agrarian dominant castes, without the cult needing to enter into any larger interpretative frameworks that necessitated tortuous dyad formations with Puranic deities. The remaining could simply visit her behind her temple in bureaucratic style.

CHAPTER 5

Rendering Women Inanimate

By the time I had come to the end of my fieldwork in Ghodegaon, most of my informants had become ambivalent about my goddess project, as I openly proposed the oppressive nature of the Satvai cult in conversations with them. They on the other hand considered goddess cults to bring equality among all their female worshippers (at least among their group of dominant caste women) by reducing interpersonal rivalry between them and bringing about equality among women. For them, the village/clan/boundary goddess cults formed a sort of rural secularism that created clan cohesion and kept them all together, while helping all women uniformly to become wives and mothers, removing afflictions and weeding out the contagious ones from amidst them. There were a lot of disagreements between my respondents and me, some who had become good friends by the end of my fieldwork, as they began to feel that I was accusing them personally of discrimination against women from the lower castes or women from Mahadev Koli groups or against childless women among their own castes like myself, while they professed friendships. They tried explaining how these 'outsider' women could be inauspicious, afflicted or dangerous and they suggested that I try performing regular Satvai rituals and go to doctors. It all grew a little helpless between us as it did between them and their clan because of disagreements about my politics, even if they personally felt my anger and pain by then. Some of these conversations grew awkward or increasingly heated, even as some women chose to remain friends.

The contradictions between different forms of caste labour and its purity defined differences between women themselves as 'different caste women' and 'different caste goddesses', stratifying them somewhat ambivalently as castes and as women lower than men, even while keeping their clan duties intact universally across the board. These created enormous overlaps between them, as upper caste women shared the impurity of the lower caste healer at certain times of the month and during affliction, producing them both as women, attached to their clans, just as I was. These in turn created spaces for the production of the goddess's power (the margins and boundaries) that transformed, socialised and deployed female bodies as caste labour, reproductive labour and sexual labour. The power of the goddess produced both the private and the public as contiguous extensions of each other in women's lives as they could hide very little from each other, with even their rituals being public, since the internal juxtapositions of private and public were created by the same unifying power.

Following de Certeau's (1984: 201) analysis of space, the study of a unified and unifying power (I was studying goddess rituals) would simply lead to the enumeration of different elements of analysis (castes, gender, religion, history or body) in an intricate manner that would form a complex whole, as all its elements would become unreadable from the same vantage point. Power within the collage of these associated fragments or elements would be like the opaque central bulwark that would unify all these concerns at a single focus point. This power would remain coded within the ritualisation of childbirth, which would release this cohesive power among all the elements to create what de Certeau refers to as 'subtle and compensatory equilibria that silently guarantee complementarities' (ibid.), somewhat like a palimpsest, even as they retained their own multi-formations. 'Thoughts' or the imagination of the central power of this system or the goddess, would then be generated by accidents and lacuna within these complementary fragments (like the death of a child that led to the loss of ownership and inheritance), and therefore could not remain divorced from its ritualisation (seeking to avoid childloss through preventive rituals at the very instant of childbirth through compulsory *paach-pauli* and establishing purity through celebrations). Accidents or lacuna formed the 'other' of an imagined regularity of everyday life, through which ownership of land, ownership of persons, extraction of duties, perpetuation of labour-related institutions, regional organization, shrines and their stories and songs were all produced as natural, everyday and unmarked. And the responsibility of keeping it unmarked and normal by averting accidents and lacuna rested on women, who had to be constantly 'purified' by the central and unifying power and its ritualisation.

It's experience for women, who performed rituals of purity, even as preventive methods to not let dharma slip, when they had children, resulted in a continuous and parallel substratum of rituals and marginalised attachments during the simultaneous gaining of motherhood. With the death of a male heir associated with women's marital clans for whose longevity and well-being they are somehow held responsible on the other hand (as wives or mothers), both these parallel lines, full of planned continuums that are held apart by superhuman effort by women, finally crash together. Expressing grief was a small and very personal question ensconced in privilege for my village respondents at such times, in comparison to the vast lacuna opening up under their feet in terms of the life accident they faced. These may have been the events, when women may have not protested too hard against or just gone under in the face of decrees that prescribed their becoming Sati or Satvai in order to redeem themselves of witchcraft accusations/ cannibalism and the death of a clan male heir, whose lives they were held responsible for, not so long back in the past.

In *Wild Goddesses in India and Nepal*, Sax (1996) writes about the humanity of goddesses, who are exactly like human women, a mixture of the good and the bad. I contend its complementary opposite for women in my field area: wild goddesses, such as the Satvai, are considered more human or are allowed to express more human emotions such as anger and the kind of motherhood that they soak up from biological mothers in rituals, exactly because real women are not allowed to express human emotions. Real women on the other hand are expected to behave in an exemplary manner that follows in the opposite path demonstrated by the goddess, since they have given up all their human weaknesses to her at ritual boundaries. In the realm of fierce goddesses of childbirth in Maharashtra, it is the women who are positioned as inanimate, while goddesses absorb their humanity.

Human Goddesses, Witches and Heroines

One of the primary means of the goddess's power lies in her ability to be accorded 'human emotions'. It is a feature that is amply demonstrated in the recounting of her stories, where her attachments, pain and rage find place and compassion. Many of my respondents recounted their compassion for goddesses in the same breath as their hatred and fear for other afflicted women, who would contaminate their purity through *vitaal*. They went into details of how the goddess experienced human emotions of having died before having experienced motherhood, while debarring childless women from auspicious celebrations in their own homes. Through the same mechanism of according goddesses emotions, they divested real women from the experience and expression of human suffering, as even attachments to children began being viewed as an impediment to Satvai dedication, impeding social motherhood. Hyper-attachments were considered to be potential symptoms of affliction or impurity that finally led to the death or illness of children. When such paradoxes and travesties were explicitly questioned, my respondents spoke of how the Satvai, Maulya or Mari-*aai* also had the power to kill their children if they were offended and how this would in turn expose mothers as malefactors and bad protectors of children in the eyes of their clans and it was this problem that led to what they termed as my accusations (*dosh dene*) of their discrimination against childless women.

It became safer for my respondents to divert their compassion to goddesses and replace real relationships of empathy with that of goddesses, since following the latter's 'opacity' also depoliticised interpersonal rivalry as part of dharma for them. According to them, the justice for this rivalry was provided by the goddess's affliction sent to women who were 'too smart' (*shining maarte*). Women did not live in a utopia of sisterhood in my field area but experienced perennial mutual tensions, conflicts and competitions of daily life that made displacing these relationships with 'bhakti' for goddesses a far safer means of expressing acceptable compassion for experiences of childlessness rather than fraught friendships with actual childless women in the village. It was then, the very primacy of the goddess cult among women and the love that they accorded it that created the compensatory equilibrium of violence in their lives. It was within its 'secular' opacity that individual women were denied existence outside collectives, even if these women were complete individuals.

It would be simplistic to assume that only those goddesses with positive stories of victory produced power. Negative stories about the goddess that denigrated her importance produced even greater power, since it produced compassion for her among my respondents. It allowed many among them to identify with her. One of my respondents cried, while recounting the story of a village goddess coming alone to the village after a war with a *rakshasa*/demon and her hardships before people accepted her, for which she had to first die and somehow become a tree. Women had sympathy for the playful goddess, who had been pushed out of the village by the powerful Natha saint, by the tip of his toenail, because she had irritated him with her small magical acts.[1] Finally, they were in complete agreement with the rage and pain of these goddesses for upholding caste rules, marriage rules, clan cohesion rules and values that glorified the brave deaths of women during childbirth, in saving the lives of their new-born sons or the souls of their dead husbands or dead kings as valorous duty. They eulogised the death of women who had died to save their husbands, sons, and their clans and society from any form of dishonour[2] and

[1] Natha saints (I was told by my informants) had barred the Satvai entry across village boundaries with the exception of the fifth and twelfth days after every childbirth in the village, when she entered to accept ritual dedications.

[2] Brubaker (1978), Nicholas (2003) and Whitehead (1921) have documented many such stories about village goddesses in south India and Bengal.

hailed it to be the goddess's right to punish all those women who broke these rules and to teach them a lesson in dharma, as had indeed been the case in many stories of village goddesses (virtuous, innocent and misunderstood women later turning into goddesses to redress their murder).

I have until now said very little about the Maulya group of goddesses independently. It remains, however, important to distinguish between the Satvai and the Maulya, since the Maulya are also important child-loss goddesses in rural Maharashtra, presiding over all sorts of instances of lacunas and accidents, with shrines that are very similar to the Satvai. Their cult is however, far more concerned with the morality of women than with the death of children.

Comparisons between the Satvai and the Maulya

The Satvai, according to my respondents, was constituted from the spirits of women, who had died in childbirth, while saving the lives of their new-born sons. There existed a short midway journey of transition for them (during which time they were considered witches) that conflated with the dead mother's death ritual period (till the thirteenth day) and the child's post-partum ritual period (of the *baaravi*), after which the mother's soul was known to have joined the goddess and become distanced and benevolent. The *paach-pauli* rituals therefore reflected the *pinda-daan* ceremony or funerary rituals for dead mothers, pushing them from their malevolent status as witches to that of the benevolent goddesses, as new mothers became their inheritors, forming dyads with them.

The Maulya, *Sati-asra* or *Apsara* on the other hand, were considered to be seven beautiful virgin-witches or nymphs, presiding over water sources, who were formed out of the spirits of overtly sexual adolescent girls, who had died before having had the chance of experiencing either marriage or childbirth. They were therefore understood as playful, capricious, cruel and sexually avaricious, leading young men and women to their deaths by inveigling and enticing them with bribes of sensual and sexual pleasures, which also led to the death of their children. One of my Muslim respondents from Ghodegaon wept as she told me of how the beautiful '*paris*' (fairies) had played with her child at the local Maulya shrine near the local stream, where she had been busy with household chores, till it had gradually wasted away and died. When I asked her how this had happened, she explained how the *paris* show their victims (and they choose whomever they like, since the prettier the better) another false and heavenly world (*jannat*) of pleasures and toys, after which the victim follows and ultimately dies to the real world that is full of limitations. After that the victim's soul joins them as a minion or if of the right gender, age-group and status (as theirs), becomes their playmate.

The Maulya were also known to be surrounded by amphibious creatures and reptiles of an unimaginable variety, since they were ultimately associated with river goddesses who had reptilian mounts (like the river Narmada flowing through Maharashtra on a crocodile).[3]

Both the Satvai and the Maulya were multitudinous and though the Satvai multitudes were broken up into castes that changed in composition depending on the variation in local population density prevalent in every region, the Maulya remained more uniform, since they were unmarried and marked only through their overt sexuality as girls. The Maulya, also remained more homogeneous as a single category of seven goddesses, even if they were essentially constituted by the number seven and hardly broke up into two-sister retinues. The sexual flavour of the Maulya cult and their cultural resistance to being translated into any kind of other social category such as caste or ecology, apart from their association with water sources, produced them as even more shadowy and malign than the Satvai in my field area. They received far less sympathy from women, since they were considered capricious, murdering, sexual and dirty, surrounded by river mud and water reptiles, while they introduced unnecessary danger and anxiety with dangerous places of inhabitation such as wells, tanks, rivers or streams where women were forced to

[3] Feldhaus (1995b) and White (2003) have written about river goddesses in connection with female fertility.

do household work alone, when near shrines. Many of my male informants and female respondents alike were of the opinion that the Maulya encouraged unhappy women to commit suicide at such places, by showing them an alternative and false world, instead of allowing them to face and solve their problems at home (*tond dene*). The Maulya's bold longing for pleasure and this longing that they evoked in those they afflicted was their only denomination that competed with women's reality and their existence within patriarchal contexts that produced humanly suffering women as too helpless, weak and vulnerable to protect themselves. Their affliction was considered to lead to the hyper-sexualisation of women, an increase in their desires and was considered to lead to the automatic failure of their duty, resulting in the death of children and the demise of passive feminine fertility. In actual terms, the Maulya affliction was associated with reproductive problems that were read deterministically. For example, an increase in white discharge (*anga varna pandhre jane*) was viewed in opposition to the more usual and normal red discharge/blood (*laal jane*) during menstruation, since an increase in white discharge was associated with semen and male sexuality. This was not specific to Maulya affliction alone but to all ritual afflictions concerning goddesses and infertility in general, as women desiring more pleasure were considered to have merged distinctions between masculinity and femininity and to have become impure.

The Satvai has brothers and minions such as the *Munja* (soul of a Brahmin boy), the *Nago-ba* (cobra), Kolhat-*ba* (fox) and *Chedoba* (soul of a Matang boy) to assist her in her village functions, while the Maulya has a brother called *Mhasoba* (soul of a Gavli Dhanga/ cattle pastoralist) or *Biroba* (soul of an ordinary Dhangar boy) to assist her. Sontheimer (1976), exploring the independent rise in the power of Dhangar cults such as Mhaskoba and Biroba, traces the way in which these deities developed aggressive and violent relationships with village goddesses such as the Maulya instead. While the Satvai cult effected surveillance over married women and upheld dharma in the villages, the Maulya, as seven goddesses, remained more playful as they were young girls, even as their childish evil remained curtailed and restricted to areas near their shrines next to waterholes, where ritual dedications were made to them by women only if and as afflictions arose.

An important difference between the Satvai and Maulya remained in the way illnesses were 'dedicated' to the Satvai in objectified forms, made out of metal, like diseased limbs of children made in metal (if these were affected). This ritual of offering limbs made in precious metals to the goddess was believed to heal and 'release' the real limbs of the child from the goddess's afflicting hold. It was also believed that a paste made out of the stump of the umbilical cord ritually dedicated to the Satvai had the power to cure pneumonia, just as the dead cells emanating from the skin of a child, after a paste of the umbilical cord was massaged on its body would prevent and heal rickets. On the other hand, no such dedications or offerings were ever made to the Maulya, since the latter were unmarried and actually reintroduced sexuality in afflicted women, thereby rendering them impure and automatically precluding fertility, pregnancy and childbirth. The Maulya did not specifically disease children in my field area, since they were not specifically connected with children; when they took beautiful looking children away, they did so only in order to play with them like toys. They were primarily connected with women and were like adolescent and sexual children themselves. When they chose anyone attractive, whom they wanted to play with, they afflicted them by evoking insatiable desires in them and gradually killed them to the real world to pull them over on to their own side.

Stories about the Satvai pair in my field area often recount how they were originally sisters, who had lost their memory of sisterhood because they had been married off at a young age into the same family of two brothers. They had gradually come to be each other's sisters-in-law and rivals. The story progresses to a saga of mutual acrimony, competition and hatred, only for them to discover their sisterhood in the end (through divine mediation). The story is always used as an injunction for sisters-in-law to live within joint families as sisters, even though it remains an unwritten prescription to not introduce real sisters within families, since this is known to harbour too much politics against and within marital families, whether these sisters gang up against the marital family or turn into mutual rivals.

The pressure, according to these Satvai stories, remains high for women to remain in ambivalent sisterhood, even when marital families take care to not introduce real sisters within their fold and despite enormous clan pressures to win at their individual feudatory tasks of achieving purity at any cost. The image of the Maulya, on the other hand, dehumanises those women who don't or cannot experience pregnancy as sexually promiscuous and violent or thoughtless women, who are addicted to sensuality. Barren, unmarried, afflicted, maddened with hatred, androgynous and those considered sexually lascivious are feared as being dangerous and inimical to children (believed to be child kidnappers, enlisting children within begging gangs, eunuch groups or brothels). This opinion led to many women in my field area constructing infertile and afflicted women into the stigmatised category of criminals and anti-society persons that led to their abandonment. There were no other options for such persons to become acceptable within rural society (according to my respondents) but to become dedicated to goddess cults that accepted prostitutes, which would redeem and forgive them and extract a recognizable form of *seva* or duty towards society out of them, giving expression to their alleged self-addiction and one day heal their affliction. Even though I heard my respondents discussing such case studies in my field area, I could never interview such women due to the extreme stigma involved in these instances.[4]

[4] I felt there were limitations in using the interview technique as an ethical form of data collection in such cases, where ethnography, due to heavy stigma, had become impossible. The cases had been about how the four women in question, stigmatised at first as afflicted and then as ill with infertility, and then as androgynous, were abandoned by their families. They were originally from different villages but had met after having migrated to nearby Manchar, where they lived together in a house and allegedly operated there as prostitutes after having dedicated themselves to Devdasi cults at the goddess Yellamma's temple at Saundhatti, Karnataka (my respondents were not sure where the dedication had exactly taken place but they were guessing that it was Saundhatti). One or two of my male informants in the village even said that they knew these women because

The Maulya are worshipped far more simply (in comparison to Satvai rituals) by dedicating baskets full of ritual offerings known as *paradi-duradi* offered at their shrines along with incense sticks. These offerings consist of seven kinds of savoury, fried and sweet foods, different kinds of fruits, differently coloured flowers, rice, milk, sweets, vegetables, differently coloured blouse pieces or *khan*, coconuts, *oti-bharan* materials and ritual offerings for their brother *Mhasoba* that consisted of a bit of blanket, a stick with a bell tied on an end and a couple of eggs. Sometimes, Maulya rituals (just as Satvai rituals) involve animal sacrifice. Women in my field area, however, never perform any preventive or normative rituals for the Maulya, since these are considered to be only affliction-based rituals.

Processes of Ritual Affliction for Village Goddesses: *How women returned to their roots*

The process of being summoned to one's roots was experienced as being very 'final' by women. A man or woman (with families in the native village) would fall inexplicably ill and would be unable to respond to any medical intervention. They would then typically consult ritual healers in the city, who would advise them to pay a visit to clan deities and village deity shrines in order to seek decisive remedies (*nikaal*). During their visit to the clan/native village goddess shrines, families would organise a ritual for the goddess. Typically, during this ritual, when drums were played (and sometimes drums were expressly played for this purpose),

the latter visited the villages in the area during the time of the year when all the *jatra* (annual festivals) of the goddesses took place. They were not disrespected by the village men, whom I spoke to, since they were considered to be 'earning members' of society, who could also get extremely aggressive like men if the need for it arose and if anybody acted 'fresh'. But they were also heavily stigmatised, hated, feared, pitied and shunned by most of my women respondents, who even crossed the street to avoid them. I found it difficult to contact these women in Manchar due to the ethical constraints of a non-ethnographical context that I would have to share with them, which was enforced upon me by my village respondents.

the woman from the summoned family would go into a trance or would take on the labour of trance for her husband (if he was ill) or other male family members and would begin to speak (or rather the goddess would begin to speak through her), of their misdemeanours and make ritual demands such as: a regular return to their respective native village or joint clan and regular worship (which also implied an increasing monetary involvement in native villages). If this demand made by the goddess along with other reprimands was accepted (which they always were, since illness was at stake), a longer ritual process of five weeks of submission (*paach-khete*) in terms of ritual visits and offerings to the shrine was demanded, wherein the woman would go into trance every time, for her clan, for her husband or for herself.

Some people made ritual promises of wish fulfilment or *navas* and built the shrine more extensively or gave expensive gifts or made endowments to the shrine once their wishes of healing were fulfilled; some promised to serve the shrine (*abdagiri*). It was considered imperative that the woman 'spoke' in goddess rituals of her demands and her afflictions and went into a trance. She was otherwise considered defiant of the goddess's will. I have witnessed healers and family members thrashing women in order to make them go into a trance and have their trances or afflictions speak so that subsequent healing rituals that can anchor a clan to the native village can take place. It is only after ritual propitiation that the woman and her family members may return to their city homes, only to have a closer relationship with the shrine and the village and its deity henceforth.

Only a clan goddess reveals the source of affliction. For example, in case a woman is unable to sustain a pregnancy and is afflicted by a Ghod-Satvai, unknown to herself during travel within another region during a picnic with friends for instance, the healer from the city will tell her to travel to her native village to meet with her clan and village goddess first and perform a ritual (usually an *abhisheka*). It will be her village goddess, who will reveal during the trance that she should do the *paach-pauli* of the Ghod-Satvai, facing the direction of the region where she had travelled during the picnic, to be healed and sustain a pregnancy. From then onwards, she would have to not only pacify the Ghod-Satvai and accept her generational worship into her own family but do the *paach-khete* of the village goddess and accept her village roots as a diagnostic tool for anchoring her body to 'her soil' and for healing her.

How Mr Jadhav became the Mari-aai's potraaj

I met Mr Jadhav from Pinnur village (Solapur district) at Ghodegaon, since the village and the surrounding regions constituted a part of his and the goddess's regular beat for asking *jogwa* (ritual alms) connected with his *potraaj-ki*. He had taken up the goddess Mari-*aai*'s *potraaj-ki* in his village and the goddess as a mobile epidemics protector was housed in a special shrine that was placed in a box, which he could carry around on his shoulders to every village, where he would ask for *jogwa* as part of his ritualised existence. He was the goddess's ritual agent and healed others by absorbing their afflictions through the grain they donated him in the villages he toured. He was immune to the affliction passed on through this grain, since he was of an absorbent caste, taking the illnesses from their clan into his body. He demonstrated his immunity to pain by whipping himself and demonstrating his agreement to accepting this feudal duty of a service provider, showing also that it did not hurt him to whip himself and absolving his spectators of guilt, while providing them entertainment of viewing his paraphernalia, dance and whipping.

According to Mr Jadhav's story, he came from a clan of practising fishermen (even if from the Matang caste) and the goddess Mari-*aai* introduced him to his caste profession of *potraaj-ki* through an accident while fishing. Once, while fishing, he cut his foot on a stone at the edge of the pond. The wound refused to heal despite medical treatment and injections at the local hospital. Mr Jadhav at last went to the local temple of Mari-*aai* after being advised to do so by a healer to ask ritual questions about his illness. There he got to know (through a trance that his mother went into) that the goddess Mari-*aai* wished him to be dedicated to her services according to his caste occupation of *potraaj-ki*. After that the family made a shrine for the goddess and Mr Jadhav underwent ritual dedication and marriage as a *potraaj* in which he became the goddess's wife. Today, he carries the mobile shrine of the goddess on his shoulders, touring villages and asking for *jogwa*, accompanied by his mother who plays the drum in rhythm to his dance as he whips himself in every neighbourhood of the village. He is dressed like the goddess and women from nearly every household come outside with winnowing fans full of grain (winnowing fans are used for Mari-*aai* because she is also the younger sister of Shitala Devi) as these grains embody the pox pustules.

He tells them of their yearly luck in terms of agricultural produce and he tells them of what is not considered *dharjin* for them in terms of colours, animals, flowers, and food for that agricultural year till the goddess's next annual visit on Mr. Jadhav's shoulders. The colours, foods, flowers and use of animals that he marks off as not *dharjin* for them that year are reserved only for the goddesses and it comes as a warning from him (in his official capacity as her agent) that they would offend the goddess if they were to use these colours, flowers, animals or foods that year, that only she (as the presiding goddess) will rightfully use. By abstaining from the goddess's *dharjin*, women and goddesses were therefore being mutually inter-related all over again as dyads as they took over compensating arenas of existence, organized in hierarchy with each other. In the year of my fieldwork in Ghodegaon, for example, the goddess, according to Mr Jadhav, had come dressed in white, was sitting on an ass holding chrysanthemum flowers and had a betel leaf tucked into her cheek. Worshipping women, therefore, would have to abstain from chewing betel, wearing or using chrysanthemum flowers in their hair, wearing pure white clothes or using the ass as a means of transportation, since these were not *dharjin* for them that year, being reserved for the goddess.

How midwives were separated from women but joined to childbirth

The midwife was often made the scapegoat of stories that my respondents from upper castes recounted about childbirth gone wrong. Midwives had been constructed as witches and scapegoats in many a mythological narrative such as the Ramayana (the figure of Manthara) or that of Goddess Jivantika that women in my field area harked back to. Women from the Matang caste at the Taljai slum in Pune, on the other hand, viewed midwives, also from the lower castes (same castes as themselves), as neighbourly helpers and simply as other women from the locality who had childbirth experiences of their own and had good luck in their hands.

The blaming of midwives was then the product of caste hierarchy that no argument about their special knowledge was ever going to be able to repair. If at all, I am afraid that claims of their special knowledge would only feed into an exotic image of the 'other' and the 'lower' that would essentialise caste and gender differences that images of the *potraaj*, for example, as the valorous, absorbing and immune magical 'other' were any ways achieving.

The midwife, constructed as a scapegoat in the village and her purported nature as a witch, exposes clan desires of controlling the very event of childbirth, the bodies of the mother and child involved within it and potentially supportive relationships between women and attachments between women and children that become embedded during this event through discourses of caste hierarchy and impositions of impurity. This caste impurity is further associated with all sorts of other anatomical products such as blood, placenta and afterbirth materials that is extended to childbirth goddess shrines that are located outside the village, where women leave their impurity behind in later rituals.

This inordinately casteist bias held by certain 'rationalist' sections of society, of midwives being unhygienic and impure and responsible for infant mortality, mimics the very desire of clan control over childbirth and makes an increasing amount of midwives even at Taljai to relinquish control over difficult childbirth cases, sending the mother to the hospital, when they can handle these cases far better than many hospitals can, while most hospitals hasten women into surgeries because it is more lucrative (according to my respondents). Midwives are simply afraid of clans joining doctors in blaming them when something goes against the clan will and in this context it is better to view their condition more realistically as experienced clans women or neighbours than imbue their practice with either a lower caste service-provider professionalism (which will get scant respect from upper caste and elite doctors) or as traditional and exotic mystique associated with quasi-magical charm, which caste impurity in any case does. The relationship of support and succour between women in childbirth and their midwives during labour is systematically sought to be politicised and effaced by dominant caste clans and this cooperates with medical systems, as some doctors are even known to abuse midwives whom they know to have actually helped in cases of childbirth.[5] Midwives, as already discussed in an earlier chapter, are already being eliminated from the public health system by paying women financial incentives for institutional births.

As a result of these biases, women from dominant castes in my field area recount ambivalences towards midwives during their pregnancy. They are viewed as harmful at several instances when pregnant woman become very afraid of them (based on some obscure notions of midwives having magical knowledge that paints them to be witches) and no amount of explaining that a midwife is simply a deeply experienced person, who is talented at child-birthing helps in this case. The 'alternative knowledge' paradigm therefore works as a bias against midwives as well and creates obstacles between them and pregnant women from the village when clans from dominant castes put them within a purity-impurity hierarchy. This bias is historic and colonial as well, demonstrated by Ram, as something that wives of British administrators perpetuated, while undermining the power that midwives had on the bodies of birthing women (Ram 2001).

Midwives nowadays are also employed by women and their clans in the village to perform dangerous home abortions and these collective memories often lead to a false consciousness about midwives being ambivalent among women from the upper castes, who want to hide clandestine pregnancies but are too ashamed of being recognised in clinics where they might want to go for safer abortions.

[5] Personal communication with Meera Sadgopal (Director, Tathapi Trust, Pune).

These home abortions that both midwives and upper-caste women are often ordered to perform, remain complicit with the clan and often lead to serious illnesses that incur medical costs and, sometimes, cost the women, if malnourished, their lives. The blame for this is almost always visited on the midwife as the clan abdicates responsibility for ill and dying woman. It is due to ambivalent upper-caste clan-centric situations such as these that midwives become dubbed witches from either side—as emissaries of birthing women (betrayers of the clan), who have to be ritually separated from women, and as emissaries of the clan (betrayers of women), who join in the torture of women from the clan side, who help to control women's bodies and reproduction.

How Gogi became a witch

A female healer from village Shinoli (district Pune) told me Gogi's story. Being a witch Gogi was very knowledgeable about diseases, affliction, healing, and witchcraft. She was known to be a powerful devotee (*bhaktin*) of the fierce cremation goddess, Mhasani, and performed witchcraft on those villagers, who had excommunicated her. She disappeared one day and people thought she had died. However, she had turned into an evil spirit and had acquired the double powers of being both a witch and an evil spirit. Since she did not have any food and peace, she was known to roam around the village stream eating whatever offal she could find. Many villagers were said to have seen her eating from the overflowing rubbish heaps outside the village near the village stream as well. It was said that even though she looked like an ordinary destitute beggar, they could feel her eyes, red hot and angry like burning coals, full of evil hatred the moment they turned on the viewer. The most problematic aspect about Gogi was that she was known to eat children if she caught them unchaperoned and alone.

The story of Gogi scared and worried women due to the implications of excommunication, destitution and cannibalism, while at the same time they protected their own children and their status as married women and mothers from her image. Gogi was different from the Satvai, who had become a goddess and who took witches into her fold and turned them into goddesses too. Gogi had done no such thing; she was afflicted, a witch, and now straddled the role of a demon. She continued to be a harmful, even after her death as she had been in life, and she did not allow herself to become redeemed, cooled or auspicious, even if she was rendered impure by her notorious reputation when alive. Neither had she started earning her livelihood as androgynous, which was nevertheless difficult because eunuchs and prostitutes, according to biases among my village respondents, were reputed to examine children for the specific reason of wanting to lure and kidnap them later to beg in bigger cities. The problem was that Gogi had turned demonic and killed and ate children outright.

Sharing the Goddess's Body in Ritual

De Certeau (1984: 202–3) writes about the primal role played by an event or accident in the life of a city that acts as a lacuna within its sense of continuity or within its 'theoretical time'. This accident produces the 'other' of theoretical time and becomes interpreted as 'causal time', which contradicts with the city's 'mythical' or imagined practice or continuity. It is, therefore, causal time that becomes the actual or real historical discourse of the city, resulting in internal differences and stratifications within its landscape that gives rise to thoughts about the power that unifies the city, its opacity preserved in rituals.

Applying this theory to the question of rituals for the Satvai and Maulya, then brings forth questions about how mythical practice in Satvai discourse can be described (if child/male death is obviously the accident or lacuna that creates stratification). Can normative imagination actually be constituted by a dyad between the Satvai and village women that explains the way in which they consist of each other's opposite attributes? Although mythical practice should not remain static and is constantly transformed by thoughts generated around the accident, it is also the enormous gendered experience of the accident that 'ritual' seeks to reverse and silence, as it tries to maintain mythical practice as universal and changeless dharma. Ritual therefore, through its visuality tries to mask accident or lacuna (in terms of experience) and recreates it, not as causal time or gender history (since women or Dalits are denied discursive individuality), but as boundary space that can be healed and integrated into mythical and theoretical time. This produces causal time as transient and ambivalent for women and Dalits and theoretical time as celebrated and timeless.

The experience of this accident that is ritually sought to be reversed by maintaining their pristine and changeless dyad relationships with the goddess is almost always silent, inarticulate and in dreams (since women are blamed for the accident), even while its obliteration takes place through the actual public rituals of reversal and its following emphatic, establishing and collective celebration. The experience of the accident of death (that has been medically controlled to some extent) has now been replaced by the accident of female immorality and witchcraft that brings them increasing shame, stigma and guilt, the fear of which cannot be erased even if their children live. It is transferred to other women in the family. Women therefore perform not just healing rituals to reverse accidents, but keep performing preventive rituals so that they may not fall from grace and disturb mythical time and theoretical dharma.

By doing so they become the inanimate aspect of the human goddess and enter into dyad relationships with the latter, so that they can share an existential vista of exclusive realms with her, where co-existence after a transfer of power between them takes place only has to adhere to the maintenance of a boundary in between. Any breaching of this boundary and there is an onset of impurity and affliction; hectic efforts are made to re-establish boundaries by retracting to the exclusive realms that can then help women resume their dyad relationships with goddesses.

The transformations back from impurity to purity among afflicted women (or the goddess's healing ritual) takes place through the ritual acceptance of this dyad relationship with goddesses through a sharing and conjoining of the body. This is done in order to give back to the goddesses what is considered the goddess's right and undo or reverse transgression that is in the first place considered the root cause of affliction; in other words it is to undertake the *dharjin* taboos especially during the ritual period. Throughout the ritual period of 'healing' of five weeks (usually a forty-day period), women have to perform the *paach-pauli* of the goddess every week at the shrine of the goddess (if the Satvai) or make ritual dedications of the *paradi-duradi* to the Maulya shrine every week or the *paach-khete* at the village goddess shrine.

During this time, women personally abstain from using all the ritual items dedicated to the goddess: food materials, flowers, fruits, and clothes in colours that have been offered to the goddess in rituals during this period. Through this abstinence of all that is not *dharjin* for them, since it is dedicated to the goddess (which usually added up to a considerable range of food materials) women undergo strict fasting by abstaining from the right to all the dedicated food materials that first belongs to the goddess. They mark their dyad relationship with the goddess by marking the boundary between them and yet remaining connected to her in these two exclusive realms.

Women also do not attend social functions at each other's homes during this ritual healing period (because the goddess was attending these) or 'eat outside' their own homes. They also do not want to risk eating at the hands of a secretly menstruating woman in this important ritual time period when they were conjoined with the goddess, as this impure contact or *vitaal* would anger the goddess further, since the goddess hated all forms of impurity. Upper-caste goddess mediums in any case are very sensitive about *vitaal*, since only the lower castes are considered immune to affliction through contagion (in contradiction to the upper castes, which made claims about getting afflicted by it, a status symbol at times). Sharing in the body of the goddess for the ritual period was considered to lead to the re-division of feminine space between castes and between purity and impurity by minimising and reducing accidents and reverting to timelessness.[6]

[6] Afflictions were manifested only after marriage even though they may have been contracted earlier. Many of my male informants accused their wives of 'running away' from their marital duties to repeatedly performing healing rituals in their natal villages (where the affliction was allegedly contracted).

Revisiting Questions of Significance and Attempting a Summary

While writing my Ph.D, I was often asked to define my work in brief or at least in as circumspect a manner as possible in order to explain why yet another book on goddesses would impact academics. Thinking of the various different levels at which a research and political enterprise such as mine engaging with multidisciplinary inputs apart from what a research about goddesses would require, I often found myself answering people differently in contexts that were specific to the location of their questioning. For example, I found myself answering anthropologists interested in my research, with descriptions of how rituals and their association with belief and cult networks constituted gendered knowledge about the body. I found myself answering activists interested in my work with descriptions of superstition-rationalism debates, struggles about issues of feminism, caste and labour, just as I told public health workers about my interest in reproductive health and poverty. On encountering questions about history and culture, I answered with data on rural settlement patterns, kingship and the importance of goddesses to the history in Maharashtra. Apart from the discrepancy of my answers being obvious to all those who had heard the different versions of my explanations directed at various strategic audiences, the seeming academic necessity of having a single focus or a relationship for intellectual exploration (reserved for one book at a time), that I obviously lacked also became confusing and distressing for me; I clung on embarrassingly to my supervisors, wanting to believe their 'take' on my work, till at a point an evaluator at a PhD student's workshop at Ghent finally observed that it seemed that I wanted to work on 'everything'.

It took me some journeying from there to gradually grow less embarrassed and more accepting of this allegation even as I began to view this 'everything' as the strength and interconnectivity of my writing on various issues that were indeed associated with a political research about goddesses. My research links various discourses and methods together with motherhood that I have had ample opportunity of exploring in this book. I would like to however end the formal discussion in this chapter with two theoretical subject matters (one external and one internal) that I have constantly tussled with through the research and writing of this book. They are flagged off as follows:

1. The first is the rather naïve claim that I held at the beginning of my research analysis that defined childbirth rituals as instruments and categories of transformations unto themselves, separate from beliefs about affliction goddesses. Nothing could have been further from the truth in the lives of the women I studied. Since they shared their bodies with the Satvai and Maulya in dyad relationships, public rituals only masked and silenced women's experiences of crisis, even if they transformed these relationships as every other relationship in their social world. Just studying rituals without studying either goddesses or feminism would have left me holding a rope without its two ends. Nor would it have made my research ethical as a feminist engaged in any kind of humanist discipline. The other big academic fallacy I confronted, while writing my data and field notes was the myth of women's personal aims for performing childbirth rituals emerging or arising from within their own culturalist frameworks, which I (as a researcher) or the Westernised world was told it could neither control, influence, understand or access. This not only absolved responsibility for culturalism, orientalism, racism and absence of empathy towards the suffering that lay obscene and silent outside acceptable dominant discourse; it was also simply untrue, since childlessness stigma and the pain of witchcraft-related denouncement for both men and women, for example, has historically been almost universally experienced by all cultures. Ritual aims for women were constructed by all forms of media, exchange and communications with the outside world that were in constant transition and interaction simultaneously, even as they transformed the very research agenda that suggested its scientific penetration. Most women shared their lives inside and outside research contexts if the research interaction

was empathetic, enduring and sincere; women's worlds did not belong to a different planet. Paradigms of relationships were definitely accessible by the sharing of experiences in the research context with them, even if besieged with varying ranges of difficulty and counter production.

Women were far more physically involved with an enmeshment of rituals, goddesses, their own reproductive and sexual bodies, their babies and their motherhood roles or given duty of healing that was all too entangled together to make their engagement with any one of the above—either ritual or simply goddesses, or just reproductive health, or just childbirth or healing—their primary focus. And understanding this already solved the first conundrum of my inter-subjectivity: too many subjects that initially hinted at a lack of focus, till I discovered that there *had* to be these many subjects within my discussion in the first place. I was exploring the lives of women that had myriad and equally important political aspects to it. My book about them would also have to have as many interlinked aspects to it that also reflected their concerns and not just mine.

2. The second conundrum concerns a pervasive assumption behind the writing of this book that can now act as a point for its closure. At the time when I was recounting my disruptive dreams to some of my friends outside the fieldwork context, the singular response they had was revulsion, horror and a feeling of shock about how I managed to articulate the most taboo of subjects in such detail that was concerned with the female body. My dreams had shattering implications for the sobriety of middle-class emotional stability that experienced a kind of secondary trauma over the exposure of the female body in such an unexpected way that it almost constituted an attack; some of them even called me an exhibitionist. In the prologue and epilogue of this book, I have, however, continued to verbalise such taboo subjects, but not in an attempt to silence readers by the perpetuation of its pain or un-speakability.

The problem I see in the articulation of women's dreams or my dreams, as I borrowed an affliction cult subjectivity from my fieldwork friends, has sometimes masked an unquestioned visual category in my text, namely the presence of the female body in univocal maternity crisis. I am sure there are many other images of childbirth that are alternative to this. I have chosen this image, due to the deliberate obliteration of child-loss, childlessness and excessive and enforced childbirths that insistently produces women as *suhasini*; due to the insistent production of Satvai and Maulya as mother and child-protecting cults, both within popular/nationalistic notions of religion and the academics of Maharashtra. But it is just that: my choice and not universal reality and I want to take the opportunity of mentioning this, so as not to create any hegemonic discourses of my own. Reading through my own texts, I have often experienced a lurking and self-accepted force of the female body in pain (that I myself shared with afflicted women) that I have assumed to be ubiquitous, harnessed as labour and mostly and essentially undergoing suffering as it resists harnessing, even as I may have sometimes overlooked the way in which my text may have created its own omnipotence that accords a 'given' status to an entire visual world of the owned 'female'.

Critiquing Kristeva's expositions about the pre-paternal maternal instinct and the biological body outside culture that could challenge its symbolic semiotics through an access to libidinous multiplicity through poetry, Butler (2006: 119–26) points to ways in which Kristeva's arguments of pre-paternal language and libidinous maternal drives become tautological, explaining how there could have been no existence of maternal, biological drives without the paternal and controlling law of symbolic ascriptions within semiotics itself.

Similarly, the afflicting and painful visual dreams of women stuck in maternity, in rebellious modes that seemingly break patriarchal taboo are all spaces structurally accorded to my respondents and to me by patriarchal systems for suffering, coping, anger and pain that are in turn diagnosed or treated and created as affliction and illness within patriarchy itself. These do not constitute healing or any kind of alternative justice mechanisms, because the goddess is entrenched within patriarchy and is herself its primary champion. These expressions and experiences are themselves a reflection of patriarchy that accords the goddess humanity, while pitting women into afflictions, when expressing the same.

The boundary space of affliction between the dyad of women and goddesses is the silent zone of rituals and dreams that tries to reverse, narrow and topple its own existence by re-establishing the purity of the dyad and the world of pristine dharma. The dark and underlined boundary between biological and real mothers represents the third angle between them of failing mothers, which deflects from their dualism and draws them both into participating in a perennial gamut of preventive rituals, even as women dying in childbirth transit to the other side in death impurity periods and mothers of dying children enter these boundary lands anew. Some face a future of abandonment, some have new babies and are re-integrated into their marital clans even if they and their clans women have to continue with their rituals, while others leave the fold to conduct feminist research on the subject.

So, just as it was entirely within the parameters of patriarchy that Kristeva's claims concerning maternal drive and subversive poetry were made, it is also within parameters of patriarchy's discursively ascribed marginal spaces that both women's wildly painful dreams and my taboo-breaking articulation of them become simultaneously subsumed and co-opted. It is the naturalisation of this co-option that includes all of us within the category of women, maternity and the various axes of feudal relationships with children, clans and goddesses that keeps the very languages of our suffering intact as both a prison and a privilege. Even while wanting and needing to escape suffering, its nature, expression and experience remained already an almost pre-plotted part of the goddess-woman dyad paradigm of affliction that operates as the third angle between them. Even as I came to realise the quality of imagined escape routes from suffering, these very routes simultaneously led back to assimilation. Nothing changed for women as far as these ways of 'rebellion' become further economised and translated into an image of women's maternity (and its association with suffering as victims) as it further contributed to a conception of weak and vulnerable womanhood that fitted conveniently with the protective paradigms of the upper and dominant castes protecting them. It was after all with deep concern that many of my upper caste audience said (to whom I had been telling my shocking dreams outside my field work context) that all I needed was love to heal an absence of a right over my body.

The book, as is clear by now, is about boundaries and how motherhood is exactly negotiated here. The boundary is an agential, vibrant and interactive parameter existing at various levels and layers simultaneously, which I have sought to explore through a complex range of theorisation and ethnography in this book. The introduction of the boundary as a concept at an epistemic level will hopefully herald the examination of many finer collaborating dynamics, without its oversimplification, which unfortunately effects more closures between complex relationships rather than facilitating the discovery of any new understanding.

EPILOGUE

Epiphany Dreams and the Impossibility of Birthing

Personal Trajectory

Recounting my own dreams and goddess-related experiences are politically important, since it seeks to counterbalance my respondents' dreams and experiences narrated in the prologue. This has been as difficult for me, as the sharing of these dream experiences was for my respondents in what started off as the idea of a 'research context' propagated by me.

These dreams often represented a spectre of humiliation and failure for my respondents, even as the recounting of dreams gradually became similar for me, re-emphasising what I began with: the exploration of a socially, ritually and medically constructed category of childless women that intensified into manifold trauma and stigma. It gradually obliterated all kinds of epistemic differences between the health sciences (mental health being different from reproductive health, as I witnessed the depression that childlessness and child-loss led to) or concepts of poverty for women. I came to understand the impoverishment of dominant caste women as more complex and immeasurable, working primarily with them, even as I came to understand the fractures within the universal axiom of all men being privileged, when I began collecting *potraaj* stories.

As I end this book, writing this epilogue is my last effort at de-rationalising my feminist escape routes from my past, even as I accept to sharing the moralist universe of the women I was researching. It is the moral universe where I grew up, even as my education and present has given me more opportunities to equalise its pain and come to terms with my experiences of loss and failed aspirations. However, given the slightest chance, I still dreamed. These dreams reminded me that I, just like these women I was 'researching' were survivors of a motherhood ideal that could never be achieved, even if children and male heirs were born. Even successful mothers or wives teetered forever on the brink of loss that they would be held responsible for; it was inescapable, since being a woman in a reproductive role/its facilitating role was existential. Only goddesses as drinkers of motherhood and the receivers of humanity and compassion from women were free like the little girl children, the *kori-savashne* who were as yet roaming the village and fed for the Satvai ritual—unknowing of their future.

My personal intellectual engagement with childbirth had begun with the rather puerile and superficial understanding of how India was a childbirth-friendly culture with a billion-mark population, where childbirth and childbirth facilitation was traditionally lauded. My naïve understanding of childbirth grew to be associated with how traditional Indian culture reserved a special place in their hearts for children, as even Hindu gods and goddesses were imagined as cherubic babies or children. This thankfully came to be offset by other forms of knowledge over time, as I informed myself more about the topic on how only upper-caste, upper-class/middle-class, legitimate (born within marriage), and preferably male children received enough preferential treatment to survive successfully and become their clan leaders. The rest—those who were very poor, of an ascribed lower caste, illegitimate and, still to a great extent, girl children—simply died, were heavily malnourished, largely underprivileged or were employed by the same child-adoring society in impossible and inhuman forms of labour, if not abused systematically. Mothers of such impoverished, dying or dead children were not just impoverished, dying or dead themselves, but mothers of rich children were also impoverished, in order to become good service providers and feudatories of their children and enriched marital clans (that had gained heirs), wherein they had to renounce their emotional hold over their children.

I was to learn through personal experience that the importance and 'social love' for children was sometimes an eyewash. Children born outside clan inheritance modalities were automatically born outside paradigms of dignity, ownership and legitimacy and then they were not only unloved but in many cases heavily underprivileged as well; their existence in a society that lauded itself on children imageries did away with them in clandestine clinics with terrific speed.

Predictably, I dreamed of 'owning' my child-to-be desperately, without wanting it to ever belong to society, even as I tried to avoid clan and social control over my body. But I lost my child in very traumatic conditions, after which my personal journey spiralled only downwards as I became consumed with rage and pain. I gradually began having ambivalent feelings about legitimate children after that as I understood how they would always belong to their clans and castes first and only last to their mothers. Being filled with anger, I began realising how I represented a classic affliction case to my village friends, as children cried when they came near me. I was too intense for them, their mothers said. And there were many like me in the village who recognised me as one among them.

Overwhelmed by social impositions and grief, I lost control and good health. Shame and guilt replaced actual loss, even as loss itself became a matter of voyeuristic interest and further shame and anger for those I confided in, who moreover believed that I was an exhibitionist suffering a madness of some sort. I remained constantly shamed, grief-stricken, enraged and anxious, and before I met my village friends I believed that I was alone in this experience of dehumanisation. I underwent long-drawn and intensive medical treatments just like my village friends underwent intensive ritual treatments, and we all clung on to our existence in the hope for better days; these hardly ever come by.

I must say that I gained a lot of patriarchal sympathy from those who viewed my misery as a woman's natural need for motherhood in order to gain 'completion'. Though I lapped up whatever scant sympathy I was getting, the real issue underlying my misery remained unaddressed. My real issue concerned my control over my reproductive body without the threat of control punishment or the imposition of shame and guilt surrounding what was considered my sexual misdemeanour. Women forced to undergo repeated childbirths within clans or sex-selective abortions or abortions because their relationships or babies were considered illegitimate face the same structural violence as women forced to relinquish their pregnancies outside marriages do. I wasn't a lifer fighting against women's rights to abortion! I was fighting for women's control over their bodies that could push out clan and dominant caste control over the female body as an owned reproductive machine.

I thought a divorce would solve my problems; it did not. I realised that I remained as fragmented outside patriarchal institutions and structures as I was within it, since it was patriarchal systems and the way it viewed the female sexual-reproductive body that had defining social power, which I had problems with, whether I lived inside or outside it; I would by default be a minority forever. I could not, for example, escape the social stigma of being a female divorcee and this had no connection whatsoever with how many people actually understood or accepted my decisions personally. Writing about patriarchal institutions, values and agents, and the manner in which all of these produced female labour in terms of caste, adherence to goddess cults and clan belonging, was the only way in which I could retain any semblance of agency against believing in my own oppression atavistically.

I found a similarly unhappy community of lonely and childless women in my field area with complicated family relationships. They were performing goddess rituals hectically, even though they were repulsed by other *suhasini* (married) women with children. I found a reflection of my own life among these women just as they found me to be afflicted like them. The affliction discourse sought to silence experiences of childlessness in much the same way as the health discourse worked to stigmatise and silence the depression I underwent. For some of them (the wealthier, for example) the medical and the goddess diagnosis actually conflated with the social, to produce them as afflicted and ill (faulty pieces, we joked!)

at the same time, along with the social stigma of being misfits, just as it did in my case. At the same time, they trusted the goddess as much as I trusted medical practitioners, since we could only have recourse to our own worlds, with its existing hierarchies, as the only source for solace. But both these kinds of practitioners were after all pro-upper caste and dominant caste clan practitioners, equally entrenched within patriarchy.

Working with issues of women, the female body, deities and rituals, the health sector, communalism and motherhood constituted the meeting ground for academic and personal interests for me. I have not intended my rationalism or the research explorations of this book to produce judgement on the lives of those women who have drawn status and pleasure through motherhood or been happily married as wives, and are in love. My objective has instead been more focused on locating an invisible and impoverished female body that is outside the discursive market back into its purview in ways that are more concrete than those suggested by mere dualisms between victimhood and agency. I am trying instead to introduce the concept of the female dyad that exists not just between goddesses and women but between mothers and childless women as well.

I have tried to demonstrate the way in which childlessness shadows motherhood constantly at boundaries between women and goddesses and between spatial organisations of territorial divisions that define private and communal ownership, wherein rituals of dedication and *paach-pauli* are simultaneous with celebrations of *paachi* and *haaravi*, for example. I am trying to suggest that between every ascription of beauty, success and purity, there also necessarily exists an ascription of the ugly, the failed, the impure and the inauspicious that is heavily imputed in terms of gender, caste and anti-poor discrimination in rural Maharashtra.

Self-hatred, Guilt, Confusion, Exhaustion, and Renunciation

During the writing of my doctoral thesis and this book, I had three sets of recurring dreams that I felt demonstrated my emotions about the goddess, my affection for my village respondents (that contradicted with my feelings about my research) and my confusion about my childlessness and its ascribed stigma.

In my first version of dreams, I was accosted by snakes, other reptiles and amphibians of various shapes, colours and sizes that crawled over me and poisoned my food. I was almost always confronted by large and threatening reptiles in what began in the dream as a mundane situation. It was a situation that was full of anxiety and dread, accompanied by visceral revulsion, even though the spectre of killing these animals (which I often had to) caused me as much wrenching pain as the reptile-type dreams did to my village friends, which in their case was a battle surrounding the children that they felt forced to give up. In both cases the pain in the dream surrounded the question of 'disguised' babies and the severing of physical connection with them for social reasons.

According to the second set, I would be followed by women who had died in childbirth, sometimes accompanied by babies. They would accost me in my hostel room or at other mundane places in different cities. I recognised them or their children to be dead, since many would at times be headless, reminding me of the Satvai (many Satvayya were imagined to be headless like the Lajja Gauri) and I connected them with my research. Their sudden menacing presence made me feel bad for having neglected or forgotten them and for having become too much of a rationalist, since I chose to write a dissertation on their experiences. I felt afraid that I would ultimately face the same fate of being pulled back to the village, on 'call' from the goddess to perform rituals of true belonging.

According to the third set of dreams, I would throw an idol of the goddess held secretly in a box or in my bag or hidden inside my clothes into a river, pond, tank or stream in order to destroy her cult and its domination over me. This exercise would be accompanied by piercing screams from the drowning goddess, who I was afraid would be rescued by others or the police and live to accuse me of wanting to murder her.

Closure

Even as I have reiterated the many mutual reflections between my village respondents and my personal trajectory and research methodology throughout this book, I have politicised the very construction of knowledge and academics as a product that is non-sacrosanct and artificially devised through unequal processes of interaction within small time-space windows that are non-general in nature, unique and hardly ever replicable when conducted by other researchers with different personal trajectories and political lenses as part of their method. I have tried to point to hegemonies of interpretation that emerge when the researchers and researched become subjects and objects of research, with no internal checks of self-reflexivity dedicated to exploring their mutual relationships of power, when taking recourse to theories of interpretation that underlie the very understanding of data, even while collecting and classifying it for consumption. For this research, my most important method has surrounded a feminist engagement with 'empathy' and possibilities for mutual transformation, amidst my deepest and the most difficult of conflicts, competitions and power struggles with my village friends, when defining motherhood in contradiction with the right to women's control over their reproductive body that they considered a sin.

I have found motherhood to be the most political of subjects, associated with demography and the state in ways tortuously implicit with policy, power, the government and religion (as a form of parallel moral government) in all manners possible, compared to those who may think of babies as cornerstones of romance; and that is already political enough! The only area in which I will have differed from my village friends is in the writing of this text in English. They will probably never read this or have access to its analytical mechanisms, wherein I have interwoven my rationalist, feminist ideas into a cause for arguing that childlessness is as necessary an aspect for facilitating social motherhood among both men and women as having biological children is, since childbirth is an opportunity I will never have again. My view still remains in central contradiction with the opinions of my respondents for whom having children was the only way in which a woman could ever achieve motherhood

This book has allowed me to approach the subject of motherhood in ways that the Satvai's ritual could never do, since that could always be reversed if the goddess became suddenly angry about some *dharjin* rule being broken inadvertently, even as I am aware of remaining within patriarchy, while agitating constantly against issues such as caste, gender and labour. This difference and separation is brought about through the act of writing itself, even as I am aware of conflicts within it. This writing of women's pain mixed with mine has represented a paradox: even as I try to liberate myself of pain, I try to do so without leaving the memory of those who introduced it to my life behind.

Bibliography

Abbot, J. 1984. *Indian Rituals and Beliefs: The Keys of Power*. New Delhi: Usha.

Anand, M.R. 2005. *The State and the Village Community in Medieval Maharashtra (17th–18th Century A.D.)*. New Delhi: Rajat Publications.

Apffel-Marglin, F. 1982. 'Kings and Wives: The Separation of Status and Royal Power', in T. N. Madan (ed.), *Way of Life: King, Householder, Renouncer*, pp. 155–181. New Delhi: Vikas Publishing House.

———. 2008. *Rhythms of Life: Enacting the World with the Goddesses of Orissa*. New Delhi: Oxford University Press.

Bell, C. 1992. *Ritual Theory, Ritual Practice*. New York: Oxford University Press.

Benjamin, G. 2002. 'On Being Tribal in the Malay World', in G. Benjamin and C. Chou (eds.), *Tribal Communities in the Malay World*, pp. 7–76. Leiden and Singapore: International Institute for Asian Studies and Institute of Southeast Asian Studies.

Bennett, L. 2002. *Dangerous Wives and Sacred Sisters: Social and Symbolic Roles of High-Caste Women in Nepal*. New York and Kathmandu: Columbia University Press and Mandala Book Point.

Bernbeck, R. and S. Pollock. 1996. 'Ayodhya, Archaeology, and Identity', *Current Anthropology*, 37(Supplement) : 138–142.

Bhattacharji, S. 1970. *The Indian Theogony: A Comparative Study of Indian Mythology from the Vedas to the Puranas*. Cambridge: Cambridge University Press.

Bhattacharyya, N.N. 1988. *Ancient Indian History and Civilization: Trends and Perspectives*. New Delhi: Manohar.

Biardeau, M. 2004. *Stories about Posts: Vedic Variations around the Hindu Goddess*. Chicago: University of Chicago Press.

Brubaker, R.L. 1978. 'The Ambivalent Mistress: A Study of South Indian

Village Goddesses and Their Religious Meaning', unpublished Ph.D. thesis, University of Chicago.

Bucher, J. 1994. *Bucher's Kannada-English Dictionary: Chiefly Based on the Labours of Dr. F. Kittel*, edited and revised by C. Watsa. New Delhi and Madras: Asian Educational Services.

Burrow, T. and M.B. Emeneau. 1998. *A Dravidian Etymological Dictionary*. New Delhi: Munshiram Manoharlal Publishers.

Butalia, U. 1998. *The Other Side of Silence: Voices from the Partition of India*. New Delhi: Penguin Books.

Butler, J. 2006. *Gender Trouble: Feminism and the Subversion of Identity*. New York and London: Routledge.

Chakravarti, U. 1998. *Rewriting History: The Life and Times of Pandita Ramabai*. New Delhi: Zubaan.

———. 2006. *Gendering Caste: Through a Feminist Lens*. Calcutta: Stree.

Chatterjee, P. 2012. 'After Subaltern Studies', *Economic and Political Weekly*, 47(35) : 44–49.

Chawla, J. 1994. *Child-Bearing and Culture: Women Centred Revisioning of the Traditional Midwife; The Dai as a Ritual Practitioner*. New Delhi: Indian Social Institute.

———. 2002. '*Hawa*, *Gola* and Mother-in-Law's Big Toe: On Understanding *Dais'* Imagery of the Female Body', in S. Rozario and G. Samuel (eds), *The Daughters of Hariti: Theory and Practice in Medical Anthropology and International Health*, pp. 147–162. London and New York: Routledge.

Childe, V.G. 2003. *Man Makes Himself*. Nottingham: Spokesman.

Clark-Deces, I. 2008. 'From Wasteland to Bus Stand: The Relocation of Demons in Tamilnadu', in I.V. Peterson and M.A. Selby (eds.), *Tamil Geographies: Cultural Constructions of Space and Place in South India*, pp. 173–198. Albany, NY: State University of New York Press.

Coburn, T.B. 1984. *Devi-Mahatmya: The Crystallization of the Goddess Tradition*. New Delhi: Motilal Banarasidass.

Connerton, P. 1989. *How Societies Remember*. Cambridge: Cambridge University Press.

Curley, D.L. 2008. *Poetry and History: Bengali Mangal-Kabya and Social Change in Precolonial Bengal*. New Delhi: Chronicle Books.

Dandekar, D. 2009. 'Satvai and the Lives of Women in Ghodegaon', in R. Badry, M. Rohrer and K. Steiner (eds.), *Liebe, Sexualität, Ehe und Partnerschaft: Paradigmen im Wandel* [Love, Sexuality, Marriage and Partnership: Changing Paradigms], pp. 281–292. Freiburg: Fördergemeinschaft wissenschaftlicher Publikationen von Frauen.

———. 2014a. 'Preserving Traditional Healing: Some Political Questions', *Economic and Political Weekly*, 49(43–44) : 19–22.

———. 2014b. 'Childlessness and Empathetic Relationships', *The Oriental Anthropologist* 14(1) [Special Number on 'Fieldwork in South Asia', ed. G. Alex]: 123–139.

———. 2015. 'Women's *Sakti* and the *Satvai*, a Folk Goddess of Childbirth in Maharashtra', in K.S. Rege, S.A. Pandit, S. Jeswani, R. Sabnis (eds), *Sakti in Indian Archaeology, Art, Literature and Philosophy*, pp. 179–188. New Delhi: Agam Kala Prakashan.

———. (Forthcoming). 'The Baaravi Ritual, the Satvai and Female Ancestor Worship in Western Maharashtra', in G. Alex and K. Polit (eds), *Childbirth and its Accompanying Rituals*. Heidelberg: Draupadi Verlag.

———. and A. Dandekar. 2011. 'The Satvai and Settlement Pattern in Rural Western Maharashtra', *South Asian Studies*, 27(2) : 221–224.

Davar, B. and M. Lohokare. 2009. 'Recovering from Psychosocial Traumas: The Place of Dargahs in Maharashtra', *Economic and Political Weekly*, 44(16) : 60–67.

de Certeau, M. 1984. *The Practice of Everyday Life*. Berkeley, Los Angeles and London: University of California Press.

———. 2000. *The Possession at Loudun*. Chicago: University of Chicago Press.

Dhavalikar, M.K. 1977. *Masterpieces of Indian Terracottas*. Bombay: Taraporevala.

———. 2002. *Environment and Culture: A Historical Perspective*. Pune: Bhandarkar Oriental Research Institute.

Dimock, E.C., Jr. 1982. 'A Theology of the Repulsive: The Myth of the Goddess Sitala', in J.S. Hawley and D.M. Wulff (eds), *The Divine Consort: Radha and the Goddesses of India*, pp. 184–203. New Delhi: Motilal Banarasidass.

Dirks, N.B. 2001. *Castes of Mind: Colonialism and the Making of Modern India*. Princeton, NJ: Princeton University Press.

Doniger, W. 2009. *The Hindus: An Alternative History*. New York: Penguin Press.

Douglas, M. 2002. *Purity and Danger*. London and New York: Routledge.

———. 2004. 'Traditional Culture: Let's Hear No More about It', in V. Rao and M. Walton (eds), *Culture and Public Action*, pp. 85–109. Stanford, CA: Stanford University Press.

Duvvury, V.K. 1991. *Play, Symbolism and Ritual: A Study of Tamil Brahmin Women's Rites of Passage* (*American University Studies*, Vol. 11). New York: Peter Lang.

Feldhaus, A. 1995a. 'Types of River Goddesses in Maharashtra', in G.D. Sontheimer (ed.), *Folk Cultures, Folk Religion and Oral Traditions as a Component in Maharashtrian Culture* (*Maharashtra: Culture and Society*, Vol. 23), pp. 31–47. New Delhi: Manohar.

———. 1995b. *Water and Womanhood: Religious Meanings of Rivers in Maharashtra*. New York: Oxford University Press.

———. 2003. *Connected Places: Region, Pilgrimage, and Geographical Imagination of India*. New York: Palgrave Macmillan.

Foucault, M. 1979. *Discipline and Punish: The Birth of the Prison*. New York: Vintage Books.

Freed, R.S. and S.A. Freed. 1993. *Ghosts: Life and Death in North India* (*Anthropological Papers of the American Museum of Natural History*, Vol. 72). Seattle, WA: University of Washington Press.

Gaikwad, L. 1998. *The Branded (Uchalya)*. New Delhi: Sahitya Academy.

Gatwood, L.E. 1985. *Devi and the Spouse Goddess: Women, Sexuality and Marriage in India*. New Delhi: Manohar.

Ghurye, G.S. 1977. *Indian Acculturation: Agastya and Skanda*. Bombay: Popular Prakashan.

Gold, A.G. 2000. 'From Demon Aunt to Gorgeous Bride: Women Portray Female Power in a North Indian Festival Cycle', in J. Leslie and M. McGee (eds), *Invented Identities: The Interplay of Gender, Religion and Politics in India* (*SOAS Studies on South Asia: Understandings and Perspectives*), pp. 203–230. New Delhi: Oxford University Press.

Gordon, S. 1993. *The Marathas 1600–1818* (*The New Cambridge History of India*, Vol. II.4). New Delhi: Cambridge University Press.

———. 1994. *Marathas, Marauders, and State Formation in Eighteenth-Century India*. New Delhi: Oxford University Press.

Guha, S. 1999. *Environment and Ethnicity in India 1200–1991* (*Cambridge Studies in Indian History and Society* 4). Cambridge: Cambridge University Press.

Guru, G. 2013. 'Freedom of Expression and the Life of the Dalit Mind', *Economic and Political Weekly*, 48(10) : 39–45.

Harlan, L. 1994. 'Perfection and Devotion: Sati Tradition in Rajasthan', in J.S. Hawley (ed.), *Sati, the Blessing and the Curse*, pp. 79–90. New York: Oxford University Press.

Hawley, J. and D.M. Wulff (eds). 1982. *The Divine Consort: Radha and the Goddesses of India*. New Delhi: Motilal Banarasidass.

Hiltebeitel, A. 1988. *The Cult of Draupadi 1: Mythologies: From Gingee to Kurukshetra*. New Delhi: Motilal Banarsidass.

———. and K.M. Erndl (eds). 2000. *Is the Goddess a Feminist? The Politics of South Asian Goddesses*. New York: New York University Press.

Jansen, R. 1995. *Die Bhavani von Tuljapur: Religionsgeschichtliche Studie des Kultes einer Göttin der Indischen Volksreligion* [The Bhavani of Tuljapur: Study in the History of Religion of the Cult of an Indian Folk Goddess] (*Beiträge zur Südasienforschung, Südasien-Institut, Universität Heidelberg* [Contributions to South Asia Research, South Asia Institute, University of Heidelberg], Vol. 168). Stuttgart: Franz Steiner Verlag.

Kakar, S. 1982. *Shamans, Mystics and Doctors: A Psychological Inquiry into India and its Healing Traditions*. New Delhi: Oxford University Press.

Kaviraj, S. 2010. *The Imaginary Institution of India: Politics and Ideas*. New York: Columbia University Press.

Kinsley, D. 1986. *Hindu Goddesses: Visions of the Divine Feminine in the Hindu Religious Tradition*. New Delhi: Motilal Banarasidass.

Kosambi, D.D. 1962. *Myth and Reality: Studies in the Formation of Indian Culture*. Bombay: Popular Prakashan.

Kosambi, M. (ed.). 2008. *Feminist Vision or 'Treason Against Men'? Kashibai Kanitkar and the Engendering of Marathi Literature*. New Delhi: Permanent Black.

Kripal, J.J. 2000. 'A Garland of Talking Heads for the Goddess: Some Autobiographical and Psychoanalytic Reflections on the Western Kali', in A. Hiltebeitel and K.M. Erndl (eds), *Is the Goddess a Feminist? The Politics of South Asian Goddesses*, pp. 239–268. New York: New York University Press.

Kurtz, S.N. 1992. *All the Mothers Are One: Hindu India and the Cultural Shaping of Psychoanalysis*. New York: Columbia University Press.

Laclau, E. 2005. *On Populist Reason*. London and New York: Verso.

Laine, J.W. 2003. *Shivaji: Hindu King in Islamic India*. New Delhi: Oxford University Press.

Leslie, J. 1991. 'Sri and Jyeshtha: Ambivalent Role Models for Women', in J. Leslie (ed.), *Roles and Rituals for Hindu Women*, pp. 107–128. New Delhi: Motilal Banarsidass.

Lewis, I.M. 1978. *Ecstatic Religion: An Anthropological Study of Spirit Possession and Shamanism*. Harmondsworth: Penguin Books.

Manicom, L. 2008. *L'inconduite arraisonnée: enferment, généalogie, événement autour du dargah d'Erwadi* [Checked Misconduct: Confinement, Genealogy, and Event around the Dargah of Erwadi]. Bordeaux: Presses Universitaires de Bordeaux.

Marriott, M. 1990. 'Constructing an Indian Ethnosociology', in M. Marriott (ed.), *India through Hindu Categories*, pp. 1–39. New Delhi: Sage Publications.

Masilamani-Meyer, E. 2004. *Guardians of Tamilnadu: Folk Deities, Folk Religion,*

Hindu themes (*Neue Hallesche Berichte* [New Reports from Halle], Vol. 5). Halle: Verlag der Franckeschen Stiftungen zu Halle.

Masselos, J. 1999. 'The Outside Inside: Incursions into the Marathi Household at the End of the Nineteenth Century', in I. Glushkova and R. Vora (eds), *Home, Family and Kinship in Maharashtra*, pp. 15–40. New Delhi: Oxford University Press.

McKean, L. 1996. 'Bharat Mata: Mother India and her Militant Matriots', in D.M. Wulff and J.S. Hawley (eds.), *Devi: Goddesses of India*, pp. 250–280. New Delhi: Motilal Banarasidass.

Molesworth, J.T. 1996. *Molesworth's Marathi-English Dictionary: Corrected Reprint*. Pune: Shubhada-Saraswat Prakashan.

Mukul, A. 2014. 'Ancient Caste System Worked Well, ICHR Head Says', *Times of India*, 15 July 2014.

Nandy, A. 2004. 'Shamans, Savages and the Wilderness: On the Audibility of Dissent and the Future of Civilizations', in *Bonfire of Creeds: The Essential Ashis Nandy*, pp. 470–87. New Delhi: Oxford University Press.

Nicholas, R.W. 2003. *Fruits of Worship: Practical Religion in Bengal*. New Delhi: Chronicle Books.

Nichter, M. 2001. 'The Political Ecology of Health in India: Indigestion as Sign and Symptom of Defective Modernization', in G.S. Linda and H. Conner (eds), *Healing Powers and Modernity: Traditional Medicine, Shamanism and Science in Asian Societies*, pp. 85–106. Westport, CT: Bergin and Garvey.

Palriwala, R. and P. Uberoi. 2008. 'Exploring the Links: Gender Issues in Marriage and Migration', in R. Palriwala and P. Uberoi (eds) *Marriage, Migration and Gender* (*Women and Migration in Asia*, Vol. 5), pp. 23–62. New Delhi: Sage Publications.

Panikkar, S.K. 1997. *Saptamatrika Worship and Sculptures: An Iconographical Interpretation of Conflicts and Resolutions in the Storied Brahminical Icons* (*Perspectives in Indian Art and Archaeology* 5). New Delhi: D.K. Printworld.

Panse, M.G. 1952. 'Index Verborum of Jnanesvari', *Bulletin of the Deccan College Research Institute*, 10: 572–762.

Parry, J.P. 1994. *Death in Banaras*. Cambridge: Cambridge University Press.

Patel, T. 2007. 'Popular Culture and Childbirth: Perceptions and Practices in Rural Rajasthan', in J.B. Bernard Bell, B. Das, V. Parthasarathi and G. Poetevin (eds), *The Social and the Symbolic* (*Communication Processes*, Vol. 2), pp. 386–412. New Delhi: Sage Publications.

Pinch, W.R. 2006. *Warrior Ascetics and Indian Empires* (*Cambridge Studies in Indian History and Society*, Vol. 12). New Delhi: Cambridge University Press.

Polke, P. 1984. *Abhraan* [Ornament]. Mumbai: Granthali Prakashan.

Quack, J. 2012. *Disenchanting India: Organized Rationalism and Criticism of Religion in India*. Oxford: Oxford University Press.

Raheja, G.G. and A.G. Gold. 1994. *Listen to the Heron's Words: Reimagining Gender and Kinship in North India*. Berkeley, CA: University of California Press.

Rairkar, H. 2007. 'Midwives: A Tradition on the Move in Maharashtra', in J.B. Bernard Bell, B. Das, V. Parthasarathi and G. Poetevin (eds), *The Social and the Symbolic* (*Communication Processes*, Vol. 2), pp. 413–472. New Delhi: Sage Publications.

Rajan, K. 2000. *South Indian Memorial Stones*. Thanjavur: Manoo Pathippakam.

Ram, K. 1991. *Mukkuvar Women: Gender, Hegemony and Capitalist Transformation in a South Indian Fishing Community*. London: Allen & Unwin.

———. 2001. 'Modernity and the Midwife: Contestations over a Subaltern Figure, South India', in G.S. Linda and H. Conner (eds), *Healing Powers and Modernity: Traditional Medicine, Shamanism and Science in Asian Societies*, pp. 64–84. Westport, CT: Bergin and Garvey.

Redij, T. and P.P. Joglekar. 2010–2011. 'The Origin and Development of Alakshmi and Lakshmi Concept', *Bulletin of the Deccan College Research Institute*, 70–71: 107–124.

Sadgopal, M. 2009. 'Can Maternity Services Open up to the Indigenous Traditions of Midwifery?' *Economic and Political Weekly*, 44(16) : 52–59.

Sax, W.S. 1991. *Mountain Goddess: Gender and Politics in a Himalayan Pilgrimage*. New York: Oxford University Press.

———. 1996. 'Draupadi and Kunti in the Pandav Lila', in A. Michaels, C. Vogelsanger and A. Wilke (eds), *Wild Goddesses in India and Nepal* (*Studia religiosa Helvetica*, Vol. 2), pp. 355–382. Bern: Peter Lang.

———. 2000. 'Gender and the Representation of Violence in Pandav Lila', in J. Leslie and M. McGee (eds), *Invented Identities: The Interplay of Gender, Religion and Politics in India* (*SOAS Studies on South Asia: Understandings and Perspectives*), pp. 252–264. New Delhi: Oxford University Press.

———. 2002. *Dancing the Self: Personhood and Performance in the Pandav Lila of Garhwal*. Oxford: Oxford University Press.

———. 2009. *God of Justice: Ritual Healing and Social Justice in the Central Himalayas*. Oxford: Oxford University Press.

———. 2010. 'Ritual and the Problem of Efficacy', in W.S. Sax, J. Quack and J. Weinhold (eds), *The Problem of Ritual Efficacy* (*Oxford Ritual Studies*), pp. 3–16. Oxford: Oxford University Press.

Scheper-Hughes, N. 1993. *Death without Weeping: The Violence of Everyday Life in Brazil*. Berkeley, CA: University of California Press.

Schuler, B. 2009. *Of Birth and Death: Icakkiyamman, a Tamil Goddess in Ritual and Story*. (*Ethno-Indology, Heidelberg Studies in South Asian Rituals*, Vol. 8). Wiesbaden: Harrassowitz Verlag.

Sen, A. 2009. *The Idea of Justice*. London: Penguin Books.

Sen, R.N. 1974. *Brahma Vaivarta Puranam (Part 1: Brahma and Prakriti Khandas)* (*The Sacred Books of the Hindus*, Vol. 24. 1). New York: AMS Press.

Sharma, R.S. 2003. *Early Medieval Indian Society: A Study in Feudalisation*. Hyderabad: Orient Longman.

Singh, U. 2011. 'Introduction', in U. Singh (ed.), *Rethinking Early Medieval India: A Reader*, pp. 1–44. New Delhi: Oxford University Press.

Skultans, V. 1987. 'The Management of Mental Illness among Maharashtrian Families: A Case Study of a Mahanubhav Healing Temple', *Man*, New Series, 22(4) : 661–679.

———. 1991. 'Women and Affliction in Maharashtra: A Hydraulic Model of Health and Illness', *Culture, Medicine and Psychiatry*, 15(3) : 321–359.

Sontheimer, G.-D. 1976. *Biroba, Mhaskoba und Khandoba: Ursprung, Geschichte und Umwelt von pastoralen Gottheiten in Maharastra* [Biroba, Mhaskoba and Khandoba: Origin, History and Ecology of Pastoral Deities in Maharastra] (Schriftenreihe des Südasien-Instituts der Universität Heidelberg [Series of the South-Asia-Institute of the University of Heidelberg] 21). Wiesbaden: Franz Steiner Verlag.

———. 1989. *Pastoral Deities in Western India*. New York and Oxford: Oxford University Press.

Srinivas, M.N. 1987. *The Dominant Caste and Other Essays*. New Delhi: Oxford University Press.

Tiwari, S.K. 2002. *Tribal Roots of Hinduism*. New Delhi: Sarup.

Turner, V. 1977. *The Ritual Process: Structure and Anti-Structure*. New York: Cornell University Press.van Gennep. A. 1977. *The Rites of Passage*. London: Routledge and Kegan Paul.

van Hollen, C. 2003. *Birth on the Threshold: Childbirth and Modernity in South India*. New Delhi: Zubaan.

Venkateswaran, T.V. 2014. 'Healing Shrines, Spirit Possession, Agency of Women: A Rationalist Revisit', *Economic and Political Weekly*, 49(28) : 170–172.

Verghese, A. 2000. 'Representations of a Fertility Goddess', in A. Verghese, *Archaeology, Art and Religion: New Perspectives on Vijayanagara*, pp. 155–170. New Delhi: Oxford University Press.

Viswanath, R. 2015. 'Silent Minority: Celebrated Difference, Caste

Difference, and the Hinduization of Independent India', in S. Vertovec (ed.), *Routledge International Handbook of Diversity Studies*, pp. 140–150. New York: Routledge.

Weigl, C. 2007. *Reproductive Health Behaviour and Decision-Making of Muslim Women: An Ethnographic Study in a Low-Income Community in Urban North India* (*Indus Ethnologische Studien* [Indus Anthropological Studies], Vol. 15). Münster: Lit Verlag.

White, D.G. 2003. *Kiss of the Yogini: 'Tantric Sex' in Its South Asian Contexts*. Chicago and London: University of Chicago Press.

Whitehead, H. 1921. *The Village Gods of South India*. Calcutta: Association Press.

Zbavitel, D. 1976. *Bengali Literature* (*A History of Indian Literature*, Vol. 9). Wiesbaden: Otto Harrassowitz.

Zelkowitz, P. 1996. 'Childbearing and Women's Mental Health', *Transcultural Psychiatry* 33(4) : 391–412.